# CRIMINAL MAN

PATTERSON SMITH REPRINT SERIES IN
CRIMINOLOGY, LAW ENFORCEMENT, AND SOCIAL PROBLEMS

*A listing of publications in the* SERIES *will be found at rear of volume*

PUBLICATION No. 134: PATTERSON SMITH REPRINT SERIES IN CRIMINOLOGY, LAW ENFORCEMENT, AND SOCIAL PROBLEMS

GINA LOMBROSO-FERRERO

# CRIMINAL MAN

## ACCORDING TO THE CLASSIFICATION OF
## CESARE LOMBROSO

WITH AN INTRODUCTION BY CESARE LOMBROSO

REPRINTED WITH A NEW INTRODUCTION
BY LEONARD D. SAVITZ

*Illustrated*

MONTCLAIR, N. J.
PATTERSON SMITH
1972

First published in 1911
as No. 27 in G. P. Putnam's Sons' Science Series
edited by Edward Lee Thorndike
and F. E. Beddard
Reprinted 1972 by Patterson Smith Publishing Corporation
Montclair, New Jersey  07042
New material copyright © 1972 by
Patterson Smith Publishing Corporation


Library of Congress Cataloging in Publication Data

Lombroso-Ferrero, Gina, 1872—1944.
    Criminal man, according to the classification of Cesare
Lombroso.

    (The science series, 27) (Patterson Smith reprint series
in criminology, law enforcement, and social problems,
publication no. 134)
    Reprint of the 1911 ed. with a new introduction.
    Includes bibliographies.
    1.  Crime and criminals.    2.  Criminal anthropology.
I. Lombroso, Cesare, 1835—1909.    II. Title.
HV6045.L83 1972            364.1            70-129338
ISBN 0-87585-134-7

## INTRODUCTION TO THE
## REPRINT EDITION

A COMMON, pleasurable and relatively harmless pastime among some professional criminologists consists of trying to discern the "true origins" of the science of criminology. Some have suggested that criminology began in the latter part of the 18th century with the armchair speculations which have come to be known as the Classical Theory or Legal Criminology. The preeminent work of this school, of course, is the Marchese di Beccaria's *Dei delitti e delle pene* (1764).

An even stronger case is made by those contending that criminology developed directly out of research undertaken in France in the second quarter of the 19th century. This Statistical (or Sociological) School produced numerous ecological studies of crime on a national level. National criminal data were first collected in France, and the first Report in 1827 analyzed the figures for 1825. In his Introduction to this Report, Guerry de Champneuf suggested that with such data, "the first symptoms of the evil [crime] would be shown with precision." Associated with this French school were Adolphe Quételet, whose most important book, *Physique sociale,* was published in 1869; and A. M. Guerry, whose *Essai sur la statistique morale de la France* (1835) measured in an extraordinarily sophisticated manner the effects of education, poverty, climate and occupation on crime. It also examined the relative frequency of 17 crimes while keeping the variables of age and sex constant. Without question, Guerry's research represents the first meaningful use of criminal statistics. Later research along similar lines was carried out in the 1850s by Frégier *(The Dangerous Classes)* and Parent-Duchatelet *(Prostitution in Paris).*

While, however, there is still contention about the earliest "sources" of criminology, one must admit that modern criminology stems directly from the activities and dedication of a single man, Cesare Lombroso. This is not the place to present a detailed biography—but, briefly, Cesare Lombroso was born in 1835, and during the course of his life was an army physician, an alienist, a professor of medical jurisprudence and a professor of psychiatry. He died in 1909. He was the founder of a school of thought and research which came to be known variously as the Italian, the Anthropological, the Modern, and, most widely, the Positivist School *(la Scuola Positiva)*.

What were the sources that seemed to coalesce and culminate in Lombroso's theory of the born criminal? First, there was the incalculable impact of the theory of evolution and of evolutionary thought, primarily derived, of course, from Charles Darwin's *The Origin of Species* (1859) and *The Descent of Man* (1871). The revolutionary nature of these works completely transformed the biological and medical sciences. In *The Descent of Man,* Darwin states that some men are closer to their primitive ancestors than others: a belief which became a central feature of Lombroso's subsequent theorizations.

Secondly, there were the early speculations on degeneracy. B. A. Morel in his *Treatise on Degeneracy* (1857) described the pathologic phenomenon of the primitive degenerate type, who represented a peculiar interplay of heredity and environment. In his *Formation of Typology in Degeneracy* (1864), Morel attempted to construct a typology of degeneracy. The degenerate race was a pathologic variety of a normal species with its own distinctive biology, including such anomalies as an asymmetrical head, deformed ears and everted lips. Similar formulations were found in Max Nordau's *Degeneration,* which concluded that many degenerates had epileptic characteristics. (Max Nordau was described by Lombroso as the "ablest and best beloved of many brothers-in-arms.")

Thirdly, the concept of "moral insanity" was extremely significant. The concept had its roots in Benjamin Rush's "The Influence of Physical Causes upon the Moral Faculty" (1786) in which he described micronomia (a weakened moral faculty) and anomia (the complete lack of a moral faculty). James Pritchard in 1857 created the descriptive label "moral insanity." The term was expanded in Henry Maudsley's *Physiology and Pathology of Mind* (1867), in which he ascribed the absence of a moral sense to a pathological condition of the brain. Moral insanity came to be the term used for an egotistical, immoral, lazy, weak-conscienced criminal whose insanity arose out of congenital and organic factors. It is important to note that moral insanity was an accepted psychiatric condition during the latter half of the 19th century (certainly until the case of Garfield's assassin, Guiteau), and Lombroso, as a trained physician and practising psychiatrist, must have been aware, and by and large accepted the existence, presence and power, of this phenomenon.

Fourthly, the rise of racism based on 19th-century scientific research was also influential in the thinking of Cesare Lombroso. Arthur de Gobineau's hugely influential tome, *Essai sur l'inégalité des races humaines* (1853–55), persuaded many of the inequality between the black and the white races, and, more significantly, of the existence of "higher" and "lower" races.

Finally, there was the impact of the burgeoning new science of physical anthropology. The early work of Pierre-Paul Broca included the invention of many basic anthropological devices and indices which were adopted with almost no modification by Lombroso, who constantly referred to Broca and openly acknowledged his debt to him.

This account of Lombroso's antecedents does not of course diminish the originality or the importance of his work, but merely indicates some of the currents, theories, and evidence already in existence which were often brilliantly blended together with his own research to formulate his theory of criminal anthropology. The contribution of Lombroso to the field of criminology has been variously evaluated. On the one hand, Leon Radzinowicz declares that "virtually every element of value in contemporary criminological knowledge owes its formulation to that very remarkable school of Italian criminologists who took pride in describing themselves as the 'positivists' " *(In Search of Criminology,* 1962). Edwin Sutherland was of an opposite mind, arguing that

Lombroso's impact had the disastrous effect of leading criminology up a blind alley for forty years.

The quintessential techniques and theory commonly associated with Lombroso are relatively few in number. He and his followers believed they had created a "new science": criminal anthropology. The basic methodology of this science comprised anthropometric measurements of the cranium and the description of anomalies of the face and of peculiarities of the bodily structure. It has been said that Lombroso, like Gall before him, embraced scientific method, but that unlike Gall he actually applied it to his subject populations.

Lombroso's theory was separate and distinct from his techniques of criminal anthropology. Essentially, it consisted of three major formulations, which changed rather dramatically over time. First of all, there was the belief in the born criminal: that is, some individuals were born to be criminals, as a result of congenital, partly pathologic, factors which impelled them to a life of crime. The criminal was a natural phenomenon, representing a distinct species, *homo delinquens.*

Secondly, the born criminal was also an atavistic being. Physiologically, he was a "throwback," a reversion to past races of mankind, who was born out of time and would have been normal had be been born at some earlier point in time. He was a "ghost from the past" or a "relic of a vanished race." Physically, emotionally and behaviorally, he was very similar to primitive races and to children, all of whom were hedonistic, non-intellectual, curious, cruel and cowardly. The criminal's behavior, morality, and phenotype was found to be remarkably similar to that of the lunatic, particularly the epileptic. In time, Lombroso came to define the born criminal as an epileptoid.

Thirdly, Lombroso contends that there is a *criminal type*—that is, the criminal demonstrates by certain physical dimensions that he is an atavism, a born criminal. The criminal was knowable, measurable and predictable, largely on the basis of cranial, facial and bodily measurements. At several junctures in his career, Lombroso suggested that the presence of a specific number of stigmata predicted, with high accuracy, the inborn predisposition to crime (at one time, the magic number was five). Later in life—in this book, for example—Lombroso discussed both born criminals and criminoloids (those who become criminals because of "vicious training" and "weak natures"), but, by and large, his reputation is indissolubly tied to the theory of the born criminal. Curiously enough, his full-blown theory was not fully explicated in any single work by Lombroso.

These theories were gathered together for the first time, under the title *L'uomo delinquente* ("Criminal Man") in 1876. The book was basically a reprinting of several previously published articles on criminal psychiatry and anthropometry. It is instructive to compare this first edition with the present volume, in which, in 1911, *L'uomo delinquente* appeared in English for the first time: this is a summary, written in English for the American public, by his devoted daughter Gina (the wife of the Italian historian Guglielmo Ferrero), of Lombroso's criminological theory and practice at the end of his career.

Chapter One was largely given over to an extremely detailed account of his studies of the cephalic indices of the skulls of sixty criminals: their circumferences, comparative sizes and degrees of microcephaly. These measurements were then compared to measurements of the cranial capacity of Hottentots and Bushmen. Both criminals and African aborigines were found to have abnormally small cranial capacities. Next, the shapes of the criminals' skulls (brachycephalic, dolichocephalic or mesocephalic) were compared, and it was found, for example, that dolichocephalics tended to dominate among robbers. More importantly, in thirteen of fifty-six skulls a median occipital depression, or fossa, was found. It was sometimes normal in size, but many of them were abnormally large.

In the case of Villella [this is the spelling Lombroso uses] of Calabria, a most skillful thief, who showed no special venereal tendency and whose [cranial] sutures were still open at the age of 70, this depression was of altogether extraordinary dimensions— 34 mm. long, 23 mm. wide and 11 mm. deep—and this was associated with atrophy of the lateral occipital depressions . . . from which appearances, comparative anatomy and human embryology have a solid reason for the deduction that in this case there was undoubtedly hypertrophy of the vermis, as much as to say a tiny median brain, in which case this organ in the sublime scale of the primates would go back . . . to the lemurs, or that of man between the third and fourth months after conception.

Data were then presented on other "regressive features" such as "the falling away of the forehead," an overabundance of Wormian bones, and abnormal cephalo-spinal and cephalo-orbital indices. While a smaller proportion of criminals had median occipital fossae than lunatics (23% to 33%), criminals were more frequently microcephalic and had lower cranial capacity, more precocious synosteosis, and greater cranial sclerosis. These physical characteristics of the criminal were said to "remind us incontestably far more of the American black and mongolian races than the white races and remind us above all of prehistoric man." "The [physical] deviations are not found in isolation, but almost always grouped in particular individuals." Villella, for example, had synosteosis, atrophy of the atlas and an enormous occipital depression.

Chapter Two of the first edition gave an exhaustive presentation of anthropometric and physiognomic data on 832 Italian delinquents, covering stature, weight, general robustness, cranial capacity and cranial circumference. A comparison is made between 390 criminals and 868 Italian soldiers with respect to eye and hair color, amount of beard, shape of ear helix, dilation of pupils, shape of nose, size of hands, and facial angles. The Italian murderer was distinguished by abundant, dark hair, and great strength as measured on Broca's dynanometer. Subsequent chapters dealt with such matters as the tatooing, emotions and passions, religion, jargon and handwriting of criminals.

In the Summary to the first edition, we are told once more of the many characteristics shared by savages, colored races, some of the higher animals, and born criminals. Atavistic analogies offer the only explanation for much criminal behavior. Thus, pederasty and infanticide are inexplicable to us only until we understand that to Romans and Greeks these were moral customs. [The pederast one supposes might be an atavism of Periclean Athens!] Even the most horrific crimes arise out of physiological and atavistic roots, which society temporarily holds in check by "upbringing, surroundings, and the fear of punishment," but which nevertheless emerge under such circumstances as sickness, changes in atmospheric conditions, or "spermatic inebriation."

In view of the closeness of the distance between the criminal and the uncouth and the savage, . . . we can appreciate why men from the lower orders . . . have so often a real predilection for crime. . . . Observe how our children, before they are educated, are unable to distinguish between vice and virtue, steal, fight, and lie . . .

The biological bases of criminal behavior render ineffective any current (and perhaps any future) system of punishment. Crime is a natural, perhaps even a necessary phenomenon, and this belief in the functional nature of crime can be traced to Plato, St. Bernard and St. Augustine.

The most interesting, and in many ways the most valuable, part of the present volume is its Introduction. Here Lombroso recalls that the first outlines of his science arose as a result of his experimental anthropometric studies of psychiatry in 1866. He indicates the traumatic impact of Villella's post-mortem, when with blinding insight he could suddenly see "lighted up as a vast plain under a flaming sky, the problem of the nature of the criminal—an atavistic being." This volume, compared to the first edition, is a more leisurely, more assured, and far less detailed summary of the mountain of research that formed the basis of the Positivist School. The born criminal, still an atavism, is said by this time to represent only about one-third of all criminals. Nor are there any longer a specific set of peculiar physical features of the born criminal which differentiate him clearly and certainly from the criminoloid. The born criminal is still found to have peculiar sensory responses, including the diminished "sensibility" to pain characteristic of primitives and children. He lacks natural affection towards relatives (but is abnormally fond of animals), is unable to differentiate right from wrong, and, as far as his emotions are concerned, he is almost completely lacking in remorse. [It would seem that the born criminal, by our present-day standards, would be either insane or psychopathic.] Significantly, at the end of his life, Lombroso concluded that the born criminal is a special type of epileptic. The theory of the etiology of crime, furthermore, was by this time extended from a relatively simple biological model to what appears to be a multi-causal model including many social variables. Thus, beyond the indirect and direct factors of heredity, such social causes of crime as population density, education, immigration, economic conditions, age, sex and (a recurring preoccupation of Lombroso's) meteoric and atmospheric conditions were mentioned.

It is interesting to note that in Part III of this book, although the physical anomalies to be looked for and measured—as determined by previous research—are described in very considerable detail, there is no longer any indication of their relative predictive value in identifying the born criminal.

The importance of Lombrosianism to the field of criminology was enormous. While its importance was less overwhelming in France and England than it was in this country, for various reasons it remained the major force in modern criminology for many years. When references to the work of A. M. Guerry and Quételet started to reappear in American texts, in the 1930s and 1940s, they came as something of a revelation to most American criminologists: so overwhelming had the triumph of Lombrosianism been that the criminal ecology of the Statistical School had for almost forty years been almost entirely lost to view.

There has been some speculation over the reasons for the success of the Positivist School. To some extent it shone in the reflected glory of the theory of human evolution, and to a much lesser extent in that of the degeneracy models of Morel and Nordau. Lombrosianism was thought to be a normal and natural adaption of Darwinism to criminology and appealed to a public already intrigued and impressed with evolution and evolutionary thought. Perhaps also the fact that it was known as the New, the Modern, the Positive School carried the implication that it was the first to use modern scientific techniques in the study of crime, and that other theories were somehow less modern, less new and less scientific. We should also remember that criminology, by the end of the 19th century, had largely become an avocation of professional people, especially physicians, whose deep involvement with problems of crime and the amelioration of prison life was replacing that of the philosophers, journalists, and social workers. Lombrosianism, therefore, represented one episode of this "seizure of power" by the medical profession. The New School of criminology, after all, was based on the theory and research of a physician, i.e. someone whom fellow doctors could respect; his pronouncements on crime were assumed to carry the same authority and validity as his medical diagnoses. Important also was Lombroso's shifting of focus from crime to the criminal. The concept of the criminal as a biological freak was simple and easily grasped. The born criminal represents a lower level of abstraction than the criminal who has to be a product of social factors. Crime rates, the product of the ecological school, were far less *interesting* than a "criminal man." Finally, the end of the 19th century saw the emergence of the "family tree" studies of crime, insanity and social pathologies of every sort. The data produced by Dugdale and those that followed him seemed independently to verify the biological or genetic basis of crime; but Dugdale never enunciated a theory of crime causation, whereas the Positivist School did.

Lombroso had his greatest impact in the United States. In the Introduction to this book, he specifically mentions that his theories have become an object of "almost fanatical adherence," especially in America. This may be due to the fact that there was no alternative tradition of research in this country. As he suggests, traditions were not important in this country. The traditional sociological approach to crime that developed before Lombroso in France, and to a lesser extent in England, acted as a bulwark against a complete capitulation to Lombrosianism and offered viable alternatives to his formulations. Then, America had no central sources of continuously collected national crime statistics such as existed in England and France. A final factor in the triumph of Lombroso in America might be that most European criminological publications, other than those of the Italian School, were not translated into English and hence were unavailable to the monoglot American criminologist. It has been pointed out that the powerful American Institute of Criminal Law and Criminology, very fierce adherents to the Positivist School, translated Lombroso, Garofalo and Ferri, but, of the French environmentalists, only Tarde and not Manouvrier and Lacassagne.

It is rather fascinating to reflect on the fundamental similarities between the now outmoded biological expositions of the Italian School and the current scientific research being carried out on the chromosomal peculiarities of some aggressive prisoners who are said to have the XYY syndrome. Both aim at ascertaining and describing genetic patterns which are outwardly manifested by peculiar bodily features ("stigmata" to Lombroso; "ectomorphic phenotype" and "poor, acned complexion" to the modern biologist). Not only are the individuals studied genetic mutants whose very existence seemingly defies normal rules of genetic distribution and diversity but their behavior, too, is uncontrollable and immutable.

If any proof can be established that the criminality of certain individuals traces to atavistic anomalies or to extra chromosomes, then, in either case, it could not be effectively prevented, nor could the criminals' behavior be significantly altered after their pathology is detected. Thus a basically Lombrosian concept of a born criminal type will still confront modern science, and with it the moral and practical dilemmas it sets for a just society.

LEONARD D. SAVITZ

Philadelphia
September 1971

# INTRODUCTION

## BY CESARE LOMBROSO

[Professor Lombroso was able before his death to give his personal attention to the volume prepared by his daughter and collaborator, Gina Lombroso Ferrero (wife of the distinguished historian), in which is presented a summary of the conclusions reached in the great treatise by Lombroso on the causes of criminality and the treatment of criminals. The preparation of the introduction to this volume was the last literary work which the distinguished author found it possible to complete during his final illness.]

IT will, perhaps, be of interest to American readers of this book, in which the ideas of the Modern Penal School, set forth in my work, *Criminal Man*, have been so pithily summed up by my daughter, to learn how the first outlines of this science arose in my mind and gradually took shape in a definite work—how, that is, combated by some, the object of almost fanatical adherence on the part of others, especially in America, where tradition has little hold, the Modern Penal School came into being.

On consulting my memory and the documents relating to my studies on this subject, I find that its two fundamental ideas—that, for instance, which claims as an essential point the study not of crime in the abstract, but of the criminal himself, in order adequately to deal with the evil effects of his wrong-doing, and that which classifies the congenital criminal as an anomaly, partly pathological and partly atavistic, a revival of the primitive savage—did not suggest themselves to me instantaneously under the spell of a single deep impression, but were the offspring of a series of impressions. The slow and almost unconscious association of these first vague ideas resulted in a new system which, influenced by its origin, has preserved in all its subsequent developments the traces of doubt and indecision, the marks of the travail which attended its birth.

The first idea came to me in 1864, when, as an army doctor, I beguiled my ample leisure with a series of studies on the Italian soldier. From the very beginning I was struck by a characteristic that distinguished the honest soldier from his vicious comrade: the extent to which the latter was tattooed and the indecency of the designs that covered his body. This idea, however, bore no fruit.

The second inspiration came to me when on one occasion, amid the laughter of my colleagues, I sought to base the study of psychiatry on experimental methods. When in '66, fresh from the atmosphere of clinical experiment, I had begun to study psychiatry, I realised how inadequate were the methods hitherto held in esteem, and how necessary it was, in studying the insane, to make the patient, not the disease, the object of attention. In homage to these ideas, I applied to the clinical examination of cases of mental alienation the study of the skull, with measurements and weights, by means of the esthesiometer and craniometer. Reassured by the result of these first steps, I sought to apply this method to the study of criminals—that is, to the differentiation of criminals and lunatics, following the example of a few investigators, such as Thomson and Wilson; but as at that time I had neither criminals nor moral imbeciles available for observation (a remarkable circumstance since I was to make the criminal my starting-point), and as I was skeptical as to the existence of those "moral lunatics" so much insisted on by both French and English authors, whose demonstrations, however, showed a lamentable lack of precision, I was anxious to apply the experimental method to the study of the diversity, rather than the analogy, between lunatics, criminals, and normal individuals. Like him, however, whose lantern lights the road for others, while he himself stumbles in the darkness, this method proved useless for determining the differences between criminals and lunatics, but served instead to

indicate a new method for the study of penal jurisprudence, a matter to which I had never given serious
thought. I began dimly to realise that the *a priori*
studies on crime in the abstract, hitherto pursued
by jurists, especially in Italy, with singular acumen,
should be superseded by the direct analytical study
of the criminal, compared with normal individuals
and the insane.

I, therefore, began to study criminals in the Italian
prisons, and, amongst others, I made the acquaintance of the famous brigand Vilella. This man
possesssed such extraordinary agility, that he had
been known to scale steep mountain heights bearing
a sheep on his shoulders. His cynical effrontery
was such that he openly boasted of his crimes. On
his death one cold grey November morning, I was
deputed to make the *post-mortem*, and on laying open
the skull I found on the occipital part, exactly on the
spot where a spine is found in the normal skull, a
distinct depression which I named *median occipital
fossa*, because of its situation precisely in the middle
of the occiput as in inferior animals, especially
rodents. This depression, as in the case of animals,
was correlated with the hypertrophy of the *vermis*,
known in birds as the middle cerebellum.

This was not merely an idea, but a revelation.
At the sight of that skull, I seemed to see all of a

sudden, lighted up as a vast plain under a flaming sky, the problem of the nature of the criminal—an atavistic being who reproduces in his person the ferocious instincts of primitive humanity and the inferior animals. Thus were explained anatomically the enormous jaws, high cheek-bones, prominent superciliary arches, solitary lines in the palms, extreme size of the orbits, handle-shaped or sessile ears found in criminals, savages, and apes, insensibility to pain, extremely acute sight, tattooing, excessive idleness, love of orgies, and the irresistible craving for evil for its own sake, the desire not only to extinguish life in the victim, but to mutilate the corpse, tear its flesh, and drink its blood.

I was further encouraged in this bold hypothesis by the results of my studies on Verzeni, a criminal convicted of sadism and rape, who showed the cannibalistic instincts of primitive anthropophagists and the ferocity of beasts of prey.

The various parts of the extremely complex problem of criminality were, however, not all solved hereby. The final key was given by another case, that of Misdea, a young soldier of about twenty-one, unintelligent but not vicious. Although subject to epileptic fits, he had served for some years in the army when suddenly, for some trivial cause, he attacked and killed eight of his superior officers and

comrades.  His horrible work accomplished, he fell
into a deep slumber, which lasted twelve hours and
on awaking appeared to have no recollection of what
had happened.  Misdea, while representing the most
ferocious type of animal, manifested, in addition,
all the phenomena of epilepsy, which appeared
to be hereditary in all the members of his family.
It flashed across my mind that many criminal characteristics not attributable to atavism, such as facial
asymmetry, cerebral sclerosis, impulsiveness, instan-
taneousness, the periodicity of criminal acts, the
desire of evil for evil's sake, were morbid characteristics common to epilepsy, mingled with others due
to atavism.

Thus were traced the first clinical outlines of my
work which had hitherto been entirely anthropological.  The clinical outlines confirmed the anthropological contours, and *vice versâ;* for the greatest
criminals showed themselves to be epileptics, and,
on the other hand, epileptics manifested the same
anomalies as criminals.  Finally, it was shown that
epilepsy frequently reproduced atavistic characteristics, including even those common to lower
animals.

That synthesis which mighty geniuses have often
succeeded in creating by one inspiration (but at
the risk of errors, for a genius is only human and in

many cases more fallacious than his fellow-men) was
deduced by me gradually from various sources—
the study of the normal individual, the lunatic, the
criminal, the savage, and finally the child. Thus,
by reducing the penal problem to its simplest expression, its solution was rendered easier, just as the
study of embryology has in a great measure solved
the apparently strange and mysterious riddle of
teratology.

But these attempts would have been sterile, had
not a solid phalanx of jurists, Russian, German,
Hungarian, Italian, and American, fertilised the
germ by correcting hasty and one-sided conclusions,
suggesting opportune reforms and applications, and,
most important of all, applying my ideas on the
offender to his individual and social prophylaxis and
cure.

Enrico Ferri was the first to perceive that the
congenital epileptoid criminal did not form a single
species, and that if this class was irretrievably
doomed to perdition, crime in others was only a
brief spell of insanity, determined by circumstances, passion, or illness. He established new
types—the occasional criminal and the criminal by
passion,—and transformed the basis of the penal
code by asking if it were more just to make laws obey
facts instead of altering facts to suit the laws, solely

in order to avoid troubling the placidity of those
who refused to consider this new element in the scientific field.  Therefore, putting aside those abstract
formulæ for which high talents have panted in vain,
like the thirsty traveller at the sight of the desert
mirage, the advocates of the Modern School came to
the conclusion that sentences should show a decrease
in infamy and ferocity proportionate to the increase
in length and social safety.  In lieu of infamy they
substituted a longer period of segregation, and for
cases in which alienists were unable to decide between
criminality and insanity, they advocated an intermediate institution, in which merciful treatment and
social security were alike considered.  They also
emphasised the importance of certain measures
which hitherto had been universally regarded as a
pure abstraction or an unattainable desideratum—
measures for the prevention of crime by tracing it
to its source, divorce laws to diminish adultery,
legislation of an anti-alcoholistic tendency to prevent
crimes of violence, associations for destitute children,
and co-operative associations to check the tendency
to theft.  Above all, they insisted on those regulations—unfortunately fallen into disuse—which in-
demnify the victim at the expense of the aggressor,
in order that society, having suffered once for the
crime, should not be obliged to suffer pecuniarily

for the detention of the offender, solely in homage to a theoretical principle that no one believes in, according to which prison is a kind of baptismal font in whose waters sin of all kinds is washed away.

Thus the edifice of criminal anthropology, circumscribed at first, gradually extended its walls and embraced special studies on homicide, political crime, crimes connected with the banking world, crimes by women, etc.

But the first stone had been scarcely laid when from all quarters of Europe arose those calumnies and misrepresentations which always follow in the train of audacious innovations. We were accused of wishing to proclaim the impunity of crime, of demanding the release of all criminals, of refusing to take into account climatic and racial influences and of asserting that the criminal is a slave eternally chained to his instincts; whereas the Modern School, on the contrary, gave a powerful impetus to the labors of statisticians and sociologists on these very matters. This is clearly shown in the third volume of *Criminal Man*, which contains a summary of the ideas of modern criminologists and my own.

One nation, however—America,—gave a warm and sympathetic reception to the ideas of the Modern School which they speedily put into practice, with the brilliant results shown by the Reformatory at

Elmira, the Probation System, Juvenile Courts, and the George Junior Republic. They also initiated the practice, now in general use, of anthropological co-operation in every criminal trial of importance.

For this reason, and in view of the fact that America does not possess a complete translation of my works—*The Criminal, Male and Female*, and *Political Crime* (translation and distribution being alike difficult on account of the length of these volumes)—I welcome with pleasure this summary, in which the principal points are explained with precision and loving care by my daughter Gina, who has worked with me from childhood, has seen the edifice of my science rise stone upon stone, and has shared in my anxieties, insults, and triumphs; without whose help I might, perhaps, never have witnessed the completion of that edifice, nor the application of its fundamental principles.

# CONTENTS

## CHAPTER IV

*PART II.—CRIME, ITS ORIGIN, CAUSE, AND CURE*

## CHAPTER I

## CHAPTER II

## CHAPTER III

*PART III.—CHARACTERS AND TYPES OF CRIMINALS*

*CONTENTS*

# ILLUSTRATIONS

# PART I

## THE CRIMINAL WORLD

# CHAPTER I

## THE BORN CRIMINAL

A CRIMINAL is a man who violates the laws decreed by the State to regulate the relations between its citizens, but the voluminous codes which in past times set forth these laws treat only of crime, never of the criminal. That ignoble multitude whom Dante relegated to the Infernal Regions were consigned by magistrates and judges to the care of gaolers and executioners, who alone deigned to deal with them. The judge, immovable in his doctrine, unshaken by doubts, solemn in all his inviolability and convinced of his wisdom, which no one dared to question, passed sentence without remission according to his whim, and both judge and culprit were equally ignorant of the ultimate effect of the penalties inflicted.

In 1764, the great Italian jurist and economist, Cesare Beccaria first called public attention to those wretched beings, whose confessions (if state-

ments extorted by torture can thus be called) formed
the sole foundation for the trial, the sole guide in the
application of the punishment, which was bestowed
blindly, without formality, without hearing the
defence, exactly as though sentence were being
passed on abstract symbols, not on human souls and
bodies.

The Classical School of Penal Jurisprudence, of
which Beccaria was the founder and Francesco
Carrara the greatest and most glorious disciple,
aimed only at establishing sound judgments and
fixed laws to guide capricious and often undiscern-
ing judges in the application of penalties. In
writing his great work, the founder of this School
was inspired by the highest of all human sentiments
—pity; but although the criminal incidentally receives notice, the writings of this School treat only
of the application of the law, not of offenders
themselves.

This is the difference between the Classical and
the Modern School of Penal Jurisprudence. The
Classical School based its doctrines on the assump-
tion that all criminals, except in a few extreme
cases, are endowed with intelligence and feelings like
normal individuals, and that they commit misdeeds
consciously, being prompted thereto by their unrestrained desire for evil. The offence alone was con-

sidered, and on it the whole existing penal system has been founded, the severity of the sentence meted out to the offender being regulated by the gravity of his misdeed.

The Modern, or Positive, School of Penal Jurisprudence, on the contrary, maintains that the anti-social tendencies of criminals are the result of their physical and psychic organisation, which differs essentially from that of normal individuals; and it aims at studying the morphology and various functional phenomena of the criminal with the object of curing, instead of punishing him. The Modern School is therefore founded on a new science, Criminal Anthropology, which may be defined as the Natural History of the Criminal, because it embraces his organic and psychic constitution and social life, just as anthropology does in the case of normal human beings and the different races.

If we examine a number of criminals, we shall find that they exhibit numerous anomalies in the face, skeleton, and various psychic and sensitive functions, so that they strongly resemble primitive races. It was these anomalies that first drew my father's attention to the close relationship between the criminal and the savage and made him suspect that criminal tendencies are of atavistic origin.

When a young doctor at the Asylum in Pavia, he

was requested to make a post-mortem examination on a criminal named Vilella, an Italian Jack the Ripper, who by atrocious crimes had spread terror in the Province of Lombardy. Scarcely had he laid open the skull, when he perceived at the base, on the spot where the internal occipital crest or ridge is found in normal individuals, a small hollow, which he called *median occipital fossa* (see Fig. 1). This abnormal character was correlated to a still greater anomaly in the cerebellum, the hypertrophy of the vermis, *i.e.*, the spinal cord which separates the cerebellar lobes lying underneath the cerebral hemispheres. This vermis was so enlarged in the case of Vilella, that it almost formed a small, intermediate cerebellum like that found in the lower types of apes, rodents, and birds. This anomaly is very rare among inferior races, with the exception of the South American Indian tribe of the Aymaras of Bolivia and Peru, in whom it is not infrequently found (40%). It is seldom met with in the insane or other degenerates, but later investigations have shown it to be prevalent in criminals.

This discovery was like a flash of light. "At the sight of that skull," says my father, "I seemed to see all at once, standing out clearly illumined as in a vast plain under a flaming sky, the problem of the nature of the criminal, who reproduces in civilised

FIG. I

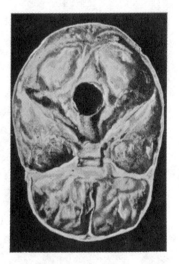

FOSSETTE OCCIPITAL

(see page 6)

times characteristics, not only of primitive savages, but of still lower types as far back as the carnivora."

Thus was explained the origin of the enormous jaws, strong canines, prominent zygomæ, and strongly developed orbital arches which he had so frequently remarked in criminals, for these peculiarities are common to carnivores and savages, who tear and devour raw flesh. Thus also it was easy to understand why the span of the arms in criminals so often exceeds the height, for this is a characteristic of apes, whose fore-limbs are used in walking and climbing. The other anomalies exhibited by criminals—the scanty beard as opposed to the general hairiness of the body, prehensile foot, diminished number of lines in the palm of the hand, cheek-pouches, enormous development of the middle incisors and frequent absence of the lateral ones, flattened nose and angular or sugar-loaf form of the skull, common to criminals and apes; the excessive size of the orbits, which, combined with the hooked nose, so often imparts to criminals the aspect of birds of prey, the projection of the lower part of the face and jaws (prognathism) found in negroes and animals, and supernumerary teeth (amounting in some cases to a double row as in snakes) and cranial bones (epactal bone as in the Peruvian Indians): all these characteristics pointed to one conclusion, the

atavistic origin of the criminal, who reproduces
physical, psychic, and functional qualities of remote
ancestors.

Subsequent research on the part of my father
and his disciples showed that other factors besides
atavism come into play in determining the criminal
type. These are: disease and environment. Later
on, the study of innumerable offenders led them
to the conclusion that all law-breakers cannot be
classed in a single species, for their ranks include very
diversified types, who differ not only in their bent
towards a particular form of crime, but also in the
degree of tenacity and intensity displayed by them
in their perverse propensities, so that, in reality, they
form a graduated scale leading from the born criminal to the normal individual.

Born criminals form about one third of the mass
of offenders, but, though inferior in numbers, they
constitute the most important part of the whole
criminal army, partly because they are constantly appearing before the public and also because the crimes
committed by them are of a peculiarly monstrous
character; the other two thirds are composed of
criminaloids (minor offenders), occasional and habitual criminals, etc., who do not show such a marked
degree of diversity from normal persons.

Let us commence with the born criminal, who as

the principal nucleus of the wretched army of law-breakers, naturally manifests the most numerous and salient anomalies.

The median occipital fossa and other abnormal features just enumerated are not the only peculiarities exhibited by this aggravated type of offender. By careful research, my father and others of his School have brought to light many anomalies in bodily organs, and functions both physical and mental, all of which serve to indicate the atavistic and pathological origin of the instinctive criminal.

It would be incompatible with the scope of this summary, were I to give a minute description of the innumerable anomalies discovered in criminals by the Modern School, to attempt to trace such abnormal traits back to their source, or to demonstrate their effect on the organism. This has been done in a very minute fashion in the three volumes of my father's work *Criminal Man* and his subsequent writings on the same subject, *Modern Forms of Crime*, *Recent Research in Criminal Anthropology*, *Prison Palimpsests*, etc., etc., to which readers desirous of obtaining a more thorough knowledge of the subject should refer.

The present volume will only touch briefly on the principal characteristics of criminals, with the object of presenting a general outline of the studies of criminologists.

## PHYSICAL ANOMALIES OF THE BORN CRIMINAL

*The Head.* As the seat of all the greatest disturbances, this part naturally manifests the greatest number of anomalies, which extend from the external conformation of the brain-case to the composition of its contents.

The criminal skull does not exhibit any marked characteristics of size and shape. Generally speaking, it tends to be larger or smaller than the average skull common to the region or country from which the criminal hails. It varies between 1200 and 1600 c.c.; *i.e.*, between 73 and 100 cubic inches, the normal average being 92. This applies also to the cephalic index; that is, the ratio of the maximum width to the maximum length of the skull [1] multiplied by 100, which serves to give a concrete idea of the form of the skull, because the higher the index, the nearer the skull approaches a spherical form, and the lower the index, the more elongated it becomes. The skulls of criminals have no characteristic cephalic index, but tend to an exaggeration of the ethnical type prevalent in their native countries. In regions where dolichocephaly (index less

[1] For a description of the methods employed in measuring skulls see Part III.

than 80) abounds, the skulls of criminals show a very low index; if, on the contrary, they are natives of districts where brachycephaly (index 80 or more) prevails, they exhibit a very high index.

In 15.5% we find trochocephalous or abnormally round heads (index 91). A very high percentage (nearly double that of normal individuals) have sub-

SKULL FORMATION

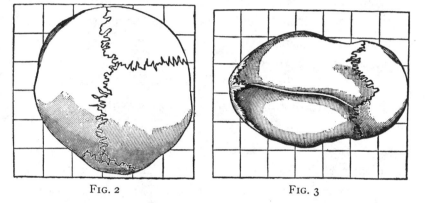

FIG. 2       FIG. 3

microcephalous or small skulls. In other cases the skull is excessively large (macrocephaly) or abnormally small and ill-shaped with a narrow, receding forehead (microcephaly, 0.2%). More rarely the skull is of normal size, but shaped like the keel of a boat (scaphocephaly, 0.1% and subscaphocephaly 6%). (See Fig. 2.) Sometimes the anomalies are still more serious and we find wholly asymmetrical skulls with protuberances on either side (plagiocephaly 10.9%, see Fig. 3), or terminating in a peak on the bregma or anterior fontanel (acrocephaly, see Fig. 4), or depressed in the middle (cymbocephaly, sphenocephaly). At times, there are crests or grooves along the sutures (11.9%) or the cranial bones are abnormally thick, a characteristic of savage peoples (36.6%) or abnormally thin (8.10%). Other anomalies of importance are the presence of Wormian bones in the sutures of the skull (21.22%), the bone of the Incas already alluded to (4%), and above all, the median occipital fossa. Of great importance also are the prominent frontal sinuses found in 25% (double that of normal individuals), the semicircular line of the temples, which is sometimes so exaggerated that it forms a ridge and is correlated to an excessive development of the temporal muscles, a common characteristic of primates and carnivores. Sometimes the forehead is receding, as in apes (19%), or low and narrow (10%).

*The Face.* In striking contrast to the narrow forehead and low vault of the skull, the face of the criminal, like those of most animals, is of disproportionate size, a phenomenon intimately connected with the greater development of the senses as compared with that of the nervous centres. Prognathism, the projection of the lower portion of the face beyond the forehead, is found in 45.7% of criminals.

Progeneismus, the projection of the lower teeth and jaw beyond the upper, is found in 38%, whereas among normal persons the proportion is barely 28%. As a natural consequence of this predominance of the lower portion of the face, the orbital arches and zygomæ show a corresponding development (35%) and the size of the jaws is naturally increased, the mean diameter being 103.9 mm. (4.09 inches) as against 93 mm. (3.66 inches) in normal persons. Among criminals 29% have voluminous jaws.

The excessive dimensions of the jaws and cheek-bones admit of other explanations besides the atavistic one of a greater development of the masticatory system. They may have been influenced by the habit of certain gestures, the setting of the teeth or tension of the muscles of the mouth, which accompany violent muscular efforts and are natural to men who form energetic or violent resolves and meditate plans of revenge.

Asymmetry is a common characteristic of the criminal physiognomy. The eyes and ears are frequently situated at different levels and are of unequal size, the nose slants towards one side, etc. This asymmetry, as we shall see later, is connected with marked irregularities in the senses and functions.

*The Eye.* This window, through which the mind

opens to the outer world, is naturally the centre of many anomalies of a psychic character, hard expression, shifty glance, which are difficult to describe but are, nevertheless, apparent to all observers (see Fig. 4). Side by side with peculiarities of expression, we find many physical anomalies—ptosis, a drooping of the upper eyelid, which gives the eye a half-closed appearance and is frequently unilateral; and strabismus, a want of parallelism between the visual axes, which is insignificant if it arises from errors of refraction, but is very serious if it betokens progressive or congenital diseases of the brain or its membranous coverings. Other anomalies are asymmetry of the iris, which frequently differs in colour from its fellow; oblique eyelids, a Mongolian characteristic, with the edge of the upper eyelid folding inward or a prolongation of the internal fold of the eyelid, which Metchnikoff regards as a persistence of embryonic characters.

*The Ear.* The external ear is often of large size; occasionally also it is smaller than the ears of normal individuals. Twenty-eight per cent. of criminals have handle-shaped ears standing out from the face as in the chimpanzee: in other cases they are placed at different levels. Frequently too, we find misshapen, flattened ears, devoid of helix, tragus, and anti-tragus, and with a protuberance on the upper part of the posterior margin (Darwin's tubercle), a relic of the pointed ear characteristic of apes. Anomalies are also found in the lobe, which in some cases adheres too closely to the face, or is of huge size as in the ancient Egyptians; in other cases, the lobe is entirely absent, or is atrophied till the ear assumes a form like that common to apes.

*The Nose.* This is frequently twisted, up-turned or of a flattened, negroid character in thieves; in murderers, on the contrary, it is often aquiline like the beak of a bird of prey. Not infrequently we meet with the trilobate nose, its tip rising like an isolated peak from the swollen nostrils, a form found among the Akkas, a tribe of pygmies of Central Africa. All these peculiarities have given rise to popular saws, of a character more or less prevalent everywhere.

*The Mouth.* This part shows perhaps a greater number of anomalies than any other facial organ. We have already alluded to the excessive development of the jaws in criminals. They are sometimes the seat of other abnormal characters,—the lemurine apophysis, a bony elevation at the angle of the jaw, which may easily be recognised externally by passing the hand over the skin; and the canine fossa, a depression in the upper jaw for the attachment of the canine muscle. This muscle, which is strongly

developed in the dog, serves when contracted to
draw back the lip leaving the canines exposed.

The lips of violators of women and murderers are fleshy, swollen and protruding, as in
negroes. Swindlers have thin, straight lips. Hare-
lip is more common in criminals than in normal
persons.

*The Cheek-pouches*. Folds in the flesh of the
cheek which recall the pouches of certain species of
mammals, are not uncommon in criminals.

*The Palate*. A central ridge (*torus palatinus*),
more easily felt than seen, may sometimes be found
on the palate, or this part may exhibit other peculiarities, a series of cavities and protuberances corresponding to the palatal teeth of reptiles. Another
frequent abnormality is cleft palate, a fissure in the
palate, due to defective development.

*The Teeth*. These are specially important, for
criminals rarely have normal dentition. The incisors show the greatest number of anomalies.
Sometimes both the lateral incisors are absent
and the middle ones are of excessive size, a
peculiarity which recalls the incisors of rodents.
The teeth are frequently striated transversely or set
very wide apart (diastema) with gaps on either side
of the upper canines into which the lower ones fit, a
simian characteristic. In some cases, these spaces

FIG. 4

HEAD OF CRIMINAL
(see page 14)

FIG. 5

HEAD OF CRIMINAL
(see page 18)

occur between the middle incisors or between these and the lateral ones.

Very often the teeth show a strange uniformity, which recalls the homodontism of the lower vertebrates. In some cases, however, this uniformity is limited to the premolars, which are furnished with tubercles like the molars, a peculiarity of gorillas and orang-outangs. In 4% the canines are very strongly developed, long, sharp, and curving inwardly as in carnivores. Premature caries is common.

*The Chin.* Generally speaking, this part of the face projects moderately in Europeans. In criminals it is often small and receding, as in children, or else excessively long, short or flat, as in apes.

*Wrinkles.* Although common to normal individuals, the abundance, variety, and precocity of wrinkles almost invariably manifested by criminals, cannot fail to strike the observer. The following are the most common: horizontal and vertical lines on the forehead, horizontal and circumflex lines at the root of the nose, the so-called crow's-feet on the temple at the outer corners of the eyes, naso-labial wrinkles around the region of the mouth and nose.

*The Hair.* The hair of the scalp, cheeks and chin, eyebrows, and other parts of the body, shows a number of anomalies. In general it may be said that in the distribution of hair, criminals of both sexes tend to exhibit characteristics of the opposite sex. Dark hair prevails especially in murderers, and curly and woolly hair in swindlers. Both grey hair and baldness are rare and when found make their appearance later in life than in the case of normal individuals. The beard is scanty and frequently missing altogether. On the other hand, the forehead is often covered with down. The eyebrows are bushy and tend to meet across the nose. Sometimes they grow in a slanting direction and give the face a satyr-like expression (see Fig. 5).

The blemishes peculiar to the delinquent are not only confined to the face and head, but are found in the trunk and limbs.

*The Thorax.* An increase or decrease in the number of ribs is found in 12% of criminals. This is an atavistic character common to animals and lower or prehistoric human races and contrasts with the numerical uniformity characteristic of civilised mankind.

Polymastia, or the presence of supernumerary nipples (which are generally placed symmetrically below the normal ones as in many mammals) is not an uncommon anomaly. Gynecomastia or hypertrophy of the mammæ is still more frequent in male criminals. In female criminals, on the contrary, we often find imperfect development or absence of the nipples, a characteristic of monotremata or lowest order of the mammals; or the breasts are flabby and pendent like those of Hottentot women.

The chest is often covered with hair which gives the subject the appearance of an animal.

*The Pelvis and Abdomen.* The abdomen, pelvis, and reproductive organs sometimes show an inversion of sex-characters. In 42% the sacral canal is uncovered, and in some cases there is a prolongation of the coccyx, which resembles the stump of a tail, sometimes tufted with hair.

*The Upper Limbs.* One of the most striking and frequent anomalies exhibited by criminals is the excessive length of the arms as compared with the lower limbs, owing to which the span of the arms exceeds the total height, an ape-like character.

Six per cent. exhibit an anomaly which is extremely rare among normal individuals—the olecranon foramen, a perforation in the head of the humerus where it articulates with the ulna. This is normal in the ape and dog and is frequently found in the bones of prehistoric man and in some of the existing inferior races of mankind.

Several abnormal characters, which point to an atavistic origin, are found in the palm and fingers. Supernumerary fingers (polydactylism) or a reduction in the usual number are not uncommon. Sometimes we find syndactylism, or palmate fingers, a continuation of the interdigital skin to the second phalanx. The length of the fingers varies according to the type of crime to which the individual is addicted. Those guilty of crimes against the person have short, clumsy fingers and especially short thumbs. Long fingers are common to swindlers, thieves, sexual offenders, and pickpockets. The lines on the palmar surfaces of the finger-tips are often of a simple nature as in the anthropoids. The principal lines on the palm are of special significance. Normal persons possess three, two horizontal and one vertical, but in criminals these lines are often reduced to one or two of horizontal or transverse direction, as in apes.

*The Lower Limbs.* Of a number of criminals examined, 16% showed an unusual development of the third trochanter, a protuberance on the head of the femur where it articulates with the pelvis. This distinctly atavistic character is connected with the position of the hind-limb in quadrupeds.

*The Feet.* Spaces between the toes like the interdigital spaces of the hand are very common, and in conjunction with the greater mobility of the toes and greater length of the big-toe, produce the prehensile foot, of the quadrumana, which is used for grasping. The foot is often flat, as in negroes. In the feet, as in the hands, there is frequently a tendency to greater strength or dexterity on the left side, contrary to what happens in normal persons, and this tendency is manifested in many cases where there is no trace of functional and motorial left-handedness.

*The Cerebrum and the Cerebellum.* The chief and most common anomaly is the prevalence of macroscopic anomalies in the left hemisphere, which are correlated to the sensory and functional left-handedness common to criminals and acquired through illness. The most notable anomaly of the cerebellum is the hypertrophy of the vermis, which represents the middle lobe found in the lower mammals. Anomalies in the cerebral convolutions consist principally of anastomotic folds, the doubling of the fissure of Rolando, the frequent existence of a fourth frontal convolution, the imperfect development of the precuneus (as in many types of apes), etc. Anomalies of a purely pathological character are still more common. These are: adhesions of the meninges, thickening of the pia mater, congestion of the meninges, partial atrophy, centres of softening, seaming of the optic thalami, atrophy of the corpus callosum, etc.

Of great importance, too, are the histological anomalies discovered by Roncoroni in the brains of criminals and epileptics. In normal individuals the layers of the frontal region are disposed in the following manner:

1. Molecular layer. 2. Superficial layer of small cells. 3. Layer of small pyramidal cells. 4. Deep layer of small nerve cells. 5. Layer of polymorphous cells (see Fig. 6).

In certain animals, the dog, ape, rabbit, ox, and domestic fowl, the superficial layer is frequently non-existent and the deep one is found only to some extent in the ape.

In born criminals and epileptics there is a prevalence of large, pyramidal, and polymorphous cells, whereas in normal individuals small, triangular, and star-shaped cells predominate. Also the transition from the small superficial to the large pyramidal cells is not so regular, and the number of nervous cells is noticeably below the average. Whereas, moreover, in the normally constituted brain, nervous cells are very scarce or entirely absent in the white substance, in the case of born criminals and epileptics they abound in this part of the brain.

The abnormal morphological arrangement described by Roncoroni is probably the anatomical expression of hereditary alterations, and reveals disorders in nervous development which lead to moral

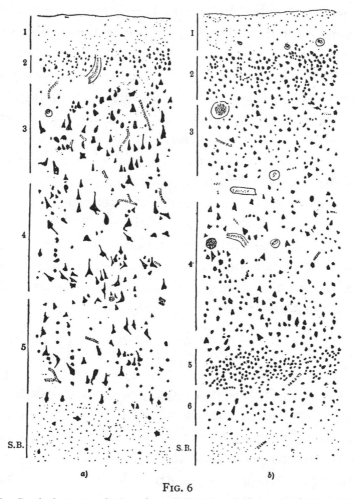

FIG. 6

*a)* Cortical strata of the circumvolutions of the parietal lobes of a
normal person.

*b)* Cortical strata of the circumvolutions of the parietal lobes of a
criminal epileptic.

1. Molecular stratum. 2. External granular stratum. 3. Stratum of the small
pyramidal cells. 4. Stratum of the large pyramidal cells. 5. Deep stratum of
the small nervous cells or the deep granular stratum. 6. Stratum of polymorphic cells.
S.B. White matter.

insanity or epilepsy according to the gravity of the morbid conditions which give rise to them.

These anomalies in the limbs, trunk, skull and, above all, in the face, when numerous and marked, constitute what is known to criminal anthropologists as the criminal type, in exactly the same way as the sum of the characters peculiar to cretins form what is called the cretinous type. In neither case have the anomalies an intrinsic importance, since they are neither the cause of the anti-social tendencies of the criminal nor of the mental deficiencies of the cretin. They are the outward and visible signs of a mysterious and complicated process of degeneration, which in the case of the criminal evokes evil impulses that are largely of atavistic origin.

## SENSORY AND FUNCTIONAL PECULIARITIES OF THE BORN CRIMINAL

The above-mentioned physiognomical and skeletal anomalies are further supplemented by functional peculiarities, and all these abnormal characteristics converge, as mountain streams to the hollow in the plain, towards a central idea — the atavistic nature of the born criminal.

An examination of the senses and sensibility of criminals gives the following results:

*General Sensibility.* Tested simply by touching

with the finger, a certain degree of obtuseness is noted. By using an apparatus invented by Du Bois–Reymond and adopted by my father, the degree of sensibility obtained was 49.6 mm. in criminals as against 64.2 mm. in normal individuals. Criminals are more sensitive on the left side, contrary to normal persons, in whom greater sensibility prevails on the right.

*Sensibility to Pain.* Compared with ordinary individuals, the criminal shows greater insensibility to pain as well as to touch. This obtuseness sometimes reaches complete analgesia or total absence of feeling (16%), a phenomenon never encountered in normal persons. The mean degree of dolorific sensibility in criminals is 34.1 mm. whereas it is rarely lower than 40 mm. in normal individuals. Here again the left-handedness of criminals becomes apparent, 39% showing greater sensibility on the left.

*Tactile Sensibility.* The distance at which two points applied to the finger-tips are felt separately is more than 4 mm. in 30% of criminals, a degree of obtuseness only found in 4% of normal individuals. Criminals exhibit greater tactile sensibility on the left. Tactile obtuseness varies with the class of crime practised by the individual. While in burglars, swindlers, and assaulters, it is double that of normal persons, in murderers, violators, and incendiaries it is often four or five times as great.

*Sensibility to the Magnet,* which scarcely exists in normal persons, is common to a marked degree in criminals (48%).

*Meteoric Sensibility.* This is far more apparent in criminals and the insane than in normal individuals. With variations of temperature and atmospheric pressure, both criminals and lunatics become agitated and manifest changes of disposition and sensations of various kinds, which are rarely experienced by normal persons.

*Sight* is generally acute, perhaps more so than in ordinary individuals, and in this the criminal resembles the savage. Chromatic sensibility, on the contrary, is decidedly defective, the percentage of colour-blindness being twice that of normal persons. The field of vision is frequently limited by the white and exhibits much stranger anomalies, a special irregularity of outline with deep peripheral scotoma, which we shall see is a special characteristic of the epileptic.

*Hearing, Smell, Taste* are generally of less than average acuteness in criminals. Cases of complete anosmia and qualitative obtuseness are not uncommon. [1]

---

[1] For a description of the methods used in measuring the acuteness of these senses, see Part III.

*Agility.* Criminals are generally agile and preserve this quality even at an advanced age. When over seventy, Vilella sprang like a goat up the steep rocks of his native Calabria, and the celebrated thief "La Vecchia," when quite an old man, escaped from his captors by leaping from a high rampart at Pavia.

*Strength.* Contrary to what might be expected, tests by means of the dynamometer show that criminals do not usually possess an extraordinary degree of strength. There is frequently a slight difference between the strength of the right and left limbs, but more often ambidexterity, as in children, and a greater degree of strength in the left limbs.

## Psychology of the Born Criminal

The physical type of the criminal is completed and intensified by his moral and intellectual physiognomy, which furnishes a further proof of his relationship to the savage and epileptic.

*Natural Affections.* These play an important part in the life of a normally constituted individual and are in fact the *raison d'être* of his existence, but the criminal rarely, if ever, experiences emotions of this kind and least of all regarding his own kin. On the other hand, he shows exaggerated and abnormal fondness for animals and strangers. La Sola, a female criminal, manifested about as much affection for her children as if they had been kittens and induced her accomplice to murder a former paramour, who was deeply attached to her; yet she tended the sick and dying with the utmost devotion.

In the place of domestic and social affections, the criminal is dominated by a few absorbing passions: vanity, impulsiveness, desire for revenge, licentiousness.

## MORAL SENSE

The ability to discriminate between right and wrong, which is the highest attribute of civilised humanity, is notably lacking in physically and psychically stunted organisms. Many criminals do not realise the immorality of their actions. In French criminal jargon conscience is called "la muette," the thief "l'ami," and "travailler" and "servir" signify to steal. A Milanese thief once remarked to my father: "I don't steal. I only relieve the rich of their superfluous wealth." Lacenaire, speaking of his accomplice Avril, remarked, "I realised at once that we should be able to work together." A thief asked by Ferri what he did when he found the purse stolen by him contained no money, replied, "I call them rogues." The notions of right and wrong appear to be completely inverted in such minds. They seem to think they have a right to rob and murder and that those who hinder them are acting unfairly. Murderers, especially when actuated by motives of revenge, consider their actions righteous in the extreme.

*Repentance and Remorse.* We hear a great deal about the remorse of criminals, but those who come into contact with these degenerates realise that they are rarely, if ever, tormented by such feelings. Very few confess their crimes: the greater number deny all guilt in a most strenuous manner and are fond of protesting that they are victims of injustice, calumny, and jealousy. As Despine once remarked with much insight, nothing resembles the sleep of the just more closely than the slumbers of an assassin.

Many criminals, indeed, allege repentance, but generally from hypocritical motives; either because they hope to gain some advantage by working on the feelings of philanthropists, or with a view to escaping, or, at any rate, improving their condition while in prison. Thus Lacenaire, when convicted for the first time, wrote in a moving strain to his friend Vigouroux in order to get money and help from him, "Repentance is the only course left open to me. You may well feel pleased at having turned a man from a path of crime for which he was not intended by nature." A few hours later he committed another theft, and before he died remarked cynically that he had never experienced remorse. When tried at the Assizes at Pavia, Rognoni pronounced a touching discourse on his repentance and refused the wine brought him in prison for some days because it reminded him of his murdered brother. But he obtained it surreptitiously from his fellow-prisoners, and when one of them grumbled at having to give up his own portion, Rognoni threatened him saying, "I have already murdered four, and shall make no bones about killing a fifth."

Sometimes remorse is advanced by criminals as a palliation of their crimes. Michelieu justified the *coup de grace* inflicted on his victim by saying, "When I saw her in that state, I felt such terrible remorse that I shot her dead in order not to meet her glance."

Sometimes an appearance of remorse is produced by hallucinations due to alcoholism. Philippe and Lucke imagined they saw the spectres of the persons they had murdered a short time before, but in reality they were suffering from the effects of drink and so little true remorse did they feel that on being sentenced, Philippe remarked, "If they had not sent me to Cayenne, I should have done it again." Generally speaking, what seems to be repentance is only the fear of death or some superstitious dread, which assumes an appearance of remorse, but is devoid of real feeling.

A typical instance of hypocrisy and cynicism is furnished by the Marquise de Brinvilliers, the notorious poisoner, who succeeded in deceiving the venerable prison-chaplain so completely that he regarded her as a model of penitence, yet in her last moments she wrote to her husband denying her guilt and exhibited lascivious and revengeful feelings.

Many criminals, when in prison, model sculptural representations of their crimes with crumbs of bread (see Fig. 7).

*Cynicism.* The strongest proof of the total lack of remorse in criminals and their inability to distinguish between good and evil is furnished by the callous way in which they boast of their depraved actions and feign pious sentiments which they do not feel. One criminal humbly entreated to be allowed to retain his own crucifix while in prison. It was subsequently discovered that the sacred image served as a sheath for his dagger (see Fig. 8).

Philippe made the following statement to one of his female companions. "My way of loving women is a very strange one. After enjoying their caresses, I take the greatest delight in strangling them or cutting their throats. Soon you will hear everyone talking about me." Shortly before he murdered his father, Lachaud said to his friends, "This evening I shall dig a grave and lay my father there to rest eternally."

Sometimes, indeed, a criminal realises dimly the depravity of his actions; he rarely judges them, however, as a normal person would, but seeks to explain and justify them after his own fashion. When asked by the magistrate if he denied having stolen a horse, Ansalone replied, "Surely you do not call that a theft; a leader of brigands could hardly be expected to go on foot!"

Others consider that their actions are less criminal if their intentions were good; like Holland, who murdered to obtain food for his wife and children. Others, again, think themselves excused by the fact that many do worse things with impunity. Any circumstance, the lack or insufficiency of evidence against them or the fact that they are accused of an offence different from the one they have really committed, is seized upon as a mitigation of their guilt, and they always manifest much resentment against those who administer the law. "London thieves," observes Mayhew, "realise that they do wrong, but think that they are no worse than ordinary bankrupts."

The constant perusal of newspaper reports leads criminals to believe that there are a great many rogues in higher circles, and by taking exceptions to

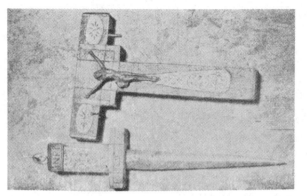

FIG. 8

CRUCIFIX POIGNARD
(see page 31)

FIG. 7

Figures made in Prison
MURDER OF A SLEEPING VICTIM
Work of a Prisoner
(see page 31)

be the rule, they flatter themselves that their own actions are not very reprehensible, because the wealthy are not censured for similar actions.

These instances show that criminals are not entirely unable to distinguish between right and wrong. Nevertheless, their moral sense is sterile because it is suffocated by passions and the deadening force of habit.

In the cant of Spanish thieves, justice is called "la justa" (the just), and this name is given in French slang to the Assizes, but, as Mayor observes, it may be applied ironically.

In alluding to the unknown author of the crimes committed in reality by himself, the murderer Prévost remarked, "Whoever it is, he is bound to end by the guillotine sooner or later." In such cases, although a sense of truth and justice exists, the desire to act according to it is lacking.

" It is one thing [observes Harwick] to possess a theoretical notion of what is right and wrong, but quite another to act according to it. In order that the knowledge of good should be transformed into an ardent desire for its triumph, as food is converted into chyle and blood, it must be urged to action by elevated sentiments, and these are generally lacking in the criminal. If, on the contrary, good feelings really exist, the individual desires to do right and his convictions are translated into action with the same energy that he displayed in doing wrong."

A philanthropist once invited a number of young London thieves to a friendly gathering, and it was noticed that the most hardened offenders were greeted with the greatest amount of applause from the company. Nevertheless, when the President requested one of them to change a gold coin outside, and he did not return, those present showed great indignation and anxiety, abusing and threatening their absent companion, whose ultimate return was hailed with genuine relief. In this case, no doubt, envy and vanity played as great a part as a sense of integrity, in the resentment shown at this fancied breach of faith.

In the prisons at Moscow, offences against discipline are dealt with by the offenders' fellow-prisoners. The convict population on the island of San Stefano compiled spontaneously a Draconian code to quell internal discord arising from racial jealousies.

*Treachery.* This species of morality and justice, which unexpectedly makes its appearance in the midst of a naturally unrighteous community, can only be forced and temporary. When, instead of reaping advantages, interests and passions are injured by acting rightly, these notions of justice, unsustained by innate integrity suddenly fail. Contrary to universal belief, criminals are very prone to betray their companions and accomplices, and are easily induced to act as informers in the hope of gaining some personal advantage or of injuring those they envy or suspect of treachery towards themselves.

"Many thieves," says Vidocq, "consider it a stroke of luck to be consulted by the police." In fact, Bouscaut, one of a notorious band of male-factors in France, was chiefly instrumental in causing the arrest of the gang; and the brigand Caruso aided the authorities in capturing his former companions.

*Vanity.* Pride, or rather vanity, and an exaggerated notion of their own importance, which we find in the masses, generally in inverse proportion to real merit, is especially strong in criminals. In the cell occupied by La Gala, the following notice was found in his handwriting: "March 24th. On this date La Gala learnt to knit." Another criminal, Crocco, tried hard to save his brother, "Lest," he said, "my race should die out." Lacenaire was less troubled by the death-sentence than by adverse criticisms of his bad verse and the fear of public contempt. "I do not fear being hated," he is reported to have said, "but I dread being despised —the tempest leaves traces of its passage, but unobserved the humble flower fades."

Thus thieves are loth to confess that they are

guilty of only petty larceny, and are sometimes prompted by vanity to commit more serious robberies. The same false shame is common to fallen women, among whom contempt is incurred, not by excess of depravity but by the failure to command high prices. Grellinier, a petty thief, boasted in court of imaginary offences, with the desire of appearing in the light of a great criminal. The crimes in the haunted castle, attributed by Holmes to himself, were certainly in part inventions. The female poisoner, Buscemi, when writing to her accomplice, signed herself, "Your Lucrezia Borgia."

One of the most frequent causes of modern crime is the desire to gratify personal vanity and to become notorious.

*Impulsiveness.* This is another and almost pathognomonical characteristic of born criminals, and also, as we shall see later on, of epileptics and the morally insane. That which in ordinary individuals is only an eccentric and fugitive suggestion vanishing as soon as it arises, in the case of abnormal subjects is rapidly translated into action, which, although unconscious, is not the less dangerous. A youth of this impulsive type, returning home one evening flushed with wine, met a peasant leading his ass and cried out, "As I have not come to blows with anyone to-day, I must vent my rage on this beast," at the same time drawing his knife and plunging it several times into the poor animal's body (Ladelci, *Il Vino*, Rome, 1868). Pinel describes a morally insane subject, who was in the habit of giving way to his passions, killing any horses that did not please him and thrashing his political opponents. He even went to the length of throwing a lady down a well, because she ventured to contradict him.

" The most trifling causes [remarks Tamburini, speaking of Sbro. . . .] that stand in the way of his wishes, provoke a fit of rage in which he appears to lose all self-control, like little children, who in resenting any offence show no sense of proportion. The most trivial reasons for disliking anyone awaken in him an irresistible desire to kill the object of his aversion, and if any new blasphemy rises to his lips, he feels constrained to repeat it."

A thief once said to my father: "It is in our very blood. It may be only a pin, but I cannot help taking it, although I am quite ready to give it back to its owner." The pickpocket Bor . . . confessed that at the age of twelve he had begun to steal in the streets and at school, to the extent of taking things from under his schoolfellows' pillows, and that it was impossible for him to resist stealing, even when his pockets were full. If he had not stolen some article before going to bed, he was unable to sleep, and when midnight struck, he felt obliged to take the first thing that came to his hand, destroying it frequently as soon as he had appropriated it.

"To give up stealing," said Deham to Lauvergne, "would be like ceasing to exist. Stealing is a passion that burns like love and when I feel the blood seething in my brain and fingers, I think I should be capable of robbing myself, if that were possible." When sentenced to the galleys, he stole the bands from the masts, nails, and copper plates, and he himself fixed the number of lashes he was to receive after each of these exploits, which did not prevent his recommencing stealing directly afterward (*Les Forçats*, p. 358).

Ponticelli once saw a thief, who was dying of consumption, steal an old slipper from his neighbour and hide it under the bedclothes.

*Vindictiveness.* Closely allied to this impulsiveness and exaggerated personal vanity, we find an extraordinary thirst for revenge. Lebuc murdered a man who had stolen some matches from him. Baron R... caused the death of a man, because he had failed to order a religious procession to halt under the windows of his palace.

> " To see expire the one you hate—
> Such is the joy of the gods.
> My sole desire is to hate and be avenged."

wrote Lacenaire.

After a slight dispute with Voit, whose hospitality he had enjoyed, Renaud threw his friend down a well. He was arrested, and when Voit, who had been rescued, pardoned him, he said, "I only regret not having finished him, but when I come out of prison, I will do so." And he kept his word.

The tattooing on the persons of criminals and their writings while in prison are full of solemn oaths of vengeance. A female thief once said, "If it were true that those who refuse to pardon will be damned eternally, I should still withhold my forgiveness."

*Cruelty* depends on moral and physical insensibility, those incapable of feeling pain being indifferent to the sufferings of others.

The post of executioner was eagerly competed for at the prison of Rochefort. Mammon used to drink the blood of his victims and when this was not to be had, he drank his own. The executioner Jean became so maddened by the sight of blood flowing beneath his lash, that guards were stationed to prevent undue prolongation of the punishment. Dippe wrote: "My chief pleasure is beheading. When I was young, stabbing was my sole pastime."

It has often been observed that the ferocity of women exceeds that of men. Rulfi killed her own niece, whom she detested, by thrusting long pins into her, and the female brigand Ciclope reproached her lover for murdering his victims too quickly.

*Idleness.* Like savages, criminals are dominated by an incorrigible laziness, which in certain cases leads them to prefer death from starvation to regular work. This idleness alternates with periods of ferocious impulsiveness, during which they display the greatest energy. Like savages, too, they are passionately fond of alcohol, orgies, and sensual pleasures, which alone rouse them to activity.

*Orgies.* Those who have observed children absorbed all day long by a game that pleases them, can understand the meaning of these words, spoken by a woman: "Criminals are grown-up children." The love of habitual debauch is so intense that, as soon as thieves have made some great haul or escaped from prison, they return to their haunts to carouse and make merry, in spite of the evident danger of falling once more into the hands of the police.

*Gambling.* The passion for gambling is so strong that the criminal is always in a penniless condition, no matter how much treasure he has appropriated, and cases of starvation in prison are not unknown, prisoners having sold their rations in order to gratify this vice.

*Games.* Many primitive and cruel amusements, similar to the pastimes of savages, have been preserved or reconstructed by criminals. Such are the games known to Italian offenders as "La Patta," in which one of the players tries to avoid being struck while passing his head between two points brought together horizontally by another, who stands with his arms outstretched; and "La Rota," in which the players run in a circle, one behind the other, seeking to escape, by dodging, the blows from a stout stick, aimed at them by one of their companions.

*Intelligence* is feeble in some and exaggerated in others. Prudence and forethought are generally lacking. A very common characteristic is recklessness, which leads criminals to run the risk of arrest for the sake of being witty, or to leave some blood-stained weapon on the very spot where they have committed a crime, notwithstanding the fact that they have taken a hundred precautions to avoid detection. This same recklessness prompts them, when the danger is scarcely past, to make verses or pictures of their exploits or to tattoo them upon their persons, heedless of consequences.

Zino relates the story of a Sicilian schoolboy, who illustrated his criminal relations with his school-fellows by a series of sketches in his album. A certain Cavaglia, called "Fusil" robbed and murdered an accomplice and hid the body in a cupboard. He was arrested and in prison decided to commit suicide a hundred days after the date of his crime, but before doing so, he adorned his water-jug with an account of his misdeed, partly in pictures and partly in writing, as though he desired to raise a monument to himself (see Fig. 9). The clearest and strangest instance of this recklessness was furnished by a photograph discovered by the police, in which, at the risk of arrest and detection, three criminals had had themselves photographed in the very act of committing a murder.

## Intellectual Manifestations

*Slang.* This is a peculiar jargon used by criminals when speaking among themselves. The syntax and grammatical construction of the language remain unchanged, but the meanings of words are altered, many being formed in the same way as in primitive languages; *i.e.*, an object frequently receives the name of one of its attributes. Thus a kid is called "jumper," death "the lean or cruel one," the soul "the false or shameful one," the body "the veil," the hour "the swift one," the moon "the spy," a purse "the saint," alms "the rogue," a sermon "the tedious one," etc. Many words are formed as among savages, by onomatopœia, as "tuff" (pistol), "tic" (watch), "guanguana" (sweetheart), "fric frac" (lottery).

FIG. 9

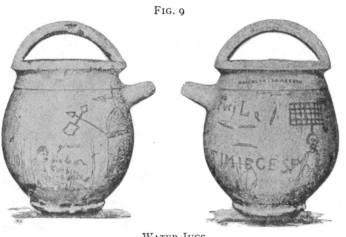

WATER-JUGS
(see page 42)

The necessity of eluding police investigations is the reason usually given for the origin of this slang. No doubt it was one of the chief causes, but does not explain the continued use of a jargon which is too well known now to serve this purpose; moreover, it is employed in poems, the object of which is to invite public attention, not to avoid it, and by criminals in their homes where there is no need for secrecy.

*Pictography.* One of the strangest characteristics of criminals is the tendency to express their ideas pictorially. While in prison, Troppmann painted the scene of his misdeed, for the purpose of showing that it had been committed by others. We have already mentioned the rude illustrations engraved by the murderer Cavaglia on his pitcher, representing his crime, imprisonment, and suicide. Books, crockery, guns, all the utensils criminals have in constant use, serve as a canvas on which to portray their exploits.

From pictography it is but an easy step to hieroglyphics like those used by ancient peoples. The hieroglyphics of criminals are closely allied to their slang, of which in fact they are only a pictorial representation, and, although largely inspired by the necessity for secrecy, show, in addition, evident atavistic tendencies.

De Blasio has explained the meaning of the hieroglyphics used by the "camorristi" (members of the *camorra* at Naples), especially when they are in prison. For instance, to indicate the President of the Tribunal, they use a crown with three points; to indicate a judge, the judge's cap (see Fig. 10).

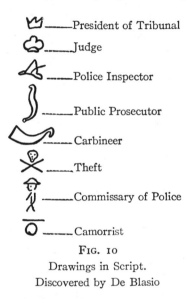

President of Tribunal

Judge

Police Inspector

Public Prosecutor

Carbineer

Theft

Commissary of Police

Camorrist

FIG. 10

Drawings in Script.
Discovered by De Blasio

The following is a list of some of the hieroglyphics mentioned by De Blasio: *Police Inspector*—a hat like those worn by the Italian soldiers who are called Alpini (a helmet with flat top and an upright feather on the left side).

*Public Prosecutor*—an open-mouthed v i p e r (see Fig. 10).

*Carabineer*—a bugle.

*Theft*—a skull and cross-bones.

*Commissary of the Police*—a dwarf with the three-cornered hat worn by the *carabinieri*.

*Arts and Industries of the Criminal.* Although habitual criminals show a strong aversion to any kind of useful labour, in prison and at large, they, nevertheless, apply themselves with great diligence to certain tasks, sometimes of an illegal nature, such as the manufacture of implements to aid them in escaping, sometimes merely artistic, such as modelling, with breadcrumbs, brickdust, or soap, the figures of persons. Sometimes they make baskets, machines, dominoes, draughts, playing-cards, etc., or form means of communication with their fellow-prisoners and construct weapons for executing their schemes of vengeance. They also devote themselves to eccentric and useless occupations, like the training of animals, such as mice, marmosets, birds, and even fleas (Lattes). This morbid and misguided activity, which frequently shows gleams of talent, might well be utilised for increasing the scope of prison industries.

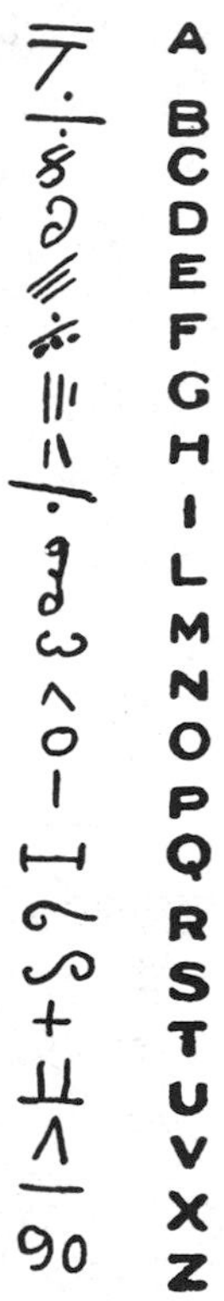

## Tattooing

This personal decoration so often found on great criminals is one of the strangest relics of a former state. It consists of designs, hieroglyphics, and words punctured in the skin by a special and very painful process.

Among primitive peoples, who live in a more or less nude condition, tattooing takes the place of decorations or ornamental garments, and serves as a mark of distinction or rank. When an

FIG. 11

Alphabet
Discovered
by
De Blasio

Eskimo slays an enemy, he adorns his upper-lip with a couple of blue stripes, and the warriors of Sumatra add a special sign to their decorations for every foe they kill. In Wuhaiva, ladies of noble birth are more extensively tattooed than women of humbler rank. Among the Maoris, tattooing is a species of armorial bearings indicative of noble birth.

According to ancient writers, tattooing was practised by Thracians, Picts, and Celts. Roman soldiers tattooed their arms with the names of their generals, and artisans in the Middle Ages were marked with the insignia of their crafts. In modern times this custom has fallen into disuse among the higher classes and only exists among sailors, soldiers, peasants, and workmen.

Although not exclusively confined to criminals, tattooing is practised by them to a far larger extent than by normal persons: 9% of adult criminals and 40% of minors are tattooed; whereas, in normal persons the proportion is only 0.1%. Recidivists and born criminals, whether thieves or murderers, show the highest percentage of tattooing. Forgers and swindlers are rarely tattooed.

Sometimes tattooing consists of a motto symbolical of the career of the criminal it adorns. Tardieu found on the arm of a sailor who had served various terms of imprisonment, the words, "Pas de chance."

The notorious criminal Malassen was tattooed on the chest with the drawing of a guillotine, under which was written the following prophecy: "J'ai mal commencé, je finirai mal. C'est la fin qui m'attend."

Tattooing frequently bears witness to indecency. Of 142 criminals examined by my father, the tattooing on five showed obscenity of design and position and furnished also a remarkable proof of the insensibility to pain characteristic of criminals, the parts tattooed being the most sensitive of the whole body, and therefore left untouched even by savages.

Another fact worthy of mention is the extent to which criminals are tattooed. Thirty-five out of 378 criminals examined by Lacassagne were decorated literally from head to foot.

In a great many cases, the designs reveal violence of character and a desire for revenge. A Piedmontese sailor, who had perpetrated fraud and murder from motives of revenge, bore on his breast between two daggers, the words: "I swear to revenge myself." Another had written on his forehead, "Death to the middle classes," with the drawing of a dagger underneath. A young Ligurian, the leader of a mutiny in an Italian Reformatory, was tattooed with designs representing all the most important episodes of his life, and the idea of revenge was paramount. On his right forearm figured two crossed swords, underneath them the initials M. N. (of an intimate friend), and on the inner side, traced longitudinally, the motto: "Death to cowards. Long live our alliance."

Tattooing, as practised by criminals, is a perfect substitute for writing with symbols and hieroglyphics, and they take a keen pleasure in this mode of adorning their skins.

Of atavistic origin, also, is the practice, common to members of the *camorra*, of branding their sweethearts on the face, not from motives of revenge, but as a sign of proprietorship, like the chiefs of savage tribes, who mark their wives and other belongings; and the form of tattooing called "Paranza," which distinguishes the various bands of malefactors,— the band of the "banner," of the "three arrows," of the "bell-ringer," of the "Carmelites," etc.

## The Criminal Type

All the physical and psychic peculiarities of which we have spoken are found singly in many normal individuals. Moreover, crime is not always the result of degeneration and atavism; and, on the other hand, many persons who are considered perfectly normal are not so in reality. However, in normal individuals, we never find that accumulation of physical, psychic, functional, and skeletal anomalies in one and the same person, that we do in the case of criminals, among whom also entire freedom from abnormal characteristics is more rare than among ordinary individuals.

Just as a musical theme is the result of a sum of notes, and not of any single note, the criminal type results from the aggregate of these anomalies, which render him strange and terrible, not only to the scientific observer, but to ordinary persons who are capable of an impartial judgment.

Painters and poets, unhampered by false doctrines, divined this type long before it became the subject of a special branch of study. The assassins, executioners, and devils painted by Mantegna, Titian, and Ribera the Spagnoletto embody with marvellous exactitude the characteristics of the born criminal; and the descriptions of great writers, Dante, Shakespeare, Dostoyevsky, and Ibsen, are equally faithful representations, physically and psychically, of this morbid type.

## THE CRIMINAL IN PROVERBIAL SAYINGS

The conclusions of instinctive observers have found expression in many proverbs, which warn the world against the very characteristics we have noted in criminals.

A proverb common in Romagna, says: "Poca barba e niun colore, sotto il cielo non vi ha peggiore (There is nothing worse under Heaven than a scanty beard and a colourless face), and in Piedmont there is a saying, "Faccia smorta, peggio che scabbia" (An ashen face is worse than the itch). The Venetians have a number of proverbs expressing distrust of the criminal type: "Uomo rosso e femina barbuta da lontan xe megio la saluta" (Greet from afar the red-haired man and the bearded woman); "Vàrdete da chi te parla e guarda in la, e vàrdete da chi tiene i oci bassi e da chi camina a corti passi" (Beware of him who looks away when he speaks to you, and of him who keeps his eyes cast down and takes mincing steps); "El guerzo xe maledetto per ogni verso" (The squint-eyed are on all sides accursed); "Megio vendere un campo e una cà che tor una dona dal naso levà" (Better sell a field and a house than take a wife with a turned-up nose); "Naso che guarda in testa è peggior che la tempesta" (A turned-up nose is worse than hail); etc.

There are innumerable cases on record, in which persons quite ignorant of criminology have escaped robbery or murder, thanks to the timely distrust awakened in them by the appearance of individuals who had tried to win their confidence. My father once placed before forty children, twenty portraits of thieves and twenty representing great men, and 80% recognised in the first the portraits of bad and deceitful people.

In conclusion, the born criminal possesses certain physical and mental characteristics, which mark him out as a special type, materially and morally diverse from the bulk of mankind.

Like the little cage-bred bird which instinctively crouches and trembles at the sight of the hawk, although ignorant of its ferocity, an honest man feels instinctive repugnance at the sight of a miscreant and thus signalises the abnormality of the criminal type.

# CHAPTER II

## *THE BORN CRIMINAL AND HIS RELATION TO MORAL INSANITY AND EPILEPSY*

NO one, before my father, had ever recognised in the criminal an abnormal being driven by an irresistible atavistic impulse to commit anti-social acts, but many had observed (cases of the kind were too frequent to escape notice) the existence of certain individuals, nearly always members of degenerate families, who seemed from their earliest infancy to be prompted by some fatal impulse to do evil to their fellow-men. They differed from ordinary people, because they hated the very persons who to normal beings are the nearest and dearest, parents, husbands, wives, and children, and because their inhuman deeds seemed to cause them no remorse. These individuals, who were sometimes treated as lunatics, sometimes as diseased persons, and sometimes as criminals, were said by the earliest observers to be afflicted with moral insanity.

*Analogy.* Those who are familiar with all that Pinel, Morel, Richard Connon, and other great alienists have written on the morally insane cannot help remarking the analogy, nay identity, of the physical, intellectual, and moral characteristics of this type of lunatic and those of the born criminal.

The same physical anomalies already observed in criminals, as described in the first chapter (cranial deformities, asymmetry, physical and functional left-handedness, anomalies in the teeth, hands, and feet), are described by these older writers as being characteristic of the morally insane, as are also those mental and moral qualities already noted in the born criminal—vanity, want of affection, cruelty, idleness, and love of orgies.

Only the analogy of the origin and early manifestations was lacking to complete the proof of the identity of the two forms. It is true that moral insanity is more often found in the descendants of insane, neurotic, or dipsomaniac forebears than in those of criminals, and that the characteristics are manifested at an earlier age than is the case with born criminals, but these differences are not of fundamental importance.

*Cases.* During many years of observation, my father was able to follow innumerable cases of moral insanity in which perversity was manifested literally from the cradle, and in which the victims of this disease grew up into delinquents in no wise distinguishable from born criminals.

A typical instance is that of a certain Rizz... who was brought to him by the mother because, while still at the breast, he bit his nurse so viciously that bottle-feeding had to be substituted. At the age of two years, careful training and medical treatment notwithstanding, this child was separated from his brothers, because he stuck pins into their pillows and played dangerous tricks on them. Two years later, he broke open his father's cash-box and stole money to buy sweets; at six, although decidedly intelligent, he was expelled from every private school in the town, because he instigated the others to mischief or ill-treated them. At fourteen, he seduced a servant and ran away, and at twenty he killed his fiancée by throwing her out of a window. Thanks to the testimony of a great many doctors, Rizz... was declared to be morally insane, but if the family had been poor instead of well-to-do, and the mother had neglected to have her child examined in infancy by a medical man, thus obtaining ample proof of the pathological nature of his perversity, Rizz... would have been condemned as an ordinary criminal, because, like all morally insane persons, he was very intelligent and able to reason clearly, like a normal individual.

Another typical case is that of a child named Rav... (see Fig. 12) a native of the Romagna, who was brought to my father at the age of eight, because his parents were convinced that his conduct was due to a morbid condition. Unlike the above-mentioned case, his evil acts were always carried out in an underhand way. He showed great spite towards his brothers and sisters, especially the smaller ones, whom he attempted to strangle on several occasions, and was expelled from school on account of the bad influence he exercised over his schoolfellows. He delighted above everything in robbing his parents, employers, and the neighbours and in falsely accusing others, and so cleverly did he manage this that he caused a great deal of mischief before his double-dealing was discovered. When only eight, on leaving home early every morning to go to work, he would secretly throw all the milk left at the neighbours' doors into the dust-bin, then he accused the janitor of stealing it and got him dismissed. A year later, he nearly succeeded in causing the arrest of a pawnbroker, whom he accused of having lent him money on a cloak, it being illegal in Italy to accept anything in pawn from a minor. The cloak, however, was discovered by his

mother hidden in the cellar.   At ten years of age, he
alleged that his father had brutally ill-treated him,
and as severe marks and bruises on his body gave
colour to the accusation, the poor man was arrested.
The marks, however, were self-inflicted.

Another boy, a certain Man..., a peasant from
the Val d' Aosta, an Alpine valley in Piedmont,
where cretinism is indigenous, exhibited perverse
tendencies from his earliest infancy.   When twelve
years old, he killed his companion in a squabble
over an egg.   (See Fig. 13.)

In the above-mentioned cases, the subjects all
belonged to well-to-do or honest families and the
pathological heredity was therefore exclusively nervous, not criminal.   For this reason, the parents
were struck by the abnormal depravity of their
sons and had them medically examined and treated,
thus discovering that they were morally insane.   If,
on the other hand, the parents had been criminals
and had, themselves, set a bad example, nobody
would have supposed that these depraved tendencies
were innate in the children or had developed precociously.   The fact of the prevalence of moral
insanity in neurotic families (with frequent cases
of lunacy, alcoholism, etc.) rather than in those of
criminal tendencies appears at first sight strange, but
according to the new theory advanced by my father,

FIG. 13

FIG. 12

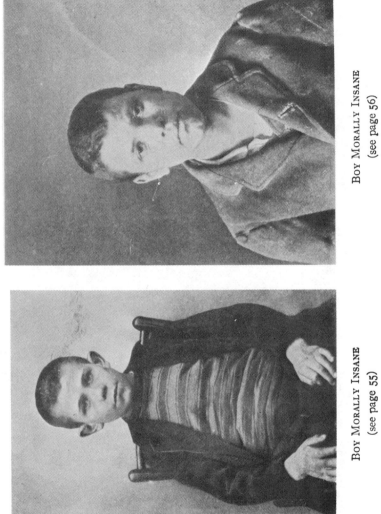

BOY MORALLY INSANE
(see page 56)

BOY MORALLY INSANE
(see page 55)

the criminal is a mentally diseased person; and we shall see in a later chapter that the heredity of insane, neurotic, and dipsomaniac parents is completely equivalent to a criminal heredity.

*Proofs of Analogy.* Thus the genesis and early manifestations, which might have been diverse, really constitute a counter-proof. Careful anamnesis shows that both born criminals and the morally insane begin at a very early age to exhibit symptoms of the morbid tendencies which make them such a danger to society, and if the general public and the police, when such cases are brought to their notice, usually fail to realise that they arise from precocious perversity, it is because atrocious actions are excused on the ground of extreme youth and attributed to this cause rather than to vicious propensities. In many cases, indeed, they are revealed only to the physician.

A counter-proof is likewise furnished by investigations of the origin of these pathological cases, since the study of born criminals shows that they, as well as the morally insane, are as frequently the offspring of insane, epileptic, neurotic, and drunken parents as of criminals, but in the latter case, the morbid origin of their perversity is seldom brought to light owing to the criminality of the parents, who naturally view with indifference symptoms of vice in their children.

## Epileptics, and their Relation to Born Criminals and the Morally Insane

We have already stated that the physical and psychic characteristics of born criminals coincide with those of the morally insane. Both are identical with those of another class of degenerates, known to the world as epileptics.

The term epilepsy was applied to a malady frequently studied but little understood by the ancient medical world, the chief symptoms of which were repeated tonic and clonic fits, preceded by the so-called "epileptic aura" and followed by a deep sleep. It was called *morbus sacer* and believed to be of divine origin.

Careful examination of epileptics by clinical and mental experts, showed that in addition to the characteristic seizure, these unfortunate beings were subject to other phenomena, which sometimes took the place of the convulsive fit and in other cases preceded or followed it. These were *pavor nocturnus*, sudden sweats, heat, neuralgia, sialorrhea, periodical cephalalgia and, above all, vertigo; and these symptoms were not always accompanied by unconsciousness nor followed by coma. Sometimes the seizure was only manifested by paroxysms of rage or ferocious and brutal impulses (devouring animals alive), which, if consciously committed, would be considered criminal. This fact led doctors and mental experts to examine other patients, and they were able to advance positive proof that a certain number of epileptics never experience the typical seizure, the disease being manifested in this milder form with cephalalgia, sialorrhea, delirious ferocity, and above all, giddiness.

The multiformity of epilepsy has been fully confirmed by the experiments of Luciani, Zehen, and others, who produced various forms of epilepsy by submitting different cerebral zones to varying degrees of irritation. By graduating the electric current, Rosenbach was able to provoke the whole series of epileptic phenomena described above, from the mildest to the most serious manifestations. A slight irritation of the motor areas gave rise to tetanic contractions and clonic convulsions in a given joint; an increase in the strength of the current produced more violent movements which spread over the whole limb, and by intensifying the current still further, to half the body. Finally, on the application of a very strong current, the typical fit was produced with clonic spasms in all the body, unconsciousness, nystagmus, and rigidity of the pupils.

By irritating the frontal lobes of dogs, Richet

and Bernard produced vertigo and certain physical phenomena (snuffing, barking, and biting).

Taking these investigations as a basis, Jackson came to the conclusion that epileptic fits are due to a rapid and excessive explosion of the grey matter, which, instead of developing its force gradually, develops it all of a sudden because it is irritated. And as it has been shown conclusively that the disease can be manifested in such varied forms— vertigo, twitching of the muscles, sialorrhea, cephalalgia, fits of rage, and ferocious actions—which appear to be the equivalent of the typical seizure, individuals subject to these forms of neurosis should be classed as epileptics, even if they never experience the typical motor attack.

It is in this category, which may be called attenuated epilepsy, that we should place criminals, who in addition to the psychic and physical characteristics of the epileptic, possess others peculiar to themselves. Physical anomalies (plagiocephaly, microcephaly, macrocephaly, strabismus, facial and cranial asymmetry, prominent frontal sinuses, median occipital fossa, receding forehead, projecting ears, progeneismus, and badly shaped teeth) are characteristic both of criminals and epileptics, as was demonstrated in certain epileptics treated by my father (Figs. 14 and 15), and the same holds

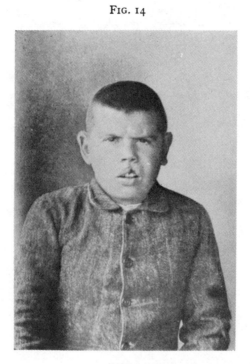

Fig. 14

An Epileptic Boy
(see page 60)

good of functional and histological anomalies. The histological anomaly discovered by Roncoroni in the frontal lobe of born criminals, consisting of the atrophy of the deep granular layer, the inversion of the pyramidal layers and small cells with enlargement and rarefaction of the pyramidal cells, and the existence of nervous cells in the white substance, is found in about the same proportion in cases of non-criminal epileptics. We find also in the same proportion in the field of vision of epileptics, as of born criminals, the anomaly discovered by Ottolenghi, consisting of peripheral scotoma intersecting the nearly uniform line of varying size common to normal eyes.

*Psychological Characteristics.* The complete identity of epileptics, born criminals and the morally insane becomes evident as soon as we study their psychology.

Epilepsy, congenital criminality, and moral insanity alone are capable of comprising in one clinical form intellectual divergencies which range from genius to imbecility. In epileptics, this divergence is sometimes manifested in one and the same person in the space of twenty-four hours. An individual at one time afflicted with loss of will-power and amnesia, and incapable of formulating the simplest notion, will shortly afterwards give expression to original ideas and reason logically.

Contradictions and exaggerations of sentiment are salient characteristics of epileptics as of born criminals and the morally insane. Quarrelsome, suspicious, and cynical individuals suddenly become gentle, respectful, and affectionate. The cynic expresses religious sentiments, and the man who has brutally ill-treated his first wife, kneels before the second. An epileptic observed by Tonnini fancied himself at times to be Napoleon; at others, he would lick the ground like the humblest slave.

The extreme excitability manifested by born criminals is shared by epileptics. Distrustful, intolerant, and incapable of sincere attachment, a gesture or a look is sufficient to infuriate them and incite them to the most atrocious deeds.

Epilepsy has a disastrous effect on the character. It destroys the moral sense, causes irritability, alters the sensations through constant hallucinations and delusions, deadens the natural feelings or leads them into morbid channels.

*Affection for Animals.* The hatred frequently manifested by criminals and epileptics towards the members of their own families is in many cases accompanied by an extraordinary fondness for animals as is shown by the cases of Caligula, Commodus, Lacenaire, Rosas, Dr. Francia, and La Sola,—who preferred kittens to her own children. A morally

Fig. 15

Fernando
Epileptic
(see page 60)

insane individual known to my father would spend months in training dogs, horses, birds, geese, and other fowls. He was wont to remark that all animals were friendly to him as though they recognised in him one of their own kind. Dostoyevsky's fellow-convicts showed great fondness for a horse, an eagle, and a number of geese. They were so attached to a goat that they wanted to gild its horns.

*Somnambulism.* This is a frequent characteristic of epileptics. Krafft–Ebing says:

" The seizure is often followed by a condition approaching somnambulism. The patient appears to have recovered consciousness, talks coherently, behaves in an orderly manner, and resumes his ordinary occupations. Yet he is not really conscious as is shown by the fact that, later he is entirely ignorant of what he has been doing during this stage. This peculiar state of mental daze may last a long time, sometimes during the whole interval between two seizures."

Many of the criminals observed by Dostoyevsky were given to gesticulating and talking agitatedly in their sleep.

Obscenity is a common characteristic. Kowalewsky (*Archivio di Psichiatria*, 1885) notes the resemblance between the reproductive act and the epileptic seizure, the tonic tension of the muscles, loss of consciousness and mydriasis in both cases, and remarks also on the frequency with which epileptic attacks are accompanied by sexual propensities.

The desire for sexual indulgence, like the taste for alcohol, is distinguished by the precocity peculiar to criminals and the morally insane. Precocious sexual instincts have been observed in children of four years, and in one case obscenity was manifested by an infant of one year.

Marro (*Annali di Freniatria*, 1890) describes a child of three years and ten months, who had exhibited signs of epilepsy from birth and was of a jealous, irascible disposition. He was in the habit of scratching and biting his brothers and sisters, knocking over the furniture, hiding things, and tearing his clothes, and when unable to hurt or annoy others, would vent his rage upon himself. If punished, he would continue his misdeeds in an underhand way.

Another child had been afflicted with convulsions from his earliest infancy, in consequence of which his character deteriorated, and while still a mere infant, he behaved with the utmost violence. He killed a cat, attempted to strangle his brother, and to set fire to the house.

Invulnerability, another characteristic common to criminals, has been observed by Tonnini in epileptics, whose wounds and injuries heal with astonishing rapidity, and he is inclined to regard this peculiarity in the light of a reversion to a stage

of evolut⁺ʲᴏn, at which animals like lizards and sala-
manders were ᵻble to replace severed joints by
new growths. This invulnerability is shared by all
degenerates: epileptics, imbeciles, and the morally
insane.

"One of these latter," says Tonnini, "tore out
his moustache bodily and with it a large piece of
skin. In a few days the wound was nearly healed."

Very characteristic is the almost automatic
tendency to destroy animate and inanimate objects,
which results in frequent wounding, suicides, and
homicides. This desire to destroy is also common to
children. Fernando P. (Fig. 15), an epileptic treated
by my father, when enraged was in the habit of
smashing all the furniture within his reach and
throwing the pieces over a wall some twenty-five
feet high.

Misdea, a regimental barber, to whom we shall
refer later, roused to fury by dismissal from his
post, broke four razors into small pieces with his
teeth. Another epileptic, Piz... used to break all
the crockery in his cell regularly every other day,
"just to give vent to his feelings."

This tendency to destroy everything in the cell
is common also to ordinary criminals.

*Cases of Moral Insanity with Latent Epileptic
Phenomena.* The following cases, which were treated

by my father and which were subject to careful observation and study, will serve to give a clear idea of the criminal form of epilepsy.

Subject: Giuliano Celestino, age 16. Yellow skin abundantly tattooed, absence of hair on face or body. Cranium: plagiocephaly on the left frontal and right parietal regions, obliquely-placed eyes, narrow forehead, prominent orbital arches, line of the mouth horizontal as in apes, lateral incisors of upper jaw resembling the canines with rugged margins, excessive zygomatic and maxillary development, tactile sensibility very obtuse, dolorific sensibility non-existent on the right, very obtuse on the left, rotular reflex action exaggerated on the right, very feeble on the left. Devoid of natural feeling. When asked if he was fond of his mother, he replied: "When she brings me cigars and money." When questioned concerning his crimes he showed neither shame nor confusion. On the contrary, he confessed with a smile that when only ten he had tried to kill his youngest brother, who was then an infant in the cradle, and when hindered by his mother, had struck and bitten her. His father was a drunkard afflicted with syphilis, and Giuliano had suffered from epilepsy from the age of seven. At this age he began to indulge in alcohol and self-abuse, and stole from his parents in order to buy sweets. He appears to have been subject to an ambulatory mania, which caused him to wander aimlessly about the country, and if kept within doors he would let himself down from the windows, climb up the chimney, or, failing in these attempts to escape, would break the furniture and attract the attention of the neighbours by his terrific yells. From the age of eight, despite his parents' efforts to apprentice him, he was always immediately dismissed by his employers. He ran away with a strolling company of acrobats, and later apprenticed himself to a butcher in order to revel in the horrors of the slaughter-house. At fifteen he was confined in a reformatory, where he twice attempted to escape and to set fire to the building, and was sentenced to two years' imprisonment. For the space of a few days, he appears to have suffered from epileptic attacks, although in a masked form, accompanied by various attempts at suicide. These were renewed every other month for a whole year. When asked what he would do for a living when released, he would reply laughingly that there was plenty of money in other people's pockets.

L... a morally insane subject, age 16, native of Turin, the son of an aged, but extremely respectable man. Height 1.50 m., weight, 46.2 kg., with abundant hair, and down on the forehead, incisors crowded together, excessive development of the canines, and exaggerated orbital angle of the frontal bone. He was entirely devoid of affection for his family, remarking cynically that he was fond of his father when he gave him money and did not worry him. Sometimes he kicked the poor old man and otherwise abused him. When unable to obtain money, he would smash all the furniture in the house, until, for the sake of economy, his family gave him what he wanted. In order to get a five-pound note from money-lenders he would sign promissory notes for ten times that amount. He changed his ideas from one hour to another. Sometimes he wanted to enter the army, at others to emigrate to France, etc. When only fourteen he frequented houses of ill-fame, where he played the bully.

Although this case may be regarded as a typical instance of moral insanity, there were apparently no symptoms of vertigo or convulsions. At the age of sixteen, however, while suffering from rheumatism, this subject tried to throw himself from the balcony of his bedroom at the same hour three nights running. After this he seems to have suffered from amnesia.

These frenzied attempts at self-destruction, which seem to have taken the place of the epileptic seizure, were related to my father casually by the boy's mother; but in other cases, similar incidents, although of the utmost importance to the criminologist, often pass unnoticed.

In the *Actes du Congrès d'Anthropologie*, Angelucci describes another typical case of epileptic moral insanity. E. G. (brother a criminal epileptic, father a sufferer from cancer) was sentenced several times for assaulting people often without motive. Tattooed with the figure of a naked woman, microcephalous (39.2 cubic inches = 589 c.c.), having cranial and facial asymmetry, he was vain, deceitful, and violent, and made great show of scepticism although he wore a great many medals of the Virgin. This subject was over twenty-five when the first epileptic seizure took place.

The connection between epilepsy and crime is one of derivation rather than identity. Epilepsy represents the genus of which criminality and moral insanity are the species.

The born criminal is an epileptic, inasmuch as he possesses the anatomical, skeletal, physiognomical, psychological, and moral characteristics peculiar to the recognised form of epilepsy, and sometimes also its motorial phenomena, although at rare intervals. More frequently he exhibits its substitutes (vertigo, twitching, sialorrhea, emotional attacks). But the criminal epileptic possesses other characteristics peculiar to himself; in particular, that desire of evil for its own sake, which is unknown to ordinary epileptics. In view of this fact this form of epilepsy must be considered apart from the purely nervous anomaly, both in the clinical diagnosis and the methods of cure and social prophylaxis.

Moreover, the nervous anomaly, which in the case of criminals appears on the scene from time to time, accentuating the criminal tendency till it reaches the atavistic form and producing morbid complications which sometimes prove fatal, serves to point out the true nature of the disease and to emphasise the fact that while it is attenuated so far as motor attacks are concerned, it is aggravated on the other hand by criminal impulses, which render the patient semi-immune and permit him a longer and less troubled existence, but provoke a constant brain irritation, which clouds and disturbs his intellectual and moral nature.

In order better to understand these two forms of epilepsy, we must recall two analogous forms of another and equally multiform disease, tuberculosis in its forms of quick consumption and scrofula. The etiology is identical and the symptoms frequently alike, but while the latter proceeds very slowly and allows the patient a long life, the former is rapid and severs life in its prime.

In motory epilepsy, the irritation is manifested on a sudden, but leaves the mind healthy in the interval, although the attacks may lead to rapid dementia. In criminal epilepsy this irritation does not break out in violent seizures and is compatible with a long life, but it changes the whole physical and psychic complexion of the individual.

The epileptic origin of criminality explains many characteristics of the criminal, the genesis of which was previously obscure. Many of the moral and physical peculiarities of born criminals and the morally insane may be classed as professional characteristics acquired through the habit of evil-doing, especially the naso-labial and zygomatic wrinkles, cynical expression, tapering fingers, etc. Many anomalies also in the bones, hair, ears, eyes, and the monstrous development of the jaws and teeth, must be explained by arrested development in the fifth or sixth month of intra-uterine existence, corresponding to the characteristics of inferior races by the usual law of ontogeny which recapitulates phylogeny. But there is a final series of anomalies, the origin of which was formerly wrapped in mystery: plagiocephaly, sclerosis, the thickening of the meninges, cranial asymmetry, and other changes in the cerebral layers, which can be explained only by a disease altering precociously the whole cerebral conformation, as is exactly the case in epilepsy.

The born criminal is an epileptic, not however afflicted with the common form of this disease, but with a special kind. The pathological basis, the etiology, and the anatomical and psychological characteristics are identical, but there are many differences. While in the ordinary form motor anomalies are very common, in the criminal form they are very rare, while in ordinary epilepsy the mental explosions are accompanied by unconsciousness, in the other form they are weakened and spread over the whole existence, and consciousness is, relatively speaking, preserved; and while, finally, the ordinary epileptic has not always the tendency to do evil for its own sake—nay, may even achieve holiness—in the hidden form the bent towards evil endures from birth to death. The perversity concentrated in one second in the motor attack, is attenuated in the second form, but spread over the whole existence. We have therefore an epilepsy *sui generis*, a variety of epilepsy which may be called criminal.

Thus the primitive idea of crime has become organic and complete. The criminal is only a diseased person, an epileptic, in whom the cerebral malady, begun in some cases during prenatal existence, or later, in consequence of some infection or cerebral poisoning, produces, together with certain signs of physical degeneration in the skull, face, teeth, and brain, a return to the early brutal egotism natural to primitive races, which manifests itself in homicide, theft, and other crimes.

# CHAPTER III

## *THE INSANE CRIMINAL*

### General Forms of Criminal Lunacy

EPILEPTIC born criminals and the morally insane may be classed as lunatics under certain aspects, but only by the scientific observer and professional psychologist. Outside these two forms, there is an important series of offenders, who are not criminals from birth, but become such at a given moment of their lives, in consequence of an alteration of the brain, which completely upsets their moral nature and makes them unable to discriminate between right and wrong. They are really insane; that is, entirely without responsibility for their actions.

Nearly every class of mental derangement contributes a special form of crime.

*The Idiot* is prompted by paroxysms of rage to commit murderous attacks on his fellow-creatures. His exaggerated sexual propensities incite him to rape, and his childish delight at the sight of flames, to arson.

*The Imbecile*, or weak-minded individual, yields to his first impulse, or, dominated by the influence of others, becomes an accomplice in the hope of some trivial reward.

The victims of *Melancholia* are driven to suicide by suppressed grief, precordial agitation, or hallucinations. Sometimes the suicidal attempt is indirect and takes the form of the murder of some important personage or their own kin, in the hope that their own condemnation may follow, or it is to save those dear to them from the miseries of life.

Persons afflicted with *General Paralysis* frequently steal, in the belief that everything they see belongs to them, or because they are incapable of understanding the meaning of property. If accused of theft, they deny their guilt or assert that the stolen articles have been hidden on their persons by others. They are inclined to forgery and fraudulent bankruptcy, and when their misdeeds are brought home to them they show no shame. Unnatural sexual offences and crimes against the authorities are also common. While they are seldom guilty of murder, they frequently commit arson, through carelessness, or with the idea of destroying their homes because they think them too small, or wish to get rid of the vermin in them, such as rats.

The sufferer from *Dementia* forgets his promises, however serious they may be. Cerebral irritability often leads him to commit violent acts, homicide, etc.

In some cases, mental alienation is manifested in a mania for litigation, which urges the sufferer to offend statesmen, state lawyers, and judges.

A common symptom of *Pellagra* is the tendency to unpremeditated murder or suicide, without the slightest cause. The sight of water suggests drowning, in the form of murder or suicide.

Young persons at the approach of puberty and women subject to amenorrhea often exhibit a tendency to arson and crimes of an erotic nature. Similar tendencies are sometimes displayed during pregnancy, and an inclination to theft is not uncommon.

Maniacs are prone to satyriasis and bacchanalian excesses. They commit rape and indecent acts in public and often appropriate strange objects, hair or wearing apparel, with the idea of obtaining means to satisfy their vices, either because they are unconscious of doing wrong or because, like true megalomaniacs, they believe the stolen goods to be their own property. Sometimes a feverish activity prompts them to steal; "I felt a kind of uneasiness, a demon in my fingers," said one, "which forced me to move them and carry off something."

Monomaniacs, especially if subject to hallucinations, frequently manifest a tendency to homicide, either to escape imaginary persecutions or in obedience to equally imaginary injunctions. The same motives prompt them to commit special kinds of theft and arson. Na . . . (see Fig. 16) murdered his friend without any reason, after suffering from delusions for one year.

The characteristics of insane criminals are so marked that it is not difficult to distinguish them from habitual delinquents. They seldom show any fear of the penalty incurred nor do they try to escape. They take little trouble to hide their misdeeds, or to get rid of any clue. If poisoners, they leave poison about in their victim's room; if forgers, they take no trouble to make their signatures appear genuine; if thieves, they exhibit stolen goods in public, or appropriate them in the presence of witnesses. They frequently manifest unbounded rage and assault those present, entirely forgetting the stolen objects. Once their crime is accomplished, not only do they give themselves no trouble to hide it, but are prone to confess it immediately, and are eager to talk about it, saying with satisfaction that they feel relieved at what they have done, that they have obeyed the order of superior beings and consider their actions praiseworthy. They deny that they are insane, or if they admit it in some cases, it is only because they are persuaded to do so by their lawyers or fellow-prisoners. And even then, they are ready at the first opportunity to contradict the idea, eulogising and exaggerating their criminal acts.

A full confession in court is not uncommon, and in the case of impulsive monomaniacs, epileptics, and insane inebriates, the descriptions are full of characteristic expressions, showing what was the offender's state of mind when dominated by criminal frenzy.

Rom..., an impulsive monomaniac, who stabbed an acquaintance, felt "the blood rushing to his head, which seemed to be in flames."

Tixier narrates that, on seeing the old man he afterward murdered pass him on a country road, "something went to his head." Frequently such criminals are quick to give themselves up to justice.

*Antecedents.* Unlike the ordinary offender, insane criminals are often perfectly law-abiding up to the moment of the crime.

*Motive.* Perhaps the greatest difference between born criminals and insane criminals lies in the motive for the act, which in the case of the latter is not only entirely disproportionate to it, but nearly always absurd and depends far less on personal susceptibility.

Here are a few typical cases: A father fancies he hears a voice bidding him kill his favourite child. He goes home, has the little victim dressed in its best clothes and cuts off its head with perfect calmness. A lady, ignorant of horticulture, plants some flowers on her husband's grave. A day or two later, noticing that they are drooping, she imagines that the gardener has watered them with boiling water, and after reproaching him bitterly, wounds him with a pair of scissors.

These unfortunate beings frequently show perfect mental clearness before the crime and even in the act of striking the fatal blow; yet their action is purely instinctive and not prompted by passion or any other cause. Although such individuals appear to reason, can it be said that they are in full possession of their mental faculties? If they are, how shall we explain the wholesale destruction of those they hold most dear? A husband kills the wife to whom he is sincerely attached; a father, the son he loves most; or a mother, the infant at her breast.

Such an extraordinary phenomenon can only be explained by a sudden suspension of the intellectual and moral faculties and of the powers of the will.

## Special Forms of Criminal Insanity

### ALCOHOLISM

In addition to these casual forms of lunacy, in which the individual is led to commit crime by a momentary alteration of his moral nature, we find other forms which might be called specific, because the criminal act forms the culminating point of the malady. The sufferers from these forms are less easily distinguished from ordinary criminals and normal persons than are the lunatics of whom we have just spoken. These mental diseases, which should be studied separately, are alcoholism, hysteria, and epilepsy.

It is well known that temporary drunkenness may transform an honest, peacable individual into a rowdy, a murderer, or a thief.

Gall narrates the case of a certain Petri, who manifested homicidal tendencies when excited by alcohol. Locatelli mentions a workman of thirty, who, when under the influence of drink, would smash everything around him and stab the companions who sought to restrain his drunken fury. Ladelci and Carmignani cite the case of a miner, who was repeatedly arrested for drunken brawls, and when reproved replied: "I cannot help it. As soon as I drink, I must start fighting."

Very characteristic is the case of a certain Papor...
who was imprisoned for some time at Turin.
His father was a drunkard and ill treated his wife.
The son became a soldier, then an excise officer,
fireman, and finally nurse in an infirmary, and was
known as a respectable, temperate man. In 1876,
he was transferred to the Island of Lipari, where
malvoisie only costs 25 centimes a litre, and there
he acquired a taste for wine, without, however,
drinking to excess. But a year later, a change in
the hospital regulations gave him longer hours of
leisure, and he began to drink deeply. In 1881, while
intoxicated, he accosted a sportsman and pretending
to be a police officer, ordered him to give up his gun.
At that moment he was arrested by a genuine
constable and taken to the barracks, where he was
sentenced, without any one's observing his drunken
condition. After his release, he committed other
offences of the same type, which were followed by
confession and repentance.

*Chronic Alcoholism.* The phenomena developed
by chronic inebriety are, however, still more important from the point of view of the criminologist
than the immediate effects of alcohol on certain
constitutions.

*Physical and Functional Characteristics of Chronic
Inebriety.* The habitual drunkard rarely exhibits

traces of congenital degeneracy, but frequently that of an acquired character, especially paresis, facial hemiparesis, slight exophthalmia (see Fig. 6), inequality of the pupils, insensibility to touch and pain, which is often unilateral, especially in the tongue, thermoanalgesia, hyperæsthesia, experienced at various points not corresponding to the nervous territories and modified spontaneously or by esthesiogenic agents (Grasset), alphalgesia (sensation of pain at contact with painless bodies), a deficiency of urea in the urine, out of proportion to the general state of nourishment, and a proneness of the symptoms to return after trauma, poisoning, agitation, or serious illness.

The gravest phenomena, however, are atrophy or degeneration in the liver, heart, stomach, seminal canaliculi, and central nervous system, which give rise to serious functional disturbances; most of all, in the digestion—as manifested by the characteristic gastric catarrh, matutinal vomit and cramp—and in the reproductive system, with resulting impotence.

*Psychic Disturbances—Hallucinations.* The most frequent and precocious symptoms are delusions and hallucinations, generally of a gloomy or even of a terrible nature, and extremely varied and fleeting, which, like dreams, in nearly every in-

Fig. 16

Italian Criminal
A Case of Alcoholism
(see page 82)

stance arise from recent and strong impressions. The most characteristic hallucinations are those which persuade the patient that he experiences the contact of disgusting vermin, corpses, or other horrible objects. He is gnawed by imaginary worms, burnt by matches, or persecuted by spies and the police.

The strange pathological conditions resulting from chronic alcoholism give rise to other fearful hallucinations. Cutaneous anæsthesia and alcoholic anaphrodisia make the sufferers fancy they have lost the generative organs, nose, legs, etc.; dyspepsia, exhaustion, and paresis, that they have been poisoned or are being persecuted. The reaction following excessively prolonged stimuli causes furious lypemania and gloomy fancies. Sometimes chronic inebriates believe that they are accused of imaginary crimes and loaded with chains amid heaps of corpses. They implore mercy and try to kill themselves in order to escape from their shame; or they remain motionless, bewildered, and terrified. Not infrequently, because of the profound faith, which, unlike many other lunatics, they have in their hallucinations, they pass from melancholy broodings to a fit of mad energy, often of a homicidal or suicidal nature. They imagine they are struggling with thieves or wild beasts and hurl themselves from the window or rush naked through the streets, killing the first person that crosses their path. In some, this delirium of energy breaks out suddenly like an epileptic attack, which it resembles in its brevity and intensity. With hair standing on end, they rush about like savage beasts, grinding their teeth, biting, rending their clothes, or tearing up the sod, or hurling themselves from some height. These symptoms are preceded by vertigo, periodical cephalalgia, and flushing of the face, and are manifested more frequently by those who are already predisposed through trauma to the head, or through typhus or heredity, or after great agitation and prolonged fasting, and often bear no relation to the quantity of alcohol imbibed, which may be small, or to the general physical state; but depend on cerebral irritation caused by chronic alcoholism. The attacks may disappear in a few hours without leaving the slightest recollection in the mind of the patient (Krafft–Ebing, p. 182). They are, in short, a species of disguised epilepsy, and thus they may well be styled, since true alcoholic epilepsy is noted in many inebriates, specially in absinthe-drinkers.

*Apathy.* Another characteristic almost invariably found in inebriates who have committed a crime, is a strange apathy and indifference, a total lack of concern regarding their state—a trait common also to ordinary criminals, but in a less marked degree. They make themselves at home in prison without showing the faintest interest in their trial or in the offence which has caused their arrest, and only when brought before the judge do they rouse themselves for a moment from their lethargy.

A well-educated man, after a varied career as doctor, chemist, and clerk, during which time he had been constantly dismissed from his posts for drunkenness, met a policeman in the street and killed him, in the belief that the officer wanted to arrest him. When taken to prison, the first thing he did was to write to his mother begging her to send him some pomade. When interrogated, he informed the examining magistrate that the interrogatory was useless, since he had already chosen a fresh trade, that of photographer. It was only after several months of total abstinence in prison, that he began to come to his senses and to realise the gravity of his situation. (Tardieu, *De la Folie,* 1870.)

*Contrast between Apathy and Impulsiveness.* This apathy alternates with strange impulses, which, although strongly at variance with the patient's former habits, he is unable to control, even when he is aware that they are criminal.

*Crimes peculiar to Inebriates.* Since modification of the reproductive organs is a common cause of hallucinations, inebriate criminals frequently suffer from a species of erotic delirium, during which they murder those whom they believe guilty of offences against themselves—generally their wives or mistresses. This is partly owing to the sexual nature of their hallucinations and partly to the wretchedness of their homes, which are in such striking contrast to the rosy dreams inspired by alcohol and which tend to increase the melancholy natural to drunkards. They imagine they are being deceived and their impotence derided, the most innocent gestures being interpreted as deadly insults.

In the prison at Turin, my father had under observation two of these unfortunate beings, one a man of sixty and the other quite young. Both had murdered their wives with the most revolting cruelty, because they believed them to be unfaithful, although in reality both the women led blameless lives.

*Course of the Disease.* The continued abuse of alcohol ends at last in complete dementia or general pseudo-paralysis. The body is at first obese, but rapidly loses flesh, the skin becomes greasy and damp, owing to hypersecretion of the sebaceous and sudoriparous glands, and soils the garments. Memory becomes enfeebled, speech uncertain and defective (dysarthria), the association of ideas sluggish, sensibility blunted, perception confused, judgment erroneous, and every species of regular and continued application impossible. The earlier hallucinations reappear, but in a less vivid form and only at long intervals; then paralysis more or less rapidly becomes general and ends in death.

### EPILEPSY

We have spoken of this disease in another chapter and have shown that the born criminal is in reality an epileptic, in whom the malady, instead of manifesting itself suddenly in strange muscular contortions or terrible spasms, develops slowly in continual brain irritation, which causes the individual thus affected to reproduce the ferocious egotism natural to primitive savages, irresistibly bent on harming others.

But besides these epileptics, who are morally insane from their birth and pass their lives in prisons and lunatic asylums, without any one being able to mark the exact boundary between their perversity and their irresponsibility; besides these individuals, whom society has a right, nay a moral obligation, to remove from its midst because they are ever a source of danger there are those who are afflicted with other forms of epilepsy;—forms in which irritation is manifested in seizures exactly similar to the typical convulsive fit, which they resemble also with regard to variation in intensity and duration. Generally speaking, they are likewise accompanied by complete loss of memory and consciousness, but in some cases there may be partial or complete consciousness, and yet the sufferer is not responsible for his actions. This variety of epilepsy, termed by Samt psychic epilepsy (epilepsy with psychic seizures), manifests itself at long intervals, sometimes only once, but more frequently twice or thrice in the course of a lifetime, and during the attack the personality of the individual undergoes a complete change.

The attack is described by Samt as follows: During the seizure, the individual behaves like a somnambulist. Sometimes he is dazed, mute, and immovable; at others, he talks incessantly; at still others, he goes on with his ordinary occupations, travelling, reading, and writing: but in every case his personality suffers a complete metamorphosis, his habits, actions, and even handwriting assume a different character. Sometimes he is seized by a mania for walking and tramps for miles; at others, he undertakes interminable railway journeys. Tissié (*Les aliénés voyageurs*, 1887) cites cases of epileptics who travelled from Paris to Bombay, who covered 71 kilometres on foot, and who wandered unconscious for 31 months.

Sometimes epilepsy is manifested only by the tendency to undertake purposeless journeys, as in the case of Ferretti and a certain M... who visited the Mahdi in Africa and from thence travelled aimlessly to Australia.

This ambulatory form of epilepsy is very common amongst lads of fourteen or fifteen. Scarcely a week passes without the police receiving information from parents that their son has disappeared from home with only a few pence in his pocket. The wanderer is discovered later, frequently in some small provincial town, which he has reached after tramping aimlessly for days, sleeping in barns, and living on charity. When questioned, the boy usually displays total ignorance regarding all that has happened to him during the interval.

Dr. Maccabruni in his *Notes on Hidden Forms of Epilepsy*, 1886, narrates the case of an epileptic, who during childhood received an injury to his skull. Later, he started out on a series of wanderings to Venice, Padua, Rome, Milan, Monaco, and Mentone. His journeys, especially those to distant parts, were undertaken in a state of unconsciousness and generally a short time before the commencement of a fit.

These attacks may last any length of time, from a few minutes to several months. In one of the cases observed by my father, the attack lasted a fortnight. The patient, a young officer with whom we were personally acquainted, was one of the quietest persons possible, but suddenly he was seized with a mania for writing innumerable letters, especially on stamped paper, in exaggeratedly large writing very different from his usual style. These letters, which were full of absurdities, were posted by the writer from the different towns he passed through on his aimless journeyings, which lasted a whole fortnight. During one of these seizures, he was arrested as a deserter and was unable to give any explanation of his conduct.

In this particular patient, the disease assumed the mild form of absurd letters and still more absurd journeys, but other individuals in the same state may commit criminal acts like homicide, equally without reason or gain to themselves. Once the fit is passed, these unfortunate individuals have generally no recollection of their past actions, and since in their normal state they are quiet, law-abiding persons, it is extremely difficult to trace back the deed to the right source, or to discover the disease, because they show no other symptoms of epilepsy, apart from the particular criminal act.

Samt describes a still more complicated form of this psychic seizure, in which the personality is

altered without there being any loss of consciousness. In a case of this kind, a servant, after forty
years of faithful service, murdered his old mistress
during the night, having previously cut all the bell-
wires to prevent communication with the other
servants. He escaped with some valuables, but
returned in a few days and gave himself up to the
police, to whom he gave a detailed account of his
crime without showing either horror or remorse.
He was tried and condemned, and a few months
later was again seized with epileptic fits during one
of which he died. Samt, who saw him in this state,
came to the conclusion that the murder had been
committed during a similar seizure and he was able
to prove that attacks of this kind are not necessarily
accompanied by loss of consciousness.

As in the above case, these psychic attacks are
sometimes accompanied by an insatiable thirst for
blood, destruction and violence of all kinds, as well
as by an extraordinary development of muscular
strength with apparent lucidity of mind. They
may last from a few minutes to half an hour, after
which the patient falls into a sound sleep and forgets everything that has happened, or else retains
only a vague recollection.

Such was the case of the epileptic Misdea, which
first suggested to my father the idea of a link between

crime and epilepsy. As this case has become famous in the annals of crime in Italy, it will perhaps be of interest to the reader. Misdea, the son of degenerate parents, manifested a series of typical epileptic anomalies—asymmetry, vaso-motor disturbances, impulsiveness, ferocity, etc. At the age of twenty, while serving in the army, for some trivial motive he suddenly attacked and killed his superior officer and eight or ten soldiers who tried to overpower him. Finally he was bound and placed in a cell, where he fell into a sound slumber and on awaking had entirely forgotten what he had done. He was condemned to death, but my father, who examined him medically, was able to prove conclusively that the crime had been committed during an attack of epilepsy.

The physical and psychic characters of this class of epileptic are those common to all non-criminal epileptics, and indeed we are justified in considering them insane rather than criminal, because, with the exception of the attack, which assumes this terrible form, they do not manifest criminal tendencies.

### HYSTERIA

Hysteria is a disease allied to epilepsy, of which it appears to be a milder form, and is much more common among women than men in the ratio of twenty to one. The disease may frequently be traced to hereditary influences, similar to those found in epilepsy, transmitted by epileptic, neurotic, or inebriate parents, frequently also, to some traumatic or toxic influence, such as typhus, meningitis, a blow, a fall, or fright.

*Physical Characteristics.* These are fewer than in epileptics. The most common peculiarities are small, obliquely-placed eyes of timid glance, pale, elongated face, crowded or loosened teeth, nervous movements of the face and hands, facial asymmetry, and black hair.

*Functional Characteristics.* These are of great importance. Hysterical subjects manifest special sensibility to the contact of certain metals such as magnetised iron, copper, and gold. Characteristic symptoms are the insensibility of the larynx or the sensation of a foreign body in it (*globus hystericus*), neuralgic pains, which disappear with extreme suddenness, reappearing often on the side opposite that where they were first felt, the prevalence of sensory and motor anomalies on one side (hemianæsthesia), the confusion of different colours (dyschromatopsia); greater sensibility in certain parts of the body, such as the ovary and the breasts, which when subjected to pressure give rise to neuropathic phenomena (hysterogenous points); a sense of pleasure in the presence of pain, the abolition of pharyngeal reflex action, the absence of the sensation of warmth in certain parts of the body and a tendency to the so-called attacks of "hysterics." These characteristics, which are closely allied, if not precisely similar to those of epilepsy, are preceded by a number of premonitory symptoms—hallucinations, sudden change of character, contractions, laryngeal spasms, strabismus, frequent spitting, inordinate laughter or yawning, cardiac palpitations, loss of strength, trembling, anæsthesia and (just before the attack,) pains in some fixed spot, generally in the head, ovary, or nape of the neck.

*Psychology.* The psychological manifestations of hysterical subjects are of still greater interest and importance.

They show, on the whole, a fair amount of intelligence, although little power of concentration. In disposition they are profoundly egotistical and so preoccupied with their own persons that they will do anything to arouse attention and obtain notoriety. They are exceedingly impressionable, therefore easily roused to anger and cruelty, and are prone to take sudden and unreasonable likes and dislikes. They are fickle and easily swayed. They take special delight in slandering others, and when unable to excite public notice by unfounded accusations, to

which they resort as a means of revenge, they em-
bitter the lives of those around them by continual
quarrels and dissensions.

*Susceptibility to Suggestion.* Of still greater importance for the criminologist is the facility with
which hysterical women are dominated by hypnotic
suggestion. Their wills become entirely subordinated to that of the hypnotiser, by whose influence
they can be induced to believe that they have
changed their sex so that they forthwith adopt
habits of the opposite sex, or to entertain *idées
fixes*—strange, impulsive, or even criminal ideas.
They are, in fact, obedient automatons when under
hypnotic influence, but they cannot be prevailed
upon to perform acts contrary to their nature, to
commit crimes or reveal secrets entrusted to them,
if they are naturally upright.

*Variability.* Mobility of mood is a still more
salient characteristic of hysteria. The subject
passes with extraordinary rapidity from laughter
to tears "like children," says Richet, "who laugh
immoderately before their tears are dry."

"For one hour," says Sydenham, "they will be
irascible and discontented; the next, they are cheer-
ful and follow their friends about with all the signs
of the old attachment."

Their sensibility is affected by the most trifling

causes. A word will grieve them like some real misfortune. Their impulses are not lacking in intellectual control, but are followed by action with excessive rapidity. Although of such changeable disposition, they are subject to fixed ideas, to which they cling with a kind of cataleptic intensity. A woman will be dumb or motionless for months, on the pretext that speech or motion would injure her. But this is the only form of constancy they exhibit, otherwise they are indolent by nature. Sometimes they will show activity for a few days only to relapse again into idleness.

*Erotomania.* This is almost a pathognomonical symptom and is shown in hallucinations and nightmares of an erotic character, preceded by epigastric aura. This erotomania is so impulsive that hysterical women frequently engage in a *liaison*, from a desire of adventure or of experiencing sudden emotions. The criminality of the hysterical is always connected with the sexual functions.

Of twenty-one women found guilty of slander, nine made false accusations of rape, four accused their husbands of sexual violence, and one of sodomy. Such accusations, when made by minors, are generally full of disgusting details, which would be repugnant to any adult.

*Mendacity.* Another peculiarity of hysterical

women is the irresistible tendency to lie, which leads them to utter senseless .falsehoods just for the pleasure of deceiving and making believe. They sham suicide and sickness or write anonymous letters full of inventions. Many, from motives of spite or vanity, accuse servants of dishonesty, in order to revel in their disgrace and imprisonment. The favourite calumny, however, is always an accusation of indecent behaviour, sometimes made against their fathers and brothers, but generally against a priest or medical man. The accusations, in most cases, are so strange and fantastic as to be quite unworthy of belief, but sometimes, unfortunately, they obtain credence. The commonest method adopted for spreading these calumnies is by means of anonymous letters. In one case, a young girl of twenty-five belonging to a distinguished family, pestered a respectable priest with love-letters and shortly afterwards accused him of seduction. Another girl of eighteen informed the Attorney for the State that she had frequently been the victim of immoral priests and accused one of her female cousins of complicity. According to her story, while praying at church, a certain Abbot R... took her into the sacristy and entreated her to elope with him to Spain. She refused indignantly, and hoping to soften her, he twice stabbed himself in her presence, whereat she fainted, and on recovering consciousness, found the priest at her feet, begging forgiveness. She further accused the same cousin of having taken her to a convent, where she was seduced by a priest, the nuns acting as accomplices. A subsequent medical examination proved that no seduction had taken place and that she was suffering from hysteria.

In another case, a girl of sixteen, the daughter of an Italian general, complained to her father that a certain lieutenant, her neighbour at table, had used indecent language to her. Shortly afterwards, a shower of anonymous letters troubled the peace of the household—declarations of love addressed to the girl's mother and threats to the daughter. It was discovered that the girl herself was the writer of all these letters.

Anonymous letter-writing is so common among hysterical persons, that it may be considered a pathognomonical characteristic. The handwriting is of a peculiar character, or rather it shows a peculiar tendency to vary from excessive size to extreme smallness, a characteristic we have noticed in epileptics.

*Delirium.* Hysterical, like epileptic, subjects often suffer from melancholia or monomaniacal delirium. Indeed, according to Morel, this symptom is more frequent when the other morbid phenomena are absent.

Psychic hysteria, like epilepsy, may exist unaccompanied by the characteristic hysterical attack, and then, as is the case with epilepsy, it is most dangerous to society.

In conclusion, although up to the present, medical men have been disposed to consider hysteria as a disease distinct from epilepsy, careful study of this malady inclined my father to class it as a variation of epilepsy, prevalent among women, who in this disease, as in many others, manifest an attenuated form.

# CHAPTER IV

## *CRIMINALOIDS*

W E have seen how, owing to disease, alcoholism and epilepsy, physically and psychically degenerate individuals make their appearance in a community of normal persons. But a large proportion of the crimes committed cannot be attributed to lunatics, epileptics, or the morally insane, nor do all criminals show that aggregate of atavistic and morbid characters,—the cruelty and bestial insensibility of the savage, the impulsiveness of the epileptic, the licentiousness, delusions, and impetuosity of the madman,—which we find united in the born criminal.

According to statistics obtained by my father, the share contributed to the sum total of criminality by this latter type is only 33%, which appears to be a magic figure for the criminal, since it corresponds to the percentage of the histological anomaly discovered by Roncoroni and to that of all important anomalies, including those of the field of vision. But besides this percentage of born criminals, doomed even before birth to a career of crime, whom all educational efforts fail to redeem and who therefore should be segregated at once; besides the epileptic, hysterical, and inebriate lunatics and those insane from alcoholisation, of whom we have already spoken, there remain a number of criminals, amounting to a full half, in whom the virus is, so to speak, attenuated, who, although they are epileptoids, suffer from a milder form of the disease, so that without some adequate cause (*causa criminis*) criminality is not manifested. The inhibitory centres are somewhat obtuse, but not altogether absent, so that a healthy environment, careful training, habits of industry, the inculcation of moral and humane sentiments may prevent these individuals from yielding to dishonest impulses, provided always that no special temptation to sin comes in their path.

We have said that education is not sufficient to convert a criminal into an honest man. Conversely, trials and difficulties and the want of education are powerless to make a criminal of an honest individual. Hypnotism, the most powerful means of suggestion possible, cannot induce a good man to commit a crime during the hypnotic sleep, but vicious training has an enormous influence on weak natures, who are candidates for good or evil according to circumstances. Such individuals were classified by my father as *criminaloids*.

*Physical Characteristics*. Criminaloids have no special skeletal, anatomical, or functional peculiarities. As the criminaloid represents a milder type of the born criminal, he may possess the same physical defects in the skull, hair, beard, ears, eyes, teeth, lips, joints, hands, and feet, as well as all the sensory anomalies, lessened sensibility to touch and pain, hyper-sensibility to the magnet and barometrical variations, etc.; but all these anomalies are never found in the same proportion as in born criminals; that is, criminaloids never manifest the aggregate of physical and psychic peculiarities which distinguish born criminals and the morally insane. On the other hand, we find in criminaloids certain characteristics, such as premature greyness and baldness, etc., which are never exhibited by the born criminal. The real distinction between the criminaloid and the born criminal is psychological rather than physical.

*Psychological Characteristics*. The difference between born criminals and criminaloids becomes apparent directly on considering the age at which the latter enter on their anti-social career and the motives which cause them to adopt it. While the born criminal begins to perpetrate crimes from the very cradle, so to speak, and always for very trivial motives, the criminaloid commits his initial offence later in life and always for some adequate reason.

A criminal of this attenuated type, a certain Salvador, without cranial or facial anomalies, had led an honest life for many years, but on returning home after a prolonged absence on business, he found his house ransacked by his wife, who had deserted him. From that time he seems to have deliberately adopted a career of dishonesty, as the leader of a band of thieves.

In another case, an engraver who showed no pathological anomalies, except excessive frontal sinuses, was ordered by a society to strike a medal for them. This happened to be exactly similar to a coin current in his country and the coincidence incited him to the making of counterfeit coin.

But the most characteristic case, which aroused much interest in its time, is that of Olivo. He was a man of handsome appearance, with normal olfactory acuteness and sensibility to touch and pain. He had, however, inherited from neurotic and insane forebears secondary epileptic phenomena, which subsequently developed into convulsive epilepsy, and certain indications of degeneracy (facial and cranial asymmetry, abnormal capillary vortices and length of arm, scotoma in the field of vision and exaggerated tendinous reflex action). Up to the age of thirty he led an irreproachable life; in fact, he was scrupulous to excess, and this, coupled with pronounced conceit and stinginess, was his only fault. He married a woman of common origin, who was not really depraved, but she was coarse and unfaithful, and, worst of all in his eyes, unscrupulous and wasteful. These defects, and her habits of lying and trickery embittered the poor man's existence. One night, feeling very ill, probably owing to an approaching seizure, he appealed to his wife for assistance and received an unfeeling reply, whereupon he sprang out of bed, picked up a knife and stabbed her. Afterwards he fell into a deep sleep. In order to obliterate all traces of the crime, he cut the corpse into small pieces, packed it into a portmanteau and threw it into the sea. Two months later, when he was arrested, he immediately made a full confession, showing deep repentance and sincere attachment to his victim, whose merits he celebrated in a poem of his own composition. At the trial, he made no attempt to defend himself; during the hearing of evidence, which appeared greatly to agitate him, he was seized with an epileptic fit. He was absolved by the jury and returned to his former peaceful occupation of bookkeeper, nor did he again come into conflict with the law.

*Reluctance to Commit Crimes.* Another trait characteristic of criminaloids is the hesitation they show before committing a crime, especially the first time, when it is not done, as in the above mentioned case, during an epileptic seizure.

Feuerbach's fine collection contains a description of the brothers Kleinroth, whose father cruelly ill-treated and starved his wife and family while lavishing his money on low women and their bastards. The sons were unwilling to run away and leave the invalid mother to bear the brunt of her husband's fury, and while they were in this terrible situation, a certain individual offered to assassinate their tormentor. After great hesitation this offer was accepted; when arrested, the youths immediately confessed their complicity and manifested deep repentance.

*Confession.* The criminaloid is easily induced to confess his misdeed.

A certain C. . . on returning from abroad, found his former mistress married to his father. The pair resumed their liaison, but after a time, fearing a scandal, the woman threatened to drown herself unless her lover could find some means of adjusting matters on a satisfactory basis. C. . ., who disliked his father, poisoned him and disappeared with the widow taking with him a few valuables belonging to his father. A year later, the woman having died meanwhile, he returned home and made full confession, first to his sister and subsequently in court.

*Moral Sense—Intelligence.* In the place of a weak, clouded, or unbalanced mind and that cynicism and absence of moral sense and natural feelings which distinguish born criminals of the most elevated type and even geniuses, criminaloids generally possess lucidity and balance of mind and may show themselves worthy of guiding the destinies of a nation. The men implicated in the French Panama Scandal and the case of the Banca Romana (Bank of Rome) are instances. When under a cloud of disgrace, instead of that insensibility, cynicism, or levity common to true criminals, they show deep sorrow, shame, and remorse, which not infrequently result in serious illness or death. Their natural affections and other sentiments are normal.

It is notorious, too, that as soon as accusations were made against those implicated in the French Panama Scandal and the affair of the Bank of Rome, the greater number became ill and two died suddenly at the end of the trial.

Unlike born criminals, criminaloids manifest deep repugnance towards common offenders. They demand solitary confinement and forego exercise, the only recreation prison life affords, in order to avoid all contact with their fellow-prisoners.

*Social Position and Culture of the Criminaloid.* Criminaloids, as we have seen, are recruited from all ranks of society and strike every note in the scale of criminality, from petty larceny to complicated and premeditated murder, from minting spurious coins to compassing gigantic frauds, which inflict incalculable damage upon the community. The magnitude of a crime does not imply greater criminality on the part of its author, but rather that he is a man of brilliant endowments, whose culture and talents multiply his opportunities and means for evil. In all cases where opportunity plays an important part, the crime must necessarily be committed by individuals exposed to special temptations: cashiers who handle other people's money, which they may be tempted to spend with the illusory idea of being able later to replace what they have taken, officials and public men, who possess a certain amount of power and an apparent impunity, and bankers who are entrusted with wealth belonging to others, of which in that capacity they are accustomed to make use. Thus is explained why men of great talent and only slight criminal tendencies have taken part in gigantic frauds, such as the affairs of the Bank of Rome and the French Panama Canal.

A characteristic case is that of Lord S——, First Lord of the Treasury, who committed forgeries to the extent of half a million sterling. "No torture," he writes, "would be an adequate punishment for my crime. Step by step, I have become the author of innumerable misdeeds and ruined more than ten thousand families. With less talent and greater uprightness, I might be now what I once was, an honest man. Now remorse is in vain."

In Lord S—— we find united all the characteristics of the criminaloid: repentance, the desire to confess, irreproachable antecedents, a strong incentive to dishonesty, and great intelligence.

Although the damage inflicted on society by this man was probably far greater than any evil wrought by a vulgar born criminal could have been, his criminality is nevertheless of an attenuated type. The mischief he wrought owed its gravity, not to the intensity of his criminal tendencies, but to his remarkable talents, which increased his power for evil as for good.

In this category of criminals must be inscribed those clever swindlers, who set the whole world talking of their exploits: Madame Humbert, Lemoine, and the cobbler-captain of Köpenick.

Sometimes, especially in political or commercial criminals, we find cases of an auto-illusion, of which the author of the crime is as much a victim as the public. Sometimes it is some device or mechanism which an inventor is convinced he has invented or is about to invent, an enterprise, in which the promoter imagines he will gain enormous wealth. Sometimes it is a trick in which the cupidity of the victims and their readiness to swallow promises of large and immediate profits play as important a part as the ability of the swindler. Sometimes it is a gigantic hoax, in which the deviser himself becomes keenly interested and for the carrying out of which he spends as much talent and energy as would suffice, if employed honestly, to acquire considerable wealth; but the swindler delights in his ingenious fraud as though he were taking part in some thrilling drama.

A typical instance is that of a certain C. . . who was imprisoned about twenty years ago for defrauding a woman. My father undertook to cure him while in prison and was able to follow him in his subsequent career. This C . . . was a young man of good family, intelligent, honest, and a good linguist. His countenance was pleasing and bore no trace of precocious criminality. At the age of twenty he developed an unrestrained love of gambling and in order to indulge this vice, promised to marry a rich woman considerably older than himself, from whom he borrowed large sums, on the understanding that they should be paid back. However, shortly afterwards, he fell in love with a young girl and married her. His ex-fiancée brought legal action against him and he was sentenced to two years' imprisonment. During this time he shrank from seeing anybody and refused to exercise in order to avoid all contact with his fellow-prisoners. He showed great affection for his wife and declared his intention of turning over a new leaf. The offence he had committed, however seemed to cause him little or no regret, because, as he said, he would never have continued the deception had not his victim shown such willingness to be gulled. From prison he went to London, where lack of funds caused him to perpetrate another swindle, but this time he was able to escape to Naples. Here for twelve years, he worked honestly in a large hotel, but once again a pressing need of money made him engage in a third fraud of considerable importance, for which he is still undergoing imprisonment.

## HABITUAL CRIMINALS

The degrading influence of prison life and contact with vulgar criminals, or the abuse of alcohol, to which better natures frequently have recourse in order to stifle the pangs of conscience, may cause criminaloids who have committed their initial offences with repugnance and hesitation, to develop later into habitual criminals,—that is, individuals who regard systematic violation of the law in the light of an ordinary trade or occupation and commit their offences with indifference.

Physically, habitual criminals do not resemble born criminals, but they exhibit some of the characteristics of those offenders from whom their ranks are recruited, besides, in a more marked degree, certain acquired characters, like sinister wrinkles and a shifty and sneaking look.

Psychologically, criminaloids tend to resemble born criminals, whose habits, tastes, slang, tattooing, orgies, idleness, etc., they gradually develop, in the same way as old couples, living isolated in the country, adopt identical habits, gestures, and tone of voice.

The type of criminaloid, who develops into an habitual criminal is well illustrated by the case of Eyraud, who in conjunction with Gabrielle Bompard, murdered Gouffré and packed the corpse in a trunk. Through his marked weakness for women, Eyraud became successively a deserter, a thief, and a murderer. He certainly possessed a few of the characteristics peculiar to degenerates—long, projecting ears, excessive development, amounting to asymmetry, of the left frontal sinus, prognathism, exaggerated brachycephaly, and the span of the arms exceeding the total height, but he had not the general criminal type, his teeth were regular, beard abundant, and hair scanty.

His psychology corresponds exactly to his physical individuality. During infancy and youth, he showed nothing abnormal, except an unusual predominance of the sexual instincts. He exhibited no signs of that love of evil for its own sake, so characteristic of criminals, above all, of murderers. According to all accounts, he was a jovial individual, fond of making merry, but at the same time, brusque and violent and easily roused to passionate fury. His extreme susceptibility to the attractions of the opposite sex made him regardless of all moral considerations. In order to gratify this weakness, he became a deserter, dissipated all the money he had earned in a distillery and as a dealer in skins, and finally committed murder. At his trial, it was shown that before his escape to America, he had attempted to kill a woman who refused to leave her husband for him. He became violently enamoured of his accomplice, Gabrielle Bompard, to whom, like many criminaloids, he was attracted by reason of her greater depravity.

The extreme levity displayed by Eyraud seems to be the strongest link between him and the born criminal. He passed with extraordinary facility from gaiety to melancholy. His intellect was well developed, he spoke three or four languages, and was successful in most things he undertook, though he seems to have been incapable of remaining constant to anything for long. As a business man he wasted his capital, and even in the execution of his crimes he showed frivolity and incoherence. At Lyons, he hired a carriage, in which he placed the corpse of Gouffré and after driving about the streets with Gabrielle Bompard like a madman, left the body of his victim in a spot near which people were constantly passing.

Eyraud appears to have been a dissolute criminaloid whose unbridled passions and connection with Gabrielle Bompard caused him to develop into an habitual criminal. This diagnosis is confirmed by the absence of morbid heredity.

It would be futile to cite a long series of cases, in which, although the details may vary, we always find the same phenomenon, the gradual development of a criminaloid into a criminal. It will suffice to name a large class of criminals, in whom this phenomenon may often be observed — the brigands common to Spain and Italy.

These outlaws, and particularly their leaders, notwithstanding the gravity of their offences, are seldom born criminals, nor do they (except in rare cases) begin their career at a very early age.    They possess, moreover, good qualities[1] and are capable of affection, generosity, and chivalry, which explains why their memories are cherished by the common people long after good and law-abiding men have been forgotten.

The brigand Mandrin, known as the "Smuggler General" is remembered with love and affection in Dauphiné and other regions of France, Switzerland, and Savoy; and this feeling is easy to understand, since he was the enemy of the "fermiers généraux," who, in the eighteenth century, leased from the French Government the right to levy excise duties, and sorely oppressed the people.

Louis Mandrin, who in early life showed no signs of perversity nor possessed criminal traits, became a bandit, because he had been unjustly treated by these same "fermiers généraux" who refused him payment for work done.    He became the chief of a small band of smugglers and spread terror among excise officers and gendarmes.    He used to bring smuggled goods openly into the vicinity of villages and towns and invite the people to buy them, and the buying and selling went on without either gendarmes' or excise officers' daring to interfere. The Administration of the "fermiers généraux"

[1] As in the case of the Sicilian brigand Salomone (see Fig. 19).

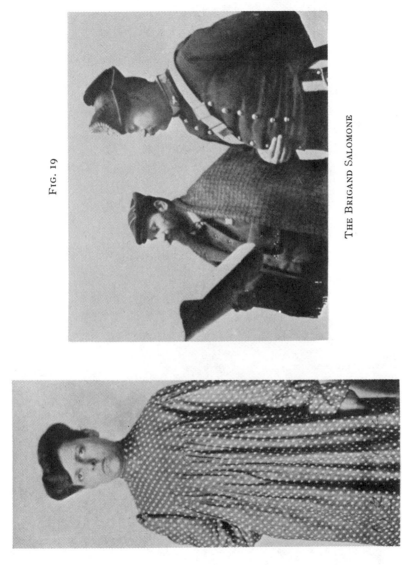

FIG. 18

CRIMINAL GIRL

FIG. 19

THE BRIGAND SALOMONE

promulgated a terrible edict against all purchasers of contraband goods; whereupon Mandrin, who was not without a sense of humour, declared he would force the Administrat on itself to buy the merchandise, and from time to time he would oblige the excise officers to buy smuggled wares at a fair price.

The brigand Gasparone (Fig. 20), whose memory is still held in great esteem by Sicilians, was an individual of much the same disposition.

## JURIDICAL CRIMINALS

This category comprises individuals who break the law, not because of any natural depravity, nor owing to distressing circumstances, but by mere accident. They may be divided into two classes:

First, the authors of accidental misdeeds, such as involuntary homicide or arson, who are not considered criminal by public opinion or by anthropologists, but who are obliged by the law to make compensation for the damage caused. Naturally, this class of law-breaker is in no way distinguishable, physically or psychically, from normal individuals, except that he is generally lacking in prudence, care, and forethought.

Second, the authors of offences, which do not cause any damage socially, nor are they considered criminal by the general public, but have been deemed such by the law, in obedience to some dominating opinion or prejudice. Bad language, seditious writings, atheism, drunkenness, evasion of customs, and any violation of petty by-laws come under this head. Instances of such offences are too well known to need citation. They may best be summed up in the words of an American judge, who pointed out how easy it would be to sentence the most honest citizen of the Republic to imprisonment for a hundred years and fines exceeding a thousand dollars for breaking a number of petty local regulations against spitting, drinking, disrobing near a window, swearing, opening places of amusement on Sunday, or employing persons on certain days or under certain conditions prohibited by the law, etc.

Although persons who commit these acts are often in no wise distinguishable from ordinary individuals, both criminals and criminaloids are more often guilty of such offences than are normal persons, who instinctively avoid coming into conflict with the law.

The difficulty of judging these misdeeds lies in the necessity for careful weighing of the motive which gives rise to them, whether, that is, they have been unwittingly committed by an honest individual, or whether they are but an item in the long list of offences perpetrated by a criminal. This differential diagnosis should be based principally on the antecedents of the offender.

To this group belong also the authors of more serious infractions of the law that are not generally considered such at the time, or in the district in which they take place. Misdeeds of this nature are: thefts of fuel in rural districts, poaching, the petty dishonesty current in commerce and in certain professions, and in countries where secret societies like the *camorra* at Naples and the *mafia* in Sicily, exist, a connection with such organisations, which to a certain extent is necessary in self-defence. Such, too, are theft and homicide during revolutions, insurrections, wars, and the conquest and exploitation of new territories and mines.

Rochefort and Whitman have pointed out that during the gold-fever in Australia and California there was an enormous increase in crime. Individuals of good antecedents engaged in deadly struggles for the possession of the most valuable territories, and unbridled orgies followed these bloody affrays.

During the expedition of Europeans to China in 1900, looting was carried on by soldiers of previously blameless career.

### CRIMINALS OF PASSION

This type of criminal, if indeed such he may be

called, represents the antithesis of the common offender, whose evil acts are the outcome of his ferocious and egotistical impulses, whereas criminals from passion are urged to violate the law by a pure spirit of altruism.   In fact, they stand in no relation whatsoever to ordinary delinquents, and it is only by a legislative compromise that they are classed together. They represent the ultra-violet ray of the criminal spectrum, of which the vulgar criminal represents the ultra-red. Not only are they free from the egotism, insensibility, laziness, and lack of moral sense peculiar to the ordinary criminal, but their abnormality consists in the excessive development of noble qualities, sensibility, altruism, integrity, affection, which if carried to an extreme, may result in actions forbidden by law, or worse still, dangerous to society.

*Physical Characteristics.*   These, too, are in complete contrast to those of the born criminal.   The countenance is frequently handsome, with lofty forehead, serene and gentle expression, and the beard is abundant.   The sensibility is extremely acute; there is a high degree of excitability and exaggerated reflex action, all characteristics of the normal (or rather hypernormal) individual, from whom nothing distinguishes the criminal of passion except the anti-social effects of his action.

*Psychology.* Here, as in all physical characteristics, criminals of passion are scarcely distinguishable from their fellow-men, except that we find in
an excessive degree those qualities we consider peculiar to good and holy persons—love, honour, noble
ambitions, patriotism. In fact, the motive of the
crime is always adequate, frequently noble, and
sometimes sublime. Love prompts certain natures to
kill those who insult their beloved ones or are the
cause of their dishonour and, in some cases, even
the object of their affection who proves unfaithful.
Crimes of this character are the murder by brothers
of the man who dishonours their sister, the murder
of an infant by its unmarried mother, the murder of
an unfaithful wife by her husband. Sometimes the
motive is a patriotic one, as in the cases of Charlotte
Corday, Orsini Sand, and Caserio (Fig. 21) all of
whom had been persons of gentle disposition and
blameless conduct up to the moment of their
crimes.

This class of offender not infrequently commits
suicide after his crime, or, if this is prevented, he
seeks to expiate it by long years of remorse and
self-inflicted martyrdom.

The deed is almost always unpremeditated and
committed publicly, without accomplices and with
the simplest means at hand—be they nails, teeth,

scissors, or a stick.   The previous career is always blameless.

Cumano, Verano, Guglielmotti, Harry, Curti, Milani, Brenner, Mari, Zucca, Bechis, Bouley, Tacco, Berruto and Sand, and Camicia, Vinci, and Leoni (these last three women), all attacked their victims single-handed and in public.

In the case of Chalanton, the woman he had rescued by marriage from a low life, not content with betraying her benefactor, covered him in public with abuse and persecuted him with anonymous accusations.   His demand for a separation was unsuccessful and at last, finding himself, in spite of his integrity, involved in a scandalous action, in which his wife figured as a go-between, and tormented by public curiosity and the implacable questionings of reporters, he murdered the cause of all his misfortunes. Another murderer, Del Prete, was prompted to kill his victim, an old woman with a reputation for witchcraft, because he believed she had caused the illness of his mother, to whom he was greatly attached.

The motive for the crime is generally a serious one and in most cases immediately precedes it. Bouley committed his crime only a few hours after receiving the news which prompted it; Bounin, Bechis, and Verano, only a few minutes; Milani,

FIG. 21

BRIGAND CASERIO
(see page 119)

twenty-four hours, Zucca eight hours; Curti, a few days. Thus the crime is seldom premeditated, or if so, for only a short space of time, never for months or years.

Homicide forms 91% of the criminality of this group of offenders. There is a certain proportion also of infanticide, owing to the prevailing prejudice which condemns immorality more harshly when the results are evident. Arson and theft form only 2%. Such cases are however possible. A young girl, whom my father had under observation in prison, seeing her family in dire poverty, committed arson in order to get the insurance money.

In another case a woman of refinement, education, and of gentle disposition, who had fallen from prosperity into extreme want, stole in order to pay her son's school-fees. When arrested, she refused to give her name so that the lad should not be dishonoured, and her identity might never have been discovered had she not been recognised by a lawyer in court. She died of a broken heart a few days after her trial.

# PART II

CRIME, ITS ORIGIN, CAUSE, AND CURE

# CHAPTER I

## *ORIGIN AND CAUSES OF CRIME*

IN order to determine the origin of actions which we call criminal, we shall be forced to hark back to a very remote period in the history of the human race. In all the epochs of which records exist, we find traces of criminal actions. In fact, if we study minutely the customs of savage peoples, past and present, we find that many acts that are now considered criminal by civilised nations were legitimate in former times, and are to-day reputed such among primitive races.

According to Pictet the Latin word *crimen* is derived from the Sanscrit *karman*, which signifies action corresponding to *kri* to do. This is contradicted by Vanicek who derives it from *kru*, to hear, *croemen* (accusation). At any rate, the Sanscrit word *apaz*, which means sin, corresponds to *apas*, work (*opus*), the Latin *facinus* derives from *facere*, and *culpa* according to Pictet and Pott, from the Sanscrit *kalp*, to do or execute. The Latin word *fur* (thief) which Vanicek derives from *bahr*, to carry, the Hebrew *ganav* and the Sanscrit *sten* only signify to put aside, to hide, to cover (*gonav*). The Greek word *peirao* ($\pi\varepsilon\iota\rho\acute{a}\omega$) from which pirate is derived, signifies to risk; the Greek *chleptein* ($\chi\lambda\acute{\varepsilon}\pi\tau\varepsilon\iota\nu$) to hide or steal, is derived from the Sanscrit *harp-hlap* to hide and steal (Vanicek).

In India, from Ceylon to the Himalayas, infanticide is sanctified by religion, not only among the more barbarous races, but also among the Rajputs, the nobles, who think themselves dishonoured if one of their daughters remains unmarried. The inhabitants of the Island of Tikopia, kill more male children than female, a fact that accounts for their practice of polygamy.

Marco Polo speaks of the infanticide practised in Japan and China, which was then, as it is now, a means of regulating the population. The same practice—common to Bushmen, Hottentots, Fijians, also existed among the natives of Hawaii and America. In the Island of Tahiti, according to the testimony of missionaries, two thirds of the children born are destroyed by their parents.

"Amongst the Guaranys," says D'Azara, "mothers kill a large proportion of their female infants, in order that the survivors may be more highly valued." (*Travels in America*, 1835.)

The Carthaginians had originally the custom of offering the noblest and most beautiful children to Kronos (Moloch), but later victims were always bought and bred for the purpose. After their defeat at the hand of Agathokles they sacrificed two hundred children belonging to the noblest Carthaginian families, in order to appease the Divine wrath.

Phœnicians, Egyptians, Cretans, Cypriotes, Rhodians, and Persians had similar practices.

Among the Lydians, the sacred courtesans were so numerous and wealthy that their contributions to the Mausoleum of Alyattes exceeded those of the artists and merchants combined (Herodotus, Book I.); in Armenia (Strabo XII.) the priestesses alone were permitted to practise polyandry, and in Media, a woman boasting of five husbands was greatly honoured, which shows that polyandry was not only allowed, but esteemed.

In Thibet, the eldest male of a family shares his wife with his brothers, the whole family live in the bride's house and the children inherit from her. Among the *Todas*, the wife espouses all her husband's younger brothers as they attain their majority, and they in their turn become the husbands of her younger sisters (Short).

Among the *Nairs*, a noble negro caste of Malabar, it is customary for one woman to have five or six husbands, the maximum number allowed being ten.

In Egypt, the business of thief was a recognised one. Those who wished to exercise this calling inscribed their names on a public tablet, collected all the stolen goods in one spot and restored them to their owners in exchange for a certain coin. The ancient Germans encouraged the youthful portion of the population to make raids on the property of neighbouring peoples, so that they should not develop habits of idleness. Thucydides states that the Greeks, as well as the barbarous peoples inhabiting the islands and along the coasts, were pirates, and the calling was a noble one.

Amongst Spartans, as is well known, theft was allowed, but the unlucky marauder who was caught in the act, was punished, not for the deed itself, but for his want of skill. In East Africa, according to Burton (*First Footsteps in East Africa*, p. 176), robbery is considered honourable. In Caramanza (Portuguese Guinea) in Africa, side by side with the peaceful rice-cultivating Bagnous dwell the Balantes who subsist upon the chase and the spoils of their raids. While they kill the individual who presumes to steal in his native village, they encourage depredations upon the other tribes (*Revue d' Anthropologie*, 1874). The cleverest thieves are greatly esteemed, are paid for instructing boys in their profession, and are chosen to lead the expeditions.

In India the tribe Zakka Khel is devoted to this dishonest calling, and at birth every male child is consecrated to thievish practices by a peculiar ceremony, in which the new-born infant is passed through a breach in the wall of his father's house, whilst the words "Become a thief" are chanted three times in chorus. Amongst the ancient Germans, according to Tacitus, thefts perpetrated outside the boundary of the tribe itself were by no means infamous. In the midst of a great assembly, the chief called upon those he wished to follow him; they showed their willingness by rising to their feet amid the applause of the crowd. Those who refused to take part were looked upon as deserters and traitors (Spencer, *Principles of Ethics*, 1895). Among the Comanches (Mülhausen, *Diary of a Journey from the Mississippi to the Pacific*) no man was considered worthy of being numbered among the warriors of the tribe, unless he had taken part in some successful pillaging expedition. The cleverest thieves were the most respected members of the tribe. No Patagonian is deemed worthy of a wife unless he has graduated in the art of despoiling a stranger (Snow, *Two Years' Cruise round Tierra del Fuego*). Among the Kukis (Dalton, *Descriptive Ethnolgy of Bengal*) skill in stealing is the most esteemed talent. In Mongolia (Gilmour, *Among the Mongols*), thieves are regarded as respectable members of the community, provided they steal cleverly and escape detection.

## CRIMINALITY IN CHILDREN

The criminal instincts common to primitive savages would be found proportionally in nearly all children, if they were not influenced by moral training and example. This does not mean that without educative restraints, all children would develop into criminals. According to the observations made by Prof. Mario Carrara at Cagliari, the bands of neglected children who run wild in the streets of the Sardinian capital and are addicted to thievish practices and more serious vices, spontaneously correct themselves of these habits as soon as they have arrived at puberty.

This fact, that the germs of moral insanity and criminality are found normally in mankind in the first stages of his existence, in the same way as forms considered monstrous when exhibited by adults, frequently exist in the fœtus, is such a simple and common phenomenon that it eluded notice until it was demonstrated clearly by observers like Moreau, Perez, and Bain. The child, like certain adults, whose abnormality consists in a lack of moral sense, represents what is known to alienists as a morally insane being and to criminologists as a born criminal, and it certainly resembles these types in its impetuous violence.

Perez (*Psychologie de l'enfant*, 2d ed., 1882) remarks on the frequency and precocity of anger in children:

"During the first two months, it manifests by movements of the eyebrows and hands undoubted fits of temper when undergoing any distasteful process, such as washing or when deprived of any object it takes a fancy to. At the age of one, it goes to the length of striking those who incur its displeasure, of breaking plates or throwing them at persons it dislikes, exactly like savages."

Moreau (*De l'Homicide chez les enfants*, 1882) cites numerous cases of children who fly into a passion if their wishes are not complied with immediately. In one instance observed by him a very intelligent child of eight, when reproved, even in the mildest manner by his parents or strangers, would give way to violent anger, snatching up the nearest weapon, or if he found himself unable to take revenge, would break anything he could lay his hands on.

A baby girl showed an extremely violent temper, but became of gentle disposition after she had reached the age of two (Perez). Another, observed by the same author, when only eleven months old, flew into a towering rage, because she was unable to pull off her grandfather's nose.  Yet another, at the age of two, tried to bite another child who had a doll like her own, and she was so much affected by her anger that she was ill for three days afterwards.

Nino Bixio, when a boy of seven (*Vita*, Guerzoni, 1880) on seeing his teacher laugh because he had written his exercise on office letter-paper, threw the inkstand at the man's face.  This boy was literally the terror of the school, on account of the violence he displayed at the slightest offence.

Infants of seven or eight months have been known to scratch at any attempt to withdraw the breast from them, and to retaliate when slapped.

A backward and slightly hydrocephalous boy whom my father had under observation, began at the age of six to show violent irritation at the slightest reproof or correction.  If he was able to strike the person who had annoyed him, his rage cooled immediately; if not, he would scream incessantly and bite his hands with gestures similar to those often witnessed in caged bears who have been teased and cannot retaliate.

The above cases show that the desire for revenge is extremely common and precocious in children. Anger is an elementary instinct innate in human beings. It should be guided and restrained, but can never be extirpated.

Children are quite devoid of moral sense during the first months or first years of their existence. Good and evil in their estimation are what is allowed and what is forbidden by their elders, but they are incapable of judging independently of the moral value of an action.

"Lying and disobedience are very wrong," said a boy to Perez, "because they displease mother." Everything he was accustomed to was right and necessary.

A child does not grasp abstract ideas of justice, or the rights of property, until he has been deprived of some possession. He is prone to detest injustice, especially when he is the victim. Injustice, in his estimation, is the discord between a habitual mode of treatment and an accidental one. When subjected to altered conditions, he shows complete uncertainty. A child placed under Perez's care modified his ways according to each new arrival. He began ordering his companions about and refused to obey any one but Perez.

Affection is very slightly developed in children. Their fancy is easily caught by a pleasing exterior or by anything that contributes to their amusement; like domestic animals that they enjoy teasing and pulling about, and they exhibit great antipathy to unfamiliar objects that inspire them with fear. Up to the age of seven or even after, they show very little real attachment to anybody. Even their mothers, whom they appear to love, are speedily forgotten after a short separation.

In conclusion, children manifest a great many of the impulses we have observed in criminals; anger, a spirit of revenge, idleness, volubility and lack of affection.

We have also pointed out that many actions considered criminal in civilised communities, are normal and legitimate practices among primitive races. It is evident, therefore, that such actions are natural to the early stages, both of social evolution and individual psychic development.

In view of these facts, it is not strange that civilised communities should produce a certain percentage of adults who commit actions reputed injurious to society and punishable by law. It is only an atavistic phenomenon, the return to a former state. In the criminal, moreover, the phenomenon is accompanied by others also natural to a primitive stage of evolution. These have already been referred to in the first chapter, which contains a description of many strange practices common to delinquents, and evidently of primitive origin—tattooing, cruel games,

FIG. 22

TERRA-COTTA BOWLS
Designed by a Criminal
(see page 135)

love of orgies, a pecuilar slang resembling in certain features the languages of primitive peoples, and the use of hieroglyphics and pictography.

The artistic manifestations of the criminal show the same characteristics. In spite of the thousands of years which separate him from prehistoric savages, his art is a faithful reproduction of the first, crude artistic attempts of primitive races. The museum of criminal anthropology created by my father contains numerous specimens of criminal art, stones shaped to resemble human figures, like those found in Australia, rude pottery covered with designs that recall Egyptian decorations (Fig. 22) or scenes fashioned in terra-cotta (Fig. 23) that resemble the grotesque creations of children or savages.

The criminal is an atavistic being, a relic of a vanished race. This is by no means an uncommon occurrence in nature. Atavism, the reversion to a former state, is the first feeble indication of the reaction opposed by nature to the perturbing causes which seek to alter her delicate mechanism. Under certain unfavourable conditions, cold or poor soil, the common oak will develop characteristics of the oak of the Quaternary period. The dog left to run wild in the forest will in a few generations revert to the type of his original wolf-like progenitor, and the cultivated garden roses when neglected show a tendency to reassume the form of the original dog-rose. Under special conditions produced by alcohol, chloroform, heat, or injuries, ants, dogs, and pigeons become irritable and savage like their wild ancestors.

This tendency to alter under special conditions is common to human beings, in whom hunger, syphilis, trauma, and, still more frequently, morbid conditions inherited from insane, criminal, or diseased progenitors, or the abuse of nerve poisons, such as alcohol, tobacco, or morphine, cause various alterations, of which criminality—that is, a return to the characteristics peculiar to primitive savages—is in reality the least serious, because it represents a less advanced stage than other forms of cerebral alteration.

The ætiology of crime, therefore, mingles with that of all kinds of degeneration: rickets, deafness, monstrosity, hairiness, and cretinism, of which crime is only a variation. It has, however, always been regarded as a thing apart, owing to a general instinctive repugnance to admit that a phenomenon, whose extrinsications are so extensive and penetrate every fibre of social life, derives, in fact, from the same causes as socially insignificant forms like rickets, sterility, etc. But this repugnance is really only a sensory illusion, like many others of widely diverse nature.

Fig. 23

ART PRODUCTION FROM PRISON
(see page 135)

Fig. 24

A COMBAT BETWEEN BRIGANDS AND GENDARMES
Designed by a Criminal
(see page 135)

*Pathological Origin of Crime.*   The atavistic origin of crime is certainly one of the most important discoveries of criminal anthropology, but it is important only theoretically, since it merely explains the phenomenon.   Anthropologists soon realised how necessary it was to supplement this discovery by that of the origin, or causes which call forth in certain individuals these atavistic or criminal instincts, for it is the immediate causes that constitute the practical nucleus of the problem and it is their removal that renders possible the cure of the disease

These causes are divided into organic and external factors of crime: the former remote and deeply rooted, the latter momentary but frequently determining the criminal act, and both closely related and fused together.

Heredity is the principal organic cause of criminal tendencies.   It may be divided into two classes: indirect heredity from a generically degenerate family with frequent cases of insanity, deafness, syphilis, epilepsy, and alcoholism among its members; direct heredity from criminal parentage.

*Indirect Heredity.*   Almost all forms of chronic, constitutional diseases, especially those of a nervous character: chorea, sciatica, hysteria, insanity, and above all, epilepsy, may give rise to criminality in the descendants.

Of 559 soldiers convicted of offences, examined by Brancaleone Ribaudo, 10 % had epileptic parents. According to Dejerine, this figure reaches 74.6% among criminal epileptics. Arthritis and gout have been known to generate criminality in the descendants. But the most serious, and at the same time most common, form of indirect heredity is alcoholism, which, contrary to general belief, wreaks destruction in all classes of society, amongst the rich and poor without distinction of sex, for alcohol may insinuate itself everywhere under the most refined and pleasant disguises, in liqueurs, sweets, and coffee.

According to calculations made by my father, 20% of Italian criminals descend from inebriate families; according to Penta the percentage is 27 and in dangerous criminals, 33%. The Jukes family, of whom we shall speak later, descended from a drunkard.

The first salient characteristic in hereditary alcoholism is the precocious taste for intoxicants; secondly, the susceptibility to alcohol, which is infinitely more injurious to the offspring of inebriates than to normal individuals; and thirdly, the growth of the craving for strong drinks, which inevitably undermine the constitution.

*Direct Heredity.* The effects of direct heredity are still more serious, for they are aggravated by environment and education. Official statistics show that 20% of juvenile offenders belong to families of doubtful reputation and 26% to those whose reputation is thoroughly bad. The criminal Galletto, a native of Marseilles, was the nephew of the equally ferocious anthropophagous violator of women, Orsolano. Dumollar was the son of a murderer; Patetot's grandfather and great-grandfather were in prison, as were the grandfathers and fathers of Papa, Crocco, Serravalle and Cavallante, Comptois and Lempave; the parents of the celebrated female thief Sans Refus, were both thieves.

The genealogical study of certain families has shown that there are whole generations, almost all the members of which belong to the ranks of crime, insanity, and prostitution (this last being amongst women the equivalent of criminality amongst men). A striking example is furnished by the notorious Jukes family, with 77 criminal descendants.

Ancestor, Max Jukes: 77 criminals; 142 vagabonds; 120 prostitutes; 18 keepers of houses of ill-fame; 91 illegitimates; 141 idiots or afflicted with impotency or syphilis; 46 sterile females.

A like criminal contingent may be found in the pedigrees of Chrêtien, the Lemaires, the Fieschi family, etc.

*Race.* This is of great importance in view of the

atavistic origin of crime. There exist whole tribes and races more or less given to crime, such as the tribe Zakka Khel in India. In all regions of Italy, whole villages constitute hot-beds of crime, owing, no doubt, to ethnical causes: Artena in the province of Rome, Carde and San Giorgio Canavese in Piedmont, Pergola in Tuscany, San Severo in Apulia, San Mauro and Nicosia in Sicily. The frequency of homicide in Calabria, Sicily, and Sardinia is fundamentally due to African and Oriental elements.

In the gipsies we have an entire race of criminals with all the passions and vices common to delinquent types: idleness, ignorance, impetuous fury, vanity, love of orgies, and ferocity. Murder is often committed for some trifling gain. The women are skilled thieves and train their children in dishonest practices. On the contrary, the percentage of crimes among Jews is always lower than that of the surrounding population; although there is a prevalence of certain specific forms of offences, often hereditary, such as fraud, forgery, libel, and chief of all, traffic in prostitution; murder is extremely rare.

### ILLNESSES, INTOXICATIONS, TRAUMATISM

These causes, although apparently as important as heredity, are in fact, decidedly less so. Both disease and trauma may intensify or call forth latent perversity, but they are less frequently the cause of it. There are, however, certain cases in which traumatism meningitis, typhus, or other diseases that affect the brain have undoubtedly evoked criminal tendencies in individuals hitherto normal. Twenty out of 290 criminals studied by my father with minute care had suffered from injury to the head in childhood; and recently a case came under his notice in which a youth of good family and excellent character received an injury to his head at the age of fourteen and became epileptic, developing subsequently into a gambler, thief, and murderer. Such cases, however, are not very common.

There is one disease that without other causes—either inherited degeneracy or vices resulting from a bad education and environment—is capable of transforming a healthy individual into a vicious, hopelessly evil being. That disease is alcoholism, which has been discussed in a previous chapter, but to which I must refer briefly again, because it is such an important factor of criminality.

Temporary drunkenness alone will give rise to crime, since it inflames the passions, obscures the mental and moral faculties, and destroys all sense of decency, causing men to commit offences in a state of automatism or a species of somnambulism. Sometimes drunkenness produces kleptomania. A slight excess in drinking will cause men of absolute honesty to appropriate any objects they can lay their hands upon. When the effects of drink have worn off, they feel shame and remorse and hasten to restore the stolen goods. Alcohol, however, more often causes violence. An officer known to my father, when drunk, twice attempted to run his sword through his friends and his own attendant.

Among Oriental sects of murderers, as is well known, homicidal fury was excited and maintained by a drink brewed for the purpose from hemp-seed.

Büchner shows that dishonest instincts can be developed in bees by a special food consisting of honey mixed with brandy. The insects acquire a taste for this drink in the same way as human beings do, and under its influence cease to work. Ants show similar symptoms after narcosis by means of chloroform. Their bodies remain motionless, with the exception of their heads, with which they snap at all who approach them.

The above cited cases show that there exists a species of alcoholic psychic epilepsy, similar to congenital epilepsy, in which after alcoholic poisoning, the individual is incited to raise his hand against himself or others without any due cause. But besides the crimes of violence committed during a drunken fit, the prolonged abuse of alcohol, opium, morphia, coca, and other nervines may give rise to chronic perturbation of the mind, and without other causes, congenital or educative, will transform an honest, well-bred, and industrious man into an idle, violent, and apathetic fellow,—into an ignoble being, capable of any depraved action, even when he is not directly under the influence of the drug.

When we were children, a frequent visitor at our house was a certain Belm . . . (see Fig. 16, Chap. III., a very intelligent man and an accomplished linguist. He was a military officer, but later took to journalism, and his writings were distinguished by vivacious style and elevation of thought. He married and had several children, but at the age of thirty some trouble caused him to take to drink. His character soon underwent a complete change. Although formerly a proud man, he was not ashamed to pester all his friends for money and to let his family sink into the direst poverty.

## SOCIAL CAUSES OF CRIME

*Education.* We now come to the second series of criminal factors, those which depend, not on the organism, but on external conditions. We have already stated that the best and most careful education, moral and intellectual, is powerless to effect an improvement in the morally insane, but that in other cases, education, environment, and example are extremely important, for which reason neglected and destitute children are easily initiated into evil practices.

At Naples, "Esposito" (foundling) is a common name amongst prisoners, as is at Bologna and in Lombardy the name "Colombo," which signifies the same thing. In Prussia, illegitimate males form 6 % of offenders, illegitimate females 1.8 %; in Austria, 10 and 2 % respectively. The percentage is considerably larger amongst juvenile criminals, prostitutes, and recidivists. In France, in 1864, 65 % of the minors arrested were bastards or orphans, and at Hamburg 30 % of the prostitutes are illegitimate. In Italy, 30 % of recidivists are natural children and foundlings.

This depends largely on hereditary influences, which are generally bad, but still more on the difficulty of finding a means of subsistence, owing to the state of neglect in which these wretched beings exist, even when herded together in charity schools and orphanages—both of which are even more anti-hygienic morally, than they are physically.

A depraved environment, which counsels or even insists on wrong-doing, and the bad example of parents or relatives, exercise a still more sinister influence on children than desertion. The criminal family Cornu, finding one of their children, a little girl, strongly averse to their evil ways, forced her to carry the head of one of their victims in her pinafore for a couple of miles, after which she became one of the most ferocious of the band.

*Meteoric Causes* are frequently the determining factor of the ultimate impulsive act, which converts the latent criminal into an effective one. Excessively high temperature and rapid barometric changes, while predisposing epileptics to convulsive seizures and the insane to uneasiness, restlessness, and noisy outbreaks, encourage quarrels, brawls, and stabbing affrays. To the same reason may be ascribed the prevalence during the hot months, of rape, homicide, insurrections, and revolts. In comparing statistics of criminality in France with those of the variations in temperature, Ferri noted an increase in crimes of violence during the warmer years. An examination of European and American statistics shows that the number of homicides decreases as we pass from hot to cooler climates. Holzendorf calculates that the number of murders committed in the Southern States of North America is fifteen times greater than those committed in the Northern States. A low temperature, on the contrary, has the effect of increasing the number of crimes against property, due to increased need, and both in Italy and America the proportion of thefts increases the farther north we go.

*Density of Population.* The agglomeration of persons in a large town is a certain incentive to crimes against property. Robbery, frauds, and criminal associations increase, while there is a decrease in crimes against the person, due to the restraints imposed by mutual supervision.

" He who has studied mankind, or, better still, himself [writes my father], must have remarked how often an individual, who is respectable and self-controlled in the bosom cf his family, becomes indecent and even immoral when he finds himself in the company of a number of his fellows, to whatever class they may belong. The primitive instincts of theft, homicide, and lust, the germs of which lie dormant in each individual as long as he is alone, particularly if kept in check by sound moral training, awaken and develop suddenly into gigantic proportions when he comes into contact with others, the increase being greater in those who already possess such criminal tendencies in a marked degree."

In all large cities, low lodging-houses form the favourite haunts of crime.

*Imitation.* The detailed accounts of crimes circulated in large towns by newspapers, have an extremely pernicious influence, because example is a powerful agent for evil as well as for good.

At Marseilles in 1868 and 1872, the newspaper reports of a case of child desertion provoked a perfect epidemic of such cases, amounting in one instance to eight in one day.

Before Corridori murdered the Head-master of his boarding-school, he is said to have declared: "There will be a repetition of what happened to the Head-master at Catanzaro" (who had been murdered in the same way).

The anarchist Lucchesi killed Banti at Leghorn shortly after the murder of Carnot by Caserio, and in a similar manner. Certain forms of crime which become common at given periods, the throwing of bombs, the cutting up of the bodies of murdered persons, particularly those of women, and frauds of a peculiar type may certainly be attributed to imitation, as may also the violence committed by mobs, in whom cruelty takes the form of an epidemic affecting even individuals of mild disposition.

*Immigration.* The agglomeration of population produced by immigration is a strong incentive to crime, especially that of an associated nature, — due to increased want, lessened supervision and the consequent ease with which offenders avoid detection. In New York the largest contingent of criminality is furnished by the immigrant population.

The fact of agglomeration explains the greater

frequency of homicide in France in thickly populated districts.

The criminality of immigrant populations increases in direct ratio to its instability. This applies to the migratory population in the interior of a country, specially that which has no fixed destination, as peddlers, etc. Even those immigrants whom we should naturally assume to be of good disposition—religious pilgrims—commit a remarkable number of associated crimes. The Italian word *mariuolo* which signifies "rogue" owes its origin to the behaviour of certain pilgrims to the shrines of Loreto and Assisi, who, while crying *Viva Maria!* ("Hail to the Virgin Mary!") committed the most atrocious crimes, confident that the pilgrimage itself would serve as a means of expiation. In his *Reminiscences* Massimo d' Azeglio notes that places boasting of celebrated shrines always enjoy a bad reputation.

*Prison Life.* The density of population in the most criminal of cities has not such a bad influence as has detention in prisons, which may well be called "Criminal Universities."

Nearly all the leaders of malefactors: Maino, Lombardo, La Gala, Lacenaire, Soufflard, and Hardouin were escaped convicts, who chose their accomplices among those of their fellow-prisoners who had shown audacity and ferocity. In fact, in prison, criminals have an opportunity of becoming acquainted with each other, of instructing those less skilled in infamy, and of banding together for evil purposes. Even the expensive cellular system, from which so many advantages were expected, has not attained its object and does not prevent communication between prisoners. Moreover, in prison, mere children of seven or eight, imprisoned for stealing a bunch of grapes or a fowl, come into close contact with adults and become initiated into evil practices, of which these poor little victims of stupid laws were previously quite ignorant.

*Education.* Contrary to general belief, the influence of education on crime is very slight.

The number of illiterates arrested in Europe is less, proportionally, than that of educated individuals. Nevertheless, although a certain degree of instruction is often an aid to crime, its extension acts as a corrective, or at least tends to mitigate the nature of crimes committed, rendering them less ferocious, and to decrease crimes of violence, while increasing fraudulent and sexual offences.

*Professions.* The trades and professions which encourage inebriety in those who follow them (cooks, confectioners, and inn-keepers), those which bring the poor (servants of all kinds, especially footmen, coachmen, and chauffeurs) into contact with wealth, or which provide means for committing crimes (brick-layers, blacksmiths, etc.) furnish a remarkable share of criminality. Still more so is this the case with the professions of notary, usher of the courts, attorneys, and military men.

It should be observed, however, that the characteristic idleness of criminals makes them disinclined to adopt any profession, and when they do, their extreme fickleness prompts them to change continually.

*Economic Conditions.*   Poverty is often a direct incentive to theft, when the miserable victims of economic conditions find themselves and their families face to face with starvation, and it acts further indirectly through certain diseases: pellagra, alcoholism, scrofula, and scurvy, which are the outcome of misery and produce criminal degeneration; its influence has nevertheless often been exaggerated.   If thieves are generally penniless, it is because of their extreme idleness and astonishing extravagance, which makes them run through huge sums with the greatest ease, not because poverty has driven them to theft.   On the other hand the possession of wealth is frequently an incentive to crime, because it creates an ever-increasing appetite for riches, besides furnishing those occupying high public offices or important positions in the banking and commercial world with numerous opportunities for dishonesty and persuading them that money will cover any evil deed.

*Sex.* Statistics of every country show that women contribute a very small share of criminality compared with that furnished by the opposite sex. This share becomes still smaller when we eliminate infanticide, in view of the fact that the guilty parties in nearly all such cases should be classed as criminals from passion. In Austria, crimes committed by females barely constitute 15 % of the total criminality; in Spain 11 %; and in Italy 8.2 %.

However, this applies only to serious crimes. For those of lesser gravity, statistics are at variance with the results obtained by the Modern School, which classes prostitutes as criminals. According to this mode of calculation, the difference between the criminality of the two sexes shows a considerable diminution, resulting perhaps in a slight prevalence of crime in women. In any case, female criminality tends to increase proportionally with the increase of civilisation and to equal that of men.

*Age.* The greater number of crimes are committed between the ages of 15 and 30, whereas, outbreaks of insanity between these ages are extremely rare, the maximum number occurring between 40 and 50. On the whole, criminality is far more precocious than mental alienation, and its precocity, which is greater among thieves than among murderers, swindlers, and those guilty of violence and assault is another proof of the congenital nature of crime and its atavistic origin, since precocity is a characteristic of savage races.

Seldom do we find among born criminals any indication of that so-called criminal scale, leading by degrees from petty offences to crimes of the most serious nature. As a general rule, they commence their career with just those crimes which distinguish it throughout, even when these are of the gravest kind, like robbery and murder. Rather may it be said that every age has its specific criminality, and this is the case especially with criminaloids. On the borderland between childhood and adolescence, there seems to be a kind of instinctive tendency to law-breaking, which by immature minds is often held to be a sign of virility. The Italian novelist and poet Manzoni describes this idea very well in his *Promessi Sposi*, when speaking of the half-witted lad Gervaso, who "because he had taken part in a plot savouring of crime, felt that he had suddenly become a man."

This idea lurks in the slang word *omerta* used by Italian criminals, which signifies not only to be a man but a man daring enough to break the law.

# CHAPTER II

## THE PREVENTION OF CRIME

THE curability of crime is an entirely novel idea, due to the Modern Penal School. As long as, in the eyes of the world, the criminal was a normal individual, who voluntarily and consciously violated the laws, there could be no thought of a cure, but rather of a punishment sufficiently severe to prevent his recidivation and to inspire others with a salutary fear of offending the law.

The penalties excogitated in past centuries were varied: flogging, hard labour, imprisonment, and exile. During the last century they have been crystallised in the form of imprisonment, as being the most humane, although in reality it is the most illogical form, since it serves neither to intimidate the offender nor to reform him. In fact, although prison with its forced separation from home and family is a terrible penalty for those honest persons, who sometimes suffer with the guilty, it is a haven of rest for ordinary criminals, or at the worst, in no wise inferior to their usual haunts. There is a certain amount of privation of air, light, and food, but these disadvantages are fully counterbalanced by the enjoyment of complete leisure and the company of men of their own stamp.

If imprisonment does not serve to intimidate instinctive criminals, still less is it a means of rehabilitation. In virtue of what law, should any man, even if he be normal, become reformed after a varying period of detention in a gloomy cell, where he is isolated from the better elements of society and deprived of every elevating influence—art, science, and high ideals; where he loses regular habits of work, the disciplining struggle with circumstances, and the sense of responsibility natural to free citizens and is tainted by constant contact with the worst types of humanity?

The autobiographies of criminals show us that far from reforming evil-doers, prison is in reality a criminal university which houses all grades of offenders during varying periods; that far from being a means of redemption, it is a hot-bed of depravity, where are prepared and developed the germs which are later to infect society, yet it is to this incubator of crime that society looks for defence against those very elements of lawlessness which it is actively fostering.

In his book *Prison Palimpsests* my father has made a collection of all the inscriptions, drawings, and allegories scratched or written by criminals while in prison, on walls, utensils, and books. Of lamentations, despair, and repentance, scarcely a trace, but innumerable imprecations, plans of revenge against enemies without, project of future burglaries and murders, and advice for the sound instruction of criminals.

Although the Modern School has demonstrated the uselessness, nay the injuriousness of prison, it has no desire to leave society suddenly unprotected and the criminal at large. Nature does not proceed by leaps, and the Modern School aims at effecting a revolution, not a revolt, in Penal Jurisprudence. It proposes, therefore, the gradual transformation of the present system, which is to be rendered as little injurious and as beneficial as possible. Such has been the course pursued by the modern science of medicine, which from the original absurd remedies and equally absurd empirical operations, has now succeeded in placing the cure of diseases on the more solid basis of experience.

The Modern School aims at preventing the formation of criminals, not punishing them, or, failing prevention, at effecting their cure; and, failing cure, at segregating such hopeless cases for life in suitable institutes, which shall protect society better than the present system of imprisonment, but be entirely free from the infamy attaching to the prison. The Modern School proposes the cure of criminals by preventive and legislative measures.

## Preventive Institutions for Destitute Children

The cure of crime, as of any other disease, has the greater chance of success, the earlier it is taken in hand. Attention, therefore, should be specially concentrated on the childhood of those likely to become criminals: orphans and destitute children, who as adults contribute the largest contingent of criminality. A community seriously resolved to protect itself from evil should, above all, provide a sound education for those unfortunate waifs who have been deprived of their natural protectors by death or vice. The greatest care must be exercised in placing them, whenever it is possible, in respectable private families where they will have careful supervision, or in suitable institutes where no pains are spared to give them a good education and, more important still, sound moral training.

In order to attain this end, the State cannot do better than follow in the footsteps of philanthropists of rare talent like Don Bosco, Dr. Barnardo, General

Booth, Brockway, and many others, who have been so successful in rescuing destitute children.

Don Bosco, the Black Pope, as he was familiarly styled at Turin, where he lived during the latter half of the last century, was a Roman Catholic priest who founded numerous institutes for orphans in all parts of Italy and many parts of both Americas, especially South America. The psychological basis on which he founded the training of children in these schools, was mainly derived from experience, and proved so successful in practice that it is worthy of quotation:

"Most neglected and abandoned children [he said], are of ordinary character and disposition, but inclined to changeableness and indifference. Brief, but frequent exhortations, good advice, small rewards, and encouragements to persevere are very efficacious, but above all the teacher must show perfect trust in his charges, while being careful never to relax his vigilance. The greatest solicitude should, however, be reserved for the unruly characters, who generally form about one fifth of the whole number. The teacher should make a special effort to become thoroughly acquainted with their dispositions and past life and to convince them that he is their friend. They should be encouraged to chatter freely, while the conversation of the master should be brief and abound in examples, maxims, and anecdotes. Above all, while showing perfect confidence in his pupils, he should never lose sight of them.

"Occasional treats of a wholesome and attractive nature, picnics and walks, will keep the boys happy and contented. Lasciviousness is the only vice that need be feared; any lad persisting in immoral practices should be expelled.

"Harsh punishments should never be resorted to. The repressive system may check unruliness, but can never influence for good. It involves little trouble on the part of those who make use of it and may be efficacious in the army, which is composed of responsible adults, but it has a harmful effect on the young, who err more from thoughtlessness than from evil disposition. Far more suitable in their case is the preventive system, which consists in making them thoroughly acquainted with the regulations they have to obey and in watching over them. In this way they are always conscious of the vigilance of the Head-master or his assistants, who are ready to guide and advise them in every difficulty and to anticipate their wants. The pupils should never be left to their own devices, yet they should have complete freedom to run, jump, and enjoy themselves in their own noisy fashion. Gymnastics, vocal and instrumental music, and plenty of outdoor exercise are the most efficacious means of maintaining discipline and improving the boys, bodily and mentally."

Only children over seven were admitted to the Institutes founded by Don Bosco. Dr. Barnardo, on the other hand, who rescued thousands of orphans and destitute children in London and was able to witness a decided decrease in the criminality of that capital, concentrated his beneficent efforts on destitute children from their earliest years, with the idea of removing them as soon as possible from the bad environment in which they were born. He was, moreover, desirous that they should share with more fortunate children the boon of happy childhood, and resolved that up to the age of seven they should be brought up without educational or other restraints, save the affection of those appointed to watch over them during the first years, so that they might imbibe sufficient love and joy for the rest of their lives. Such is the rule followed in the buildings set apart for the infants, Bird Castle, Tiny House, and Jersey House, which are perfect nests of happy birds.

In spite of the seeming impossibility of obtaining individual education in a school, thanks to a system devised by Dr. Barnardo, the older children actually enjoy this advantage. New-comers are placed in a special department until facts relative to their past life are ascertained and an idea formed of their individuality. The results of these preliminary inquiries determine in which school the boy shall be placed and what trade he shall follow. Moreover, any boy desiring to change his occupation is encouraged to do so. Every year a re-distribution is made according to the aptitudes shown by the lads in study and manual work and their physical and intellectual development, special care being taken that the younger children should not be put with those who have arrived at a more advanced stage of physical and mental evolution. Free development of the various individual aptitudes is thus secured, while avoiding that common defect of schools, the turning out of numerous lads all made after one regulation pattern.

Having come to the conclusion that life in an institute, in spite of all these precautions, is unsuited to girls, Dr. Barnardo founded a village at a short distance from London with cottage homes for children of both sexes. Each cottage contains from fifteen to twenty children and forms a family, the domestic duties of the homes being discharged by the girls.

Dr. Barnardo realised, however, that the placing of children in private families is the best means of effecting their salvation, and he made great efforts in private and public to induce benevolent persons to adopt his protégés. Finally, he organised a regular emigration of lads to Canada, where a special agent provides them with situations on farms or in factories.

America certainly does not lag behind Europe in the number and excellence of its organisations for rescuing the little derelicts of its cities. In every town of the United States visited by me, I had the pleasure of inspecting such institutions, all of which are kept with extraordinary care, and in some cases, with elegance. Amongst others, I may mention the Hebrew Sheltering Guardian Society in New York City and the George Junior Republic at Freeville, near Ithaca, both of which seemed to me the most original of their kind.

The Hebrew Sheltering Guardian Society is an orphanage for the Jews, managed with rare insight and intelligence by Mr. Lewisohn. The Institute being founded for orphans only, there is no limit as to age or condition. Infants and young people, diseased and healthy, intelligent and mentally deficient, normal and abnormal, good and bad, are all welcome. In order to prevent the overcrowding of the institution and to provide homes for as many children as possible, a committee has been organised for the purpose of finding homes in private families for all children under six years of age and for those who are sickly and delicate. A certain proportion are adopted, and others are boarded out, but the sum paid for their keep is always less than it would cost to place them in a school; and there is, moreover, always a chance of their being adopted later. At the age of six, all healthy and robust children enter the Institute, which becomes their home, providing them with board, lodging, clothing, moral and religious instruction, and training in some kind of work, but in order that they shall mix with other children, they are educated at the public schools, and the consequent saving in money and space enables the Institute to receive a larger number of children than it otherwise could.

Instead of the uniform customary in such insti-

tutions which serves to accentuate in a humiliating
way the contrast between the inmates and more fortunate children who possess parents and homes, the
clothing worn by the orphans of the Hebrew Sheltering Guardian Society is varied in colour and style.
Girls skilled in the use of their needle alter their
dresses to suit their individual tastes, and are allowed
to sew, either gratis or for payment, for the boys and
other girls of the Institute, who are unable or unwilling to make these alterations themselves.   When
school-tasks are finished, boys and girls of over
twelve are allowed to engage in light occupations—
needlework, writing, etc., supplied by the Institute to
enable them to earn a little pocket-money and learn
to spend it properly.

When the boys and girls have passed all the
standards of the elementary schools, they enter trade
schools, where they remain until they are proficient
in some craft which will enable them to earn a living.
Those who show decided intellectual or business
aptitudes are sent to colleges or commercial schools.

The children are encouraged to take an interest
in social and political life by the foundation of a
miniature republic, or rather two separate republics,
one for the boys and the other for the girls, each with
its president, a boy or a girl according to the case.
In reality, however, they are under the management

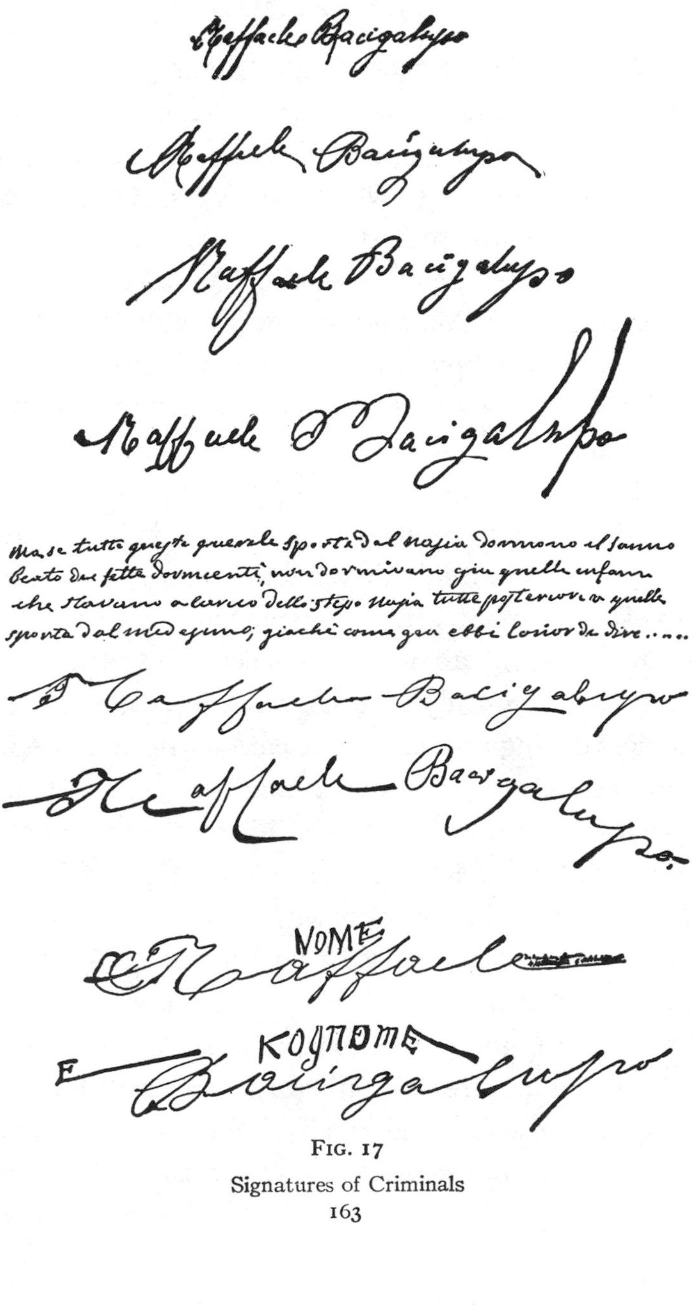


FIG. 17

Signatures of Criminals

of a lady, who devises various amusements for the children, reading, games, etc., teaches them music and drawing, and helps the little President to organise entertainments to which outsiders, relatives, and schoolfellows are invited.

The George Junior Republic (America) is a very different institution, having been founded for unruly and turbulent boys, who are beyond their parents' control. It is a species of Reformatory, not a Home for Waifs.

Mr. George, the founder of the Republic, a man of original and intelligent cast of mind, if I may judge of his individuality from hearsay, decided on its establishment after many attempts of a similar nature. Being anxiously concerned for the future of so many unruly youths who, left to their own devices during the summer vacations, degenerate into rowdies, he invited about a hundred of these lads to spend the summer months on his estate at Freeville, near Ithaca, and tried to influence them for good. The attempt did not meet with much success at first. Mr. George soon realised that however easy it is to exercise a beneficial influence on one or two boys by adopting gentle methods, it is extremely difficult to manage hundreds in this way. He had, however, observed how fair and rigidly honest boys generally are in their games and how ready they are to condemn any meanness, and he conceived the idea of making his charges look after each other. Thus each one would feel himself a responsible judge of his companions' actions.

At the end of the summer holidays in 1895, when the time came for the boys to return home, five remained behind at Freeville in a cottage standing on three acres of land; the next year the number of lads remaining was doubled or trebled. A miniature Republic was founded, of which the lads were the citizens, and in this capacity, were obliged to make laws and to insist on their being respected. The Republic proved to be a great success, the temporary colony became a permanent one capable of reforming wild, unruly boys, who if allowed to wander about in the streets and to mix with older and more vicious lads, would possibly have been ruined. A recent census of the Republic showed that it possessed 150 citizens, 82 boys and 68 girls, three hundred acres of land, twenty-four buildings, a chapel, prison, school, and court of justice.

In order that the colonists should not completely lose touch with the outside world, but should in some measure be prepared for the social exigencies of their future lives, the colony is organised like a miniature town. The children, boys and girls, are divided into so many families, each consisting of ten or twelve

members presided over by two adults, who take the
place of parents and look after the household. The
greater part of the population is engaged in agriculture, in cultivating the land belonging to the Republic,
but a certain proportion adopt the arts and crafts
necessary to every community: joinery, book-bind-
ing, printing, shoemaking, or shop-keeping. The
colony coins its own money and possesses a bank run

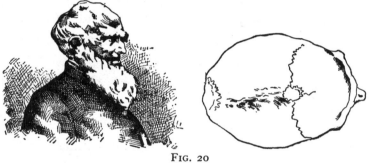

FIG. 20

Brigand Gasparone

by the boys themselves, where the colonists can de-
posit their savings. All labour and produce are paid
for separately. The colony has its own laws sanc-
tioned by its Parliament, its Tribunal, the members of which, chosen from amongst the citizens, are
charged with enforcing the laws. The Parliament,
composed without distinction of sex, of boys and
girls, decrees the holidays, organises the games and
entertainments, and establishes the public expendi-

ture, revenue, and taxes, etc. (see Figs. 19 and 20).

The results of this system appear to be excellent; most of the ex-colonists have turned out well, and in view of this fact, republics on similar lines are being organised in various parts of the United States. This Republic admits only children over twelve, who remain in the colony about three years.

## PREVENTIVE INSTITUTIONS FOR DESTITUTE ADULTS

Besides institutions for the careful training of the young, methods for preventing crime also include all attempts to help young or adult persons at any crisis in their lives when they are friendless and out of work, for it is precisely then that they are most exposed to temptation.

People's hotels, shelters for emigrants or strangers, reading-rooms, inexpensive but wholesome entertainments, evening classes for instruction in manual work, labour bureaus, organisations for assisting emigrants, etc., are the most efficacious institutions of this kind. And in this connection, I must refer to the work done by the Salvation Army, which from what I was able to observe in America, seems to me the best organised of all existing benevolent associations, since by means of a thousand arms it reaches every form of poverty and misery and seeks to make all its institutions self-supporting. It fights drunkenness by lectures, recreation rooms, and temperance hotels; it fights poverty by investigating each individual case of destitution, visiting poor families, dispensing sympathy and help, providing shelter for the night at a minimum price and industrial homes for those who are out of work. Sometimes the rooms are turned into recreation halls for drunkards or industrial schools for the girls of poor mothers who are obliged to go out to work, or temporary hospitals for some urgent case which, owing to bureaucratic formalities, the hospitals are unable to attend to immediately, or rooms with moving pictures for friendly gatherings on holidays, thus grafting one benevolent work on to another so as to obtain the best results at the smallest cost.

That interesting book *Where the Shadows Lengthen* gives an account of the different institutions founded by the Salvation Army in the United States. There are sixty-five Industrial Homes, where unemployed of all classes can apply for work. In these Homes refuse and worn-out articles collected from individual homes of their respective towns are disinfected and transformed into useful articles, which are sold at low prices to the neighbouring poor, thus benefiting purchasers, work-people, and society in general. During one year these Homes gave employment to 8696 men, distributed 1,318, 044 meals (work-people who are temporarily employed in these Homes have a right only to board and lodging), and gave a night's shelter to 463,550 persons.

In addition, the Army has seventy-seven Hotels where the working-classes find a night's lodging at a low price (just sufficient to cover the maintenance of the Shelter), and 7990 Accommodations which in one year supplied a night's rest to 2,114,037 persons. It has, besides, three colonies with 420 inhabitants, two boarding-houses for servants and shop-girls out of employment, where for a few pence they may have a bed, cook their own meals, wash and mend their clothes, and are assisted to find work.

The Salvation Army has also 22 Rescue Homes, where young girls condemned by the Juvenile Court and generally more neglected than vicious, are reformed with a little care and affection, and 3599 Accommodations to which during one year 1701 girls were admitted.

To ensure careful supervision of all the poor quarters, the Salvation Army has divided them into twenty slums, in each of which they have established their Headquarters and send out their soldiers to investigate and assist cases of poverty and misery of every kind. Each slum Headquarters is provided with halls for meetings, rooms for the officials, a

Kindergarten, and Dormitories which also serve as shelters or hospitals for urgent cases. In one year 26,290 families were visited by the Army and 38,290 received assistance. Employment, temporary and permanent, was found for 66,621 persons.

All poor of whatever condition, nationality, or religion, whether honest or criminal, on applying to the nearest of these Headquarters may be sure of finding sympathy and help.

Five Homes have been founded by the Army for waifs and children whose mothers are obliged to go out to work, and 225 Accommodations where children may find a temporary or permanent home.

A special squad of soldiers has recently undertaken work amongst prisoners with great success. In two months they visited 43 prisons, wrote 1732 letters to prisoners, and distributed 10,000 pamphlets. 19,882 prisoners attended meetings held in the prisons, 194 articles of clothing were distributed, 128 persons provided with work on their release and 300 with sleeping accommodation.

In South America the Army has founded similar institutions, which embrace others, such as hospitals, etc., suited to the needs of each place.

Other benevolent organisations which seem to me admirable, are the Sisterhoods founded twenty years ago by the Rabbi Gottheil. These Sisterhoods, as may be assumed from the name, are entirely directed by women. They consist of premises, sometimes annexed to the synagogue; at others, situated independently, which form a species of Headquarters for the philanthropical work done in the surrounding districts. The Sisterhood is open day and night to all the poor who are in need of help of any kind. There is a resident Directress, under whose orders a number of ladies take turns in helping applicants. The Sisterhoods were founded on the principle that human beings are capable of doing the maximum amount of good to others when they follow their own particular tendencies and try to utilise their individual talents in satisfying the intellectual, moral, or recreative needs of the poor. Some of the ladies devote themselves to simple legal questions, tracing an absent husband or wife, registering births, taking unruly children to the Juvenile Courts, or looking after them, etc. Others take charge of medical matters, arrange for the admission of children or adults to the hospitals, etc.; others organise entertainments, teach singing, drawing, needlework, and cooking classes. The premises are used in turn by working-girls learning sewing, or others rehearsing some play or opera chorus. Almost all the Sisterhoods possess a permanent Kindergarten for the children of women who are obliged to work outside their homes, and an employment bureau. All the ladies, except the Directress, give their services gratis. For all help given by the Sisterhood, except in the case of the very poor, a small fee is demanded, and this enables the Sisterhood to pay its way without depending much on donations and subscriptions from private persons, and to spread and increase its work without difficulty.

" The Educational Alliance" of New York, founded to give assistance to Jewish emigrants arriving at that city from all parts of the world, is another institution deserving of mention. This " Alliance" has a large building in the Jewish quarter near the docks, where emigrants can obtain instruction in gymnastics, cookery, domestic economy, English, needlework, etc. There are also recreation rooms, baths, a library, and rooms where school children can prepare their lessons. Men and women are assisted in obtaining employment and receive medical and legal aid. There is also a species of tribunal for settling petty disputes in cases where the parties interested object to applying to the ordinary courts. It was crowded when I saw it, and I was not surprised to learn that it is of great service to the emigrants. For public holidays, the Alliance organises concerts, excursions, and lectures, and during the summer vacations it opens a number of boarding-houses in the country.

All these benevolent institutions, schools, rescue homes, orphanages, and shelters, organised with so much care for the prevention of crime and adopted in America by all communities of whatever religion, regardless of cost, have given excellent results. Bosco and Rice (*Les Homicides aux Etats-Unis*) and my father (*Crimes, Ancient and Modern*) have demonstrated statistically that in States like Massachusetts, where there is no great influx of immigration nor a large coloured population, the diminution in the number of crimes has been very rapid, the percentage of homicides being about equal to those of England, that is, lower than the majority of European States.

It must be confessed in honour to the people of the United States, that they are very ready to admit their own short-comings and constantly regret the large proportion of crimes in their country. But when they reflect that the constant stream of immigration contains many lawless elements, that the different laws in force in the different States make evasions of justice in many cases easy, that the construction of houses with the fire-escape communicating directly with the public thoroughfare provides an easy means of ingress and egress, and that an enormous proportion of the dense population of their cities is composed of people from all parts of the world, accustomed to varying moral codes, they may realise with pride that the percentage of crime in the United States is certainly lower than it would be in any Continental State under similar conditions.

# CHAPTER III

## *METHODS FOR THE CURE AND REPRESSION OF CRIME*

PREVENTIVE methods, the careful training of children, and assistance rendered to adults in critical moments of their lives, may diminish crime, but cannot suppress it entirely. Such methods should be supplemented by institutions which undertake to cure criminals, while protecting society from their attacks, and by others for the segregation of incurable offenders, who should be rendered as useful as possible in order to minimise in every way the injury they inflict on the community.

Although unjustly accused of desiring to revolutionise penal jurisprudence, criminal anthropologists realised from the very beginning that laws cannot be changed before there is a corresponding change in public opinion, and that even equitable modifications in the laws, if too sudden, are always fraught with dangerous consequences. Therefore, instead of a radical change in the penal code, their aim was to effect a few slight alterations in the graduation of penalties, in accordance with age, sex, and the degree of depravity manifested by culprits in their offences. They also counselled certain modifications in the application of the laws, the reformation according to modern ideas, of prisons, asylums, penal colonies, and all institutions for the punishment and redemption of offenders, and an extensive application of those penalties devised in past ages as substitutes for imprisonment, which have the advantage of corrupting the culprit less, and costing the community very little.

*Juvenile Offenders.* Young people, and, above all, children, should be dealt with separately by special legislative methods.

With the exception of England, where quite recently a children's court has been opened at Westminster, special tribunals for the young are unknown in Europe. However, in modern times, the penal codes of nearly every European State make marked allowance for the age of offenders, and where there is no differentiation in the laws, the magistrate uses his own discretion and refuses in many cases to convict juvenile offenders, even when they are guilty of serious offences.

These instinctive methods of dealing with the young have many drawbacks:

1. Without special courts, children guilty of simple acts of insubordination or petty offences (thefts of fruit or riding in trams and trains without paying the fare) which cannot be separated by a hard and fast line from ordinary childish pranks, come into contact with criminal types in court or in prison, and this is greatly detrimental to them morally. If naturally inclined to dishonesty, they run the risk of developing into occasional criminals and of losing all sense of shame: or if really honest, contact with bad characters cannot fail to shock and perturb them, even though their stay in prison be only a short one.

2. The magistrate has no legal powers to supervise juvenile offenders, nor when their actions show grave depravity, to segregate and cure them to prevent their developing into criminals. It has already been shown that born criminals begin their career at a very early age. In one case cited in a previous chapter, a morally insane child of twelve killed one of his companions for a trifling motive— a dispute about an egg; in another, a child of ten caused the arrest of his father by a false accusation; he had previously attempted to strangle a little brother. Children of this type, notwithstanding their tender age, are a social danger, and the moral disease from which they

suffer should be taken in hand at once.   In any case they should be carefully segregated until a cure appears to be effected.

Minors require a special code, which takes into consideration the fact that certain offences are incidental to childhood and that children who have committed these offences may still develop into honest men.   It should also contain provisions for dealing with born criminals, epileptics, and the morally insane at an early age, by segregation in special reformatories where they cannot corrupt juvenile offenders of a non-criminal type, and where a thorough-going attempt to cure them may be made.

An excellent reform of this character has been effected in many of the United States of America with the adoption of the probation system and juvenile courts which protect children from the corruption of prison life and contact with habitual offenders.   The juvenile court, this tribunal exclusively instituted for minors, has been brought to great perfection in many of the United States.   In some, special buildings have been erected for the hearing of cases against children, by which means all contact with adult criminals is avoided: in others, where this is not practicable, a part of the ordinary court is set aside for them with a separate entrance.

Nor are juvenile offenders judged according to

the common law; their offences are tried by special magistrates, who deal with them in a paternal, rather than in a strictly judicial spirit, and the penalties are slight, varied, and suited to children. The magistrates are assisted by officers, who obtain information from teachers, parents, and neighbours as to the character, conduct, faults, and good qualities of the culprit, and with these indications the magistrate is able to essay the correction, not of the particular offence which has brought the child within his jurisdiction, but his general organic defects. The punishments do not include imprisonment, and are drawn from practical experience and common-sense, not from any article of the penal code.

I was present at the hearing of a case against a lad, who was accused of having travelled on a subway without paying. He was sentenced to copy out the by-laws twenty times, to learn them by heart and repeat them a month later at the same court. In the case of more serious offences, children may be sent to some public or private reformatory, according to the circumstances of the parents. However, none of these punishments are infamous, and parents themselves, when unable to control their children, have recourse to the juvenile court.

It is supplemented in a very efficacious manner by the probation system, the organisation of a number of men and women who undertake the super-vision of children when the court decides that they require it. These protectors use every means at their disposal to prevent their charges falling into bad ways and assist them in every possible way to correct their defects.

This system has proved to be so efficacious, and at the same time so devoid of any drawbacks, that its unconditional adoption by all the States of Europe and America would be of great social advantage.

### INSTITUTIONS FOR FEMALE OFFENDERS

The weighty reasons which call for separate courts and reformatories for juvenile offenders are equally valid in the case of female law-breakers, for whom special tribunals and legislation should be provided.

The percentage of criminality among women is considerably lower than that of men, and in nearly all cases offenders belong to the category of criminaloids.

My father's work *The Female Offender* demon-strates that prostitution is the true equivalent of criminality. When we except this class of unfor-tunates, there remain only hysterical and occasional offenders, guilty generally of petty larceny (particu-larly of a domestic nature) or of harbouring criminals and acting as more or less passive accomplices; and criminals from passion, who commit infanticide or kill faithless husbands and lovers. In all these cases, imprisonment should not be resorted to; in fact, the greater number might be dealt with by a magisterial reprimand or the granting of conditional liberty. In view also, of the important part played by dress, ornaments, etc., in the feminine world, penalties inflicted on vanity—the cutting off of the hair, the obligation to wear a certain costume, etc., might with advantage be substituted for imprisonment.

The milder nature of feminine criminality, the usefulness of women in the home, and the serious injury inflicted on the family and society in general by the segregation of the wife and mother (if only for a short period), are reasons for advocating the institution of special tribunals for dealing with the offences of women and special legislation which would take into consideration their position in the family and the fact that they are rarely a violent social danger.

At present, in Europe at least, no such differential treatment exists. The reduction of penalties is left entirely to the discretion and humanity of judges, who in many cases, it is true, are instinctively disposed to be more indulgent towards women and to take these conditions into account. But it would be a far more satisfactory state of things if legislation paid due regard to such circumstances, just as in Italy in enrolling recruits for compulsory military service, allowance is made for social and family relations, the only sons of widowed mothers, men of delicate constitution, etc., being exempted.

In spite of the low percentage and, generally speaking, trifling importance of the crimes committed by women, there are a small number of female delinquents, some of whom show an extraordinary degree of depravity, as though all the perversity lacking in the others were concentrated in these few. They are true born criminals, epileptics, and morally insane subjects.

These serious anti-social elements, murderers, poisoners, and swindlers, might be secluded in a small reformatory with compulsory labour and silence as additional penalties. Separate cells, however, are not necessary. All reformatories for women should be provided with a nursery where children born in prison could be nursed by their mothers, thereby diminishing the social injury which must result from the imprisonment of any mother, and fostering the growth of the sublime and sacred maternal sentiment, which is unfortunately so often lacking in criminals.

The Reformatory Prison for Women at South Framingham, near Boston, under the management of Mrs. Morton, is an excellent example of an institution conducted on the lines laid down by criminologists.    The Reformatory is situated at about an hour's journey by rail from Boston, in the midst of fields which are cultivated by a part of the convict population.    No high walls surround the building and separate it from the outer world, nor is it watched by guards.    A broad avenue leads to the entrance, where, in answer to my ring, I was welcomed by neat white-clad attendants and shown into a charming room looking out upon a lovely garden.    I passed through corridors, unmolested by the sound of keys grating in locks, from this room to the dining-rooms, dormitories, recreation and work rooms.

As soon as prisoners enter the Reformatory, they are carefully examined by an intelligent and pleasant woman physician, who is in charge of the infirmary where the anthropological examination takes place. When the prisoner has been declared able-bodied, she is placed in one of the work-rooms to learn and follow the trade indicated by the medical officer as the best adapted to her constitution and aptitude. At night, she is conducted to a second-class cell situated in a large, well-lighted corridor.    The cell is furnished with a table, bed, chair, pegs to hang clothes on, a calendar, a picture, and a book or two.

Work is compulsory and done by the piece, and when each prisoner has finished her allotted task, she is at liberty to work for herself or to read books supplied from the library.   If unskilled, she receives instruction in some manual work, and the payment for her labour is put aside and handed over to her on her release, with the small outfit she has prepared and sewed during detention.

Women with children under a year, or those who give birth to a child in the Reformatory, are allowed to have their little ones with them during the night and part of the day.   When they go to work every morning, the babies are left in the nursery, which adjoins the infirmary, and is under the direct supervision of the doctor.   The nursery, a large, well-lighted room, spotlessly clean and bright with flowers, is a veritable paradise for the little ones.

At noon, the prisoner is permitted to fetch her baby, feed, and keep it near her during dinner-hour. At two o'clock she resumes work until five, when she again takes charge of her baby till next morning. A cradle is placed in her cell for the infant, and she is provided with a small bath.

A series of trifling rewards encourage moral improvement.   Those who show good conduct during the first two months are transferred to the first class with its accompanying privileges, a better and more spacious cell, a smart collar, the right to correspond with friends and to receive visitors more frequently, to have an hour's recreation in company with other good-conduct prisoners and to receive relatives in a pretty sitting-room instead of in the common visitors' room.

The final reward for uninterrupted improvement and untiring industry on the part of the prisoner is her ultimate release, which since the sentence is unlimited, may take place as soon as the Directress considers her competent to earn an honest living. But released prisoners are not left to their own devices with the risk of speedily succumbing to temptation. A commission of ladies interested in the Reformatory (one of whom, Mrs. Russell, was my guide on the occasion of my visit there) are consulted before the release of each prisoner and undertake to furnish her with suitable employment, and to guide and watch over her during the first few months so that she may be sure of advice and assistance in any difficulties.

## INSTITUTIONS FOR MINOR OFFENDERS

Punishments should vary according to the type of criminal, distinction being made between criminals of passion, criminaloids, and born criminals.

*Criminals of Passion.* The true criminal of passion suffers more from remorse than from any penalty the law can inflict. Additional punishments should be: exile of the offender from his native town or from that in which the person offended resides; indemnity for the injury caused, in money, or in compulsory labour if the offender is not possessed of sufficient means. Recourse should never be had to imprisonment, which has an injurious effect even upon the better types of law-breakers; and criminals from passion do not constitute a menace to society. On the contrary, they are not infrequently superior to average humanity and are only prompted to crime by an exaggerated altruism which with care might be turned into good channels.

This applies equally to political offenders, for whom exile is the oldest, most dreaded, and most efficacious punishment, and the disuse into which it has fallen does not appear to be justified, since it admits of graduation, is temporary, and an adequate check on any attempt at insurrection.

*Criminaloids.* Repeated short terms of detention in prison should be avoided and other penalties substituted for petty offences against police regulations, cheating the Customs, etc., when committed by criminaloids who are not recidivists and have no accomplices. A short term of imprisonment, which brings this type of offender into contact with habitual criminals, not only does not serve as a deterrent, but generally has an injurious effect, because it tends to lessen respect for the law, and, in the case of recidivists, to rob punishment of all its terrors; and because criminaloids, when once branded with the infamy of prison and corrupted by associaton with worse types, are liable to commit more serious crimes.

For all minor offences, fines are more efficacious than imprisonment and, in the case of the poor, should be replaced by compulsory labour at the discretion of the magistrate.   Binding over under a guarantee to make good the injury done, corporal punishment, confinement to the house, judicial reprimands and cautions are applicable to offenders of this type, as is also the system of remitting first offences used in France with great success by Magnaud.   Under this system, the offender is sentenced to an adequate penalty, which, however, is only inflicted in the case of recidivation.

An efficacious, and at the same time, more serious method of dealing with criminaloids, is by means of the probation system and indeterminate sentence. The offender is sentenced to the maximum penalty applicable to his particular offence, but it may be diminished after a certain time if he shows signs of improvement.   During this interval he is on probation, that is, under supervision, much in the same way as juvenile offenders.

The probation system is extensively and successfully adopted in America, either singly or in conjunction with other penalties, as shown above.

## THE PROBATION SYSTEM

This is an ideal manner of dealing with offenders of a less serious type, minors and criminaloids, who have fallen into bad ways, since, instead of punishing them, it seeks to encourage in them habits of integrity and to check the growth of vices by means of a benevolent but strict supervision. The offender is placed under the guidance of a respectable person, who tries in every way to smooth the path of reform by providing his charge with employment if he has none, or putting him in the way of learning some trade if he is unskilled, by isolating him from bad company, by rewarding any improvement, and reporting progress to the central office, which has to decide whether the period of probation is sufficient, or, in cases where it has not been efficacious, to have recourse to sterner measures.

The only drawback to this system is the difficulty of applying it, because it is not always possible to find in every town a number of persons of high moral standing, who are able and willing to exercise vigi-

lance over offenders. However, to the honour of the
United States it must be said that in many States
this supervision is organised in a truly admirable
manner. At Boston I visited the Probation Office
organised and managed by Miss Mary Dewson, which
undertakes the supervision of girls and is a model
worthy of imitation from the general arrangement
down to the smallest details.

The relations between the officers and their
charges are in most cases very cordial. The little girls
write most affectionate letters, in which they narrate
their joys and sorrows, express penitence for their
shortcomings and ask advice and help as of guardian
spirits. The officers in their turn show themselves
to be affectionate protectors and are scrupulous in
the fulfilment of their duties towards the central
office. Upwards of one hundred lockers were opened
at my request, and I was able to examine the documents relating to each of the children with their
antecedents, improvement, or the reverse, methodically entered up to a few days previous to my visit.

The splendid results obtained everywhere by
this system are leading to its gradual adoption in
nearly all the States of the Union and in many parts
of Australia and England, in dealing with young
people, adults, and all first offenders convicted of
petty infractions of the law, drunkenness, disturbance

of the peace, and disorderly conduct, and also for prisoners released on ticket-of-leave. The probationer is obliged to report himself every fortnight, or at any time the probation officer may desire. The officer is empowered to supervise the conduct of the probationer at home and in his place of employment, and to threaten him with legal proceedings should his conduct be unsatisfactory.

The supervision of adults, as may be supposed, is a far more delicate and complicated matter than that of children, and however discreetly the officer proceeds in order to keep the matter hidden from neighbours and employers, the position is such a humiliating one for adults that many prefer imprisonment to supervision. I was told that special reformatories have been established at Boston for the detention of those who prefer prison to vigilance.

Perhaps this aversion of adult offenders in America to the probation system is due to the fact that the probation officer is vested with powers almost exceeding those of any magistrate. If he thinks fit, he may extend the period of supervision almost indefinitely or convert it into imprisonment. Moreover, the feeling that every movement and action, however innocent, is being watched is very galling to a grown-up person. However, these drawbacks could no doubt be remedied.

In England, supervision is replaced by a pledge of good behaviour guaranteed by the culprit or a surety, who is induced to exercise vigilance by the knowledge that he will lose the sum deposited in the case of recidivation. The magistrate is obliged by English law to fix the period of probation, which cannot be extended without another sentence. In France, Belgium, and Australia, the probation system appears to have given good results.

*Corporal Punishment.* Although repugnant to civilised ideas, the various forms of corporal punishment, fasting, cold shower-bath, or even the rod, are very suitable substitutes for imprisonment in the case of children guilty of petty offences, because not only are these punishments inexpensive and have the advantage of creating a deeper and more immediate impression, but they do not corrupt minor offenders nor do they interrupt their regular occupations, whether work or study. Fines should always be inflicted for slight infractions of the law and in all cases of petty larceny, frauds, and forgeries committed by minors. The fines should be proportioned to the means of the individual and the gravity of the offence, and replaced by compulsory labour in the case of those who refuse to pay.

*Indemnity.* The obligation to make adequate compensation for the injury caused would be an ideal punishment, but is extremely difficult to put into practice. The magistrate, however, should do his utmost to make suitable use of this penalty, and the victim should be legally entitled to receive a part of the proceeds from work done by the culprit during detention.

## REFORMATORIES

Minors convicted for the first time of such serious offences that supervision becomes an insufficient guarantee against recidivation, should be relegated to reformatories or other institutions which undertake to punish offences and to segregate and correct offenders.

For the truly magnificent scale on which such reclaiming institutions are conducted in North and South America, both continents merit special mention.

The oldest and most celebrated of these reformatories, that founded at Elmira by Brockway, owed its inspiration to my father's book *Criminal Man* and is the first reformatory that has been instituted on similar principles.

The convicts admitted to Elmira are young men between the ages of sixteen and thirty, convicted for the first time of any offence, except those of the most serious kind. The Administrative Council is invested with unlimited powers for determining the period of detention and may release prisoners long before the expiration of their sentence.

Each newcomer has a bath, dons the uniform of the Institute, is photographed, registered, medically examined, and finally shut up in a cell to meditate upon his offence. During this time the superintendent obtains all the available information concerning his character, environment, and the probable causes that have led to his crime, and this information serves as a basis for the cure. According to the aptitude and culture of the prisoner, he is placed in a technical or industrial class, where he learns some trade which will enable him to become honestly self-supporting on his release. He is immediately acquainted with his duties and rights and the conditions under which he may regain his liberty.

Education in the Reformatory consists of instruction in general knowledge and special training in some trade. Moral and intellectual progress is stimulated by the publication of a weekly review, *The Summary*, which gives a report on political matters and the news of the Reformatory.

The convicts are divided into three categories: good, middling, and bad. The transference from the second to the first class entails certain privileges, especially those respecting communication with the outer world, the right to receive visitors, to have books, and to eat at a common table instead of partaking of a solitary meal in a cell.   Those who obtain the highest marks for good conduct are at liberty to walk about the grounds and are entrusted with confidential missions, such as the supervision of the other convicts.   Bad conduct marks cause prisoners to be transferred from a higher to the lowest division, where they are obliged to perform the rudest labour.

First-class convicts are purposely exposed to temptations of various kinds, and when they have passed through this ordeal triumphantly, they obtain a conditional release.   This cannot take place, however, until the prisoner is provided with regular employment of some kind, procured by his own exertions, through friends, or by the director of the Reformatory.

For six months after his release he is obliged to give an account of himself regularly in the manner prescribed by the Director; after one year absolute liberty is regained.

In order to reduce the working expenses of the Reformatory as much as possible, all posts, even that of superintendent or teacher in the technical schools, are filled by the convicts.

### PENITENTIARIES

Although born criminals, habitual criminals, and

recidivists should be carefully isolated from minor offenders, they nevertheless require institutes conducted on nearly similar principles. A prison, which is to punish, but at the same time to correct and redeem, demands strict discipline: in fact, milder punishments have very little effect and their constant repetition is harmful, although any exaggeration of brute force is more injurious than useful. Harshness may cow criminals, but does not improve them: on the contrary, it only serves to irritate them or to convert them into hypocrites. Even the adult offender should be looked upon in the light of a child or a moral invalid, who must be cured by a mixture of gentleness and severity, but gentleness should predominate, since criminals are naturally prone to vindictiveness and are apt to regard even slight punishments as unjust tortures. Even a too rigid adherence to the rule of silence may have a detrimental effect on the character of the prisoners. An old convict once said to Despine: "When you winked at slight offences against the rules, we used to talk more, but there was no harm in what we said. Now we talk less, but when we do, we blaspheme and plot evil."

In Danish prisons under rigorous discipline, infractions of prison regulations amounted to 30%;

more recently under milder rule such infractions only amount to 6%.

In order to strengthen the sense of justice which, as we have said, is little developed in criminals, if indeed it is not altogether suffocated by ignoble passions, it is often advisable to appeal to their vanity and self-esteem to aid in maintaining discipline and increasing industry, by constituting them judges of each other's conduct. Obermayer used to divide the convicts into small groups and ask them to elect their own superintendents and teachers, thus establishing a spirit of good-comradeship and rendering possible a system of detailed and individual instruction, the sole kind that is really efficacious. The 385 convicts at Detroit showed the highest percentage of efficiency, because they were divided into 21 classes with 28 teachers, all of whom, with the exception of one, were prisoners. It was noticed that the worst convicts were the best teachers (Pears, *Prisons and Reform*, 1872), which proves that even the most perverse elements may often be utilised for the improvement of others.

Equally good was Despine's method of letting a certain time elapse before inflicting punishment, so that it should not be attributed to mere anger on his part. As soon as the infraction was noted, the prisoner was left to reflect on his conduct, and an hour later the teacher and Director came to show him the penalty prescribed by the regulations. Sometimes it was found efficacious to administer a rebuke and punishment to the whole group to which the offender belonged. Obermayer considered this method to be advantageous.

Work should be the motive force, aim, and recreation of every institute of this kind, in order to stimulate flagging energies, to accustom prisoners to useful pursuits after release, to reinforce prison discipline and to compensate the State for the expense incurred. This latter object should, however, always be subordinated to the others, and lucrative trades must occasionally be avoided. Occupations which might pave the way for other crimes: lockmaking, brass-work, engraving, photography, and calligraphy should not be adopted, but choice made, instead, of those agricultural employments which show the lowest mortality and are much in demand. The manufacture of articles in straw, esparto, and string, printing, tailoring, the making of pottery, and building are all suitable trades, but those which require dangerous tools—shoemaking, cabinet-making, and carpentering — should be resorted to last of all. The rush baskets made by the convicts at Noto (Sicily) obtained several medals.

The tasks allotted to prisoners should always be

proportioned to their strength and tastes. Unskilled or physically weaker individuals who conscientiously do their best, should be rewarded in some way, if not pecuniarily, at least by a reduction of their sentences. In this way work becomes profitable and a spirit of comradeship and friendly emulation develops among the prisoners.

## INSTITUTES FOR HABITUAL CRIMINALS

To protect society against the repeated misdeeds of these offenders and those of born criminals, segregation is essential. However, the institutions set apart to receive these classes should still regard the redemption of the inmates as their chief aim, and only when all attempts have proved futile should they be replaced by almost perpetual isolation in a penal colony.

The Penitenciario Nacional of Buenos Ayres is a splendid instance of an institute founded for the redemption of adult offenders as well as for the punishment of their offences. The inmates of this penitentiary comprise offenders of all types—criminaloids, habitual and born criminals—belonging to the Province of Buenos Ayres. It was established a few years after the Reformatory at Elmira, the fundamental principles of which it has imitated with certain wise modifications to suit diverse circumstances.

Externally, it has nothing in common with the gloomy European prisons. It is a large, white edifice with a broad flight of steps leading to the street and is devoid of all signs of force, soldiers, sentry-boxes, etc.

After passing through a wide vestibule, I reached a large, shady court-yard with low walls almost hidden beneath a wealth of flowers and foliage. A corridor opening on to the court-yard was flanked on each side by a row of open, white cells, each well lighted by a fair-sized window during the day, and by electricity at night. Each cell is furnished with book-shelves, a table with paper, pen and inkstand, and a chair. All the corridors, which are gay with plants, converge towards a central glass-room, whence the sub-inspector surveys all the radiating corridors under his jurisdiction. Each corridor ends in a workshop, where printing, lithography, shoemaking, metal and steel work are carried on, and between the corridors are garden plots in which fruit, vegetables, and flowers are cultivated. The workshops are reckoned among the best the Republic contains. The printing-office turns out many weekly papers, illustrated magazines, and scientific and literary reviews. Footgear of the finest and most elegant quality is manufactured in the shoe-factory, and the foundry and workshop produce lathes, boilers, industrial and agricultural machines and implements. All the cooking in the Penitentiary is done by steam, and the plant is installed in a large building erected by the prisoners themselves.

Work in the Penitentiary is compulsory. On arrival, each convict receives instruction in some handicraft, chosen by himself or one of the foremen. Of course swindlers and forgers are not admitted to trades like lithography, for reasons easy to understand.

The convicts receive regular wages which vary according to their abilities and are about equal to the standard wages in each particular trade. All earnings are put aside and handed to the convict on his release when he is also provided with suitable employment.

Work is finished at five o'clock in the evening and after a substantial supper the prisoners are divided into nine classes, six elementary and three secondary, according to their culture and intelligence. If illiterate, they are taught reading and writing and later, arithmetic, geography, history, languages, and drawing,—this latter being adapted to the particular trade of each individual. When school is finished, prisoners are allowed to go to the library to return the books they have read and take others for the night.

Instead of a weekly newspaper like that published at Elmira, intellectual development is stimulated by means of lectures delivered each week by the prisoners or their teachers and attended by the Director, Vice-Director, and all the convicts.

In addition to the care lavished by the Director, Señor Ballvé, on the work and education of his charges, he spares no pains to encourage moral progress by rewarding good conduct. As each convict enters the Penitentiary, his name, trial, sentence, and antecedents are entered in a book with his photograph and particulars of his physical and psychic individuality, and these data are supplemented by remarks on his conduct and good actions, if any, so that on his release a clear idea is obtained of the moral progress he has made while in prison.

## PENAL COLONIES

When after unsparing efforts for the redemption of a criminal, repeated convictions prove him to be a hopeless recidivist, the community should decline to allow him to perfect his anti-social abilities at their expense in prisons or at large, and should segregate him permanently, unless, indeed, there is any hope of reform, or circumstances render him harmless. Perpetual confinement in a prison, even of an improved type is, however, both cruel and expensive, but an excellent substitute may be found in the Penal Colony. Here the chief object should be, not to educate, elevate, or redeem the criminal, but to render him as useful as possible, so that he does not prove too great a burden on the community.

Penal colonies should be situated on islands or in remote territories, that is, completely isolated from populous districts. The agricultural colony at Meseplas founded by the Belgian Government is a model worthy of imitation.

In this colony the convict population is divided into four categories:

1. Turbulent and dangerous individuals, who exercise an injurious influence over the other inmates of reformatories and prisons;

2. Recidivists, ticket-of-leave men, escaped and mutinous convicts;

3. Persons of bad reputation, who have hitherto avoided conviction;

4. The better types, who have been convicted three or four times only and although not depraved, lack moral stamina and are constantly yielding. to temptation when at large.

All the common necessities of life are supplied by the colonists themselves, beginning with the dwellings which are erected as they are required and according to the resources available. In this way, extensive building operations are carried out at a very slight cost to the State. Cattle and crops are raised on the land, which is cultivated by a number of the convicts, while others manufacture articles which find a ready market in the vicinity and for which they possess suitable tools.

Any convict refusing to work is imprisoned on bread and water. All work is paid for in special coin current only in the colony itself, but which, on the release of the owner, is exchanged for the coin of the country.

The "Open Door," an institution on similar lines, was founded by Professor Cabred for the insane of the Province of Buenos Ayres, and judging from what I was able to observe during my short visit, it fulfils its purpose admirably. It consists of a large village populated by some ten or twelve thousand lunatics. With the exception of the price of the land and the cost of erecting the first buildings, this colony does not cost the community anything; on the contrary, the colonists are able to make large profits.

The ultimate plan of the village with streets and edifices has already been mapped out, and the patients are continually occupied in erecting new buildings, etc. There is a brick-kiln, a carpenter shop, and a smithy, which produce all the materials used in building and furnishing the dwellings. Only the less dangerous patients are employed in these operations: those of weaker mind make brushes and wicker articles.

The colony is situated in the midst of a vast stretch of land in the Province of Buenos Ayres, on which fruit and vegetables are grown by a number of the patients. Others are occupied in raising fowls and pigs, which supply the colony with eggs and meat and yield a large profit when sold outside.

Professor Cabred wisely prefers agriculture of this kind to the raising of large crops of wheat or maize, because it simplifies the task of supervision necessary in any colony, and gives the colonists, whose toil is compulsory, a continual and regular occupation of an almost unvarying character. (This applies equally to the case of a penal colony.) Workmen, foremen, engineers, builders, mechanics, gardeners,—all are patients, with the exception of the Director, the doctor, and about a hundred mounted warders, who pass rapidly from one part to another and are able to intervene in suicidal or homicidal outbreaks.

A colony on these lines would be suitable for the large mass of habitual criminals, who, although unable to resist the temptations of ordinary life, are capable of useful work under supervision, and under such conditions may prove beneficial to themselves and to the community.

## INSTITUTIONS FOR BORN CRIMINALS AND THE MORALLY INSANE

*Asylums for Criminal Insane.* We have still to consider born criminals, epileptics, and the morally insane, whose crimes spring from inherited perverse instincts. These unfortunate beings cannot be consigned to ordinary prisons, since, owing to their state of mental alienation, they do not possess even the modesty of the vicious—hypocrisy—and they never fail to pervert those criminaloids with whom they come in contact. Malcontents by nature, they distrust everybody and everything, and as they see an enemy in every warder and official, they are the centres of constant mutinies.

To confine them in common asylums would be still more injurious, for they preach sodomy, flight, and revolt and incite the others to robbery, and their indecent and savage ways, as well as the terrible reputation which often precedes them, make them objects of terror and repulsion to the quieter patients and their relatives, who dread to see their kin in such company.

Ordinary asylums are equally unsuited to those victims of mental derangement who, although devoid of the depraved instincts of the morally insane and generally of blameless career up to the moment in which they are led to commit a crime by some isolated evil impulse, have a bad influence on the other inmates. Unlike other lunatics, they do not shrink from the company of others, whom they torment with their violence and contaminate with that spirit of restlessness and discontent which distinguished them even before they became insane or criminals. Firm in the belief that they are always being ill treated and insulted, they instil these ideas into their companions and suggest thoughts of flight and revolt, which would never occur to ordinary lunatics, absorbed as they are by their own world of fancies. The condition of the inmates is thereby aggravated, and it becomes impossible to accord them that large measure of freedom advocated by all modern alienists.

To leave these madmen at large would be more dangerous still. Beneath an appearance of perfect calm and mental lucidity are hidden morbid impulses, which may give terrible results at some unexpected moment.

All these offenders—insane criminals and the morally insane whose irresistible tendencies are detrimental to the community—should be confined in special institutes to be cured, or at any rate segregrated for life. No infamy would attach to their names, because their irresponsibility would be clearly recognised, and society would be secure from their attacks.

England was the first country to provide asylums for the criminal insane. In 1840 a portion of Bedlam was set aside for this purpose. Fisherton House, a special private asylum of this kind, was opened in 1844, and later others were instituted at Dundrum (Ireland) in 1850, at Broadmoor in 1863, and at Perth (Scotland) in 1858, to receive criminals who commit crimes in a state of insanity, or become insane during their trial, and all prisoners whose state of lunacy or imbecility renders them unable to conform to the discipline of a prison. Of course sanguinary and violent scenes often occur in these asylums, where the pernicious influence this type of lunatic exercises over his surroundings in ordinary asylums or prisons is multiplied and intensified a hundred-fold. Conspiracies, almost unknown in common asylums, and the murder of warders or officials are very common. Despairing of release and conscious of their irresponsibility, these wretched beings attack the warders, destroy the walls which confine them, murder and wound others and themselves; but at any rate the injury is limited to a small circle, and both harmless lunatics and common criminals are not contaminated. Moreover, even in criminal asylums, long experience with these strange pathological types and the adoption of subdivisions like those recently introduced into Broadmoor by Orange have done much towards improving the general condition and eliminating many drawbacks. According to this classification insane criminals are divided into two classes, *unconvicted* and *convicted*, the former class being subdivided into *untried* and *tried*. Untried offenders, those who are considered to have been insane before committing the crime, are sent to a common county asylum, where are also confined persons convicted of minor offences and declared insane (the percentage of cures in this class is considerable) and others suspected of shamming insanity. In this way, the better elements are eliminated and the inmates of the criminal insane asylum reduced to the worst and most dangerous types only.

## Capital Punishment

When, notwithstanding prisons, deportation, and criminal asylums, individuals of ineradicable anti-social instincts make repeated attempts on the lives of others, whether honest men or their own companions in evil-doing, the only remedy is the application of the extreme penalty—death.

Amongst barbarous peoples, on whom prison makes but slight impression, or in primitive communities that do not possess criminal asylums, penitentiaries, and other means of social defence and redemption, the death penalty has always been considered the most certain and at the same time the most economical means of common protection. But criminal anthropologists realise that the desire to abolish this penalty, which so often finds expression in civilised countries, arises from a noble sentiment and one they have no wish to destroy.

Capital punishment, according to the opinion of my father, should only be applied in extreme cases, but the fear of it, suspended like a sword of Damocles above their heads, would serve as a check to the murderous proclivities displayed by some criminals when they are condemned to perpetual imprisonment.

We have, it is true, no right to take the lives of others but if we refuse to recognise the legitimacy of self-defence, exile and imprisonment are equally unjustifiable.

When we realise that there exist beings, born criminals, who are organised for evil, who reproduce the instincts common to the wildest savages and even those of ferocious carnivora, and are destined by nature to injure others, our resentment becomes softened; but notwithstanding our sense of pity, we feel justified in demanding their extermination when they prove to be dangerous and absolutely irredeemable.

## Penalties Proposed by the Modern School

The following tables, compiled by Senator Garofalo, a celebrated jurist of the Modern School and inserted in *Criminal Man*, vol. iii, show the distribution of penalties systematically arranged.

I. Born Criminals who are utterly devoid of the sentiment of pity.

| Offender | Crime | Penalty |
|---|---|---|
| Murderers exhibiting moral insensibility and instinctive cruelty, convicted of | Murder for lucre or some other egotistical object Murder without provocation on the part of the victim Murder with ferocious execution | Prison, penal colony, criminal insane asylum, or capital punishment if recidivists. |

II. Violent and Impulsive Criminals, Criminaloids, and those guilty through insufficiency of pity, of decency, of inhibitory power, and through prejudiced notions of honor.

| Offender | Crime | Penalty |
|---|---|---|
| Adults convicted of | Cruelty, assault and battery, rape, kidnapping | Criminal insane asylum for epileptics, or Indefinite seclusion for a period equal to one of the natural divisions of a man's life, with period of supervision. |
| Minors convicted of | Murder, cruelty and other offences against the person without provocation Offences against decency | Special reformatories, criminal insane asylum if there are congenital tendencies. Penal colony and deportation in cases of recidivation. |

| Offender | Crime | Penalty |
|---|---|---|
| Adults convicted of | Homicide provoked by injury or genuine grievances | Exile from native place and from the town in which the victim's family live. |
| Adults convicted of | Homicide in self-defence<br>Homicide to avenge some wrong or personal dishonour | Exile, segregation for an indefinite period in some remote town or settlement. |
| Adults convicted of | Assault in quarrels, or ill-treatment when intoxicated, blows, insults, or slander | Compensation for injury caused, fines, reprimand, security, conditional liberty. |
| Adults convicted of | Mutiny and revolt | Reprimand, security, imprisonment for a definite period. |

### III. Criminals Devoid of a Sense of Honesty

| Offender | Crime | Penalty |
|---|---|---|
| Adults (habitual offenders) convicted of | Theft, fraud, arson, forgery, blackmail | Criminal lunatic asylums (if insane or epileptic), deportation (for sane offenders). |
| Adults (occasional offenders) convicted of | Theft fraud, forgery, blackmail, arson | Reformatories, conditional liberty, exclusion from particular profession. |
| Adults convicted of | Peculation, concussion | Loss of office, exclusion from all public offices, fines, compensation for damage done. |
| Adults convicted of | Arson, malicious damage to property | Compensation, or as a substitute, imprisonment. Criminal lunatic asylums (if insane). Penal colonies (for recidivists). |

| Offender | Crime | Penalty |
|---|---|---|
| Adults convicted of | Fraudulent bankruptcy | Compensation for damage caused, exclusion from business and public offices. |
| Adults convicted of | Counterfeiting, forging cheques, public title-deeds, etc. | Reformatories, fines, compensation for damage, exclusion from office. |
| Adults convicted of | Bigamy, substitution or suppression of child | Seclusion for an indefinite period. |
| Minors convicted of | Theft, fraud, and picking pockets | Magisterial reprimand, probation, reformatory, or agricultural colony. |

IV. Offenders Lacking in Industry

| Offender | Penalty |
|---|---|
| Beggars, vagabonds, loafers | Agricultural colony for country offenders, workshop for city offenders. |

V. Offenders Deficient in Misoneism (Hatred of Change)

| Offender | Penalty |
|---|---|
| Political, social, and religious rebels | Temporary exile. |

## Symbiosis

The punishment of offenders and the protection of society from the insane are the two chief objects of criminal jurisprudence, but criminal anthropologists aim at something higher, the utilisation of anti-social elements, thus redeeming them completely and justifying their existence in the eyes of mankind and in the scheme of nature.

We find, in fact, in nature numerous instances of a partnership for mutual benefit between animals and plants of very diverse species and tendencies. Lichens are a living symbiosis of algæ and fungi: the pagurus allows the actiniæ to settle on his dwelling, where they attract his prey and in return are housed and conveyed from place to place.

In imitation of this principle, criminal anthropologists seek to devise a means of making offenders serviceable to civilisation by carefully analysing their tendencies and psychology, and fitting them into some suitable groove in the social scheme, where they may be useful to themselves and to others. Side by side with depraved instincts, criminals frequently possess invaluable gifts: an abnormal degree of intelligence, great audacity, and love of innovation. The wonderful galleries and fortifications cut out in the rocks at Gibraltar and Malta by English convicts and the complete transformation of parts of Sardinia have led criminologists to the conclusion that the ancient penalty of enforced labour was more logical, useful, and advantageous both for the culprit and the community than all modern punishments. The Mormons of America and the religious sects persecuted in Russia by an omnipotent bureaucracy, have by their energy transformed uninhabitable regions into lands of extraordinary fertility. Still greater results might be obtained, if the abnormal tendencies of certain individuals were turned into useful channels, instead of being pent up until they manifest themselves in anti-social acts, and this beneficent and lofty task should devolve on teachers and protectors of such of the young as show physical and psychic anomalies at an early age.

The colonisation of wild regions and all professions (motoring, cycling, acrobatic and circus feats) which demand audacity, activity, love of adventure, and intense efforts followed by long periods of repose are eminently suited to criminals. There are cases on record in which young men have actually become thieves and even murderers in order to gain sufficient means to become comedians or professional cyclists, and there is every reason to suppose that these crimes would never have been committed had the youths been able to obtain the required sums honestly. On the other hand, men of bad character, ready to develop into criminals, often undergo a complete transformation when they find some outlet for their intelligence and aptitudes, in becoming pioneers in virgin regions or soldiers. War, the original, perpetual and exclusive occupation of our ancestors, is emi-

nently suited to the tendencies of criminals.  All the
characteristics of the criminal, impulsiveness, cynicism, physical and moral insensibility, and invulnerability are valuable qualities in the soldier in times
of war, especially when waged against savage and
barbarous nations, when cunning and ability have
to be employed against primitive races who laugh at
the rules and ethics of civilised warfare.

Amongst brigands, we find a few badly-armed
individuals performing marvels of valour, and the
leaders, although ignorant men, manifesting an
intelligence and tactical skill that puts trained armies
to shame.  Could not the tendencies of criminals be
used for the good of their country?  The qualities
developed in primitive races by constant warfare
against the forces of nature are characteristic also
of criminals.  Let those whom nature has destined
to reproduce impulsive and brutal instincts in a
civil and industrial age be permitted to employ them
in defending civilisation with true primitive valour
against external and internal enemies, against barbarous peoples who would restrict its boundaries, or
reactionary elements who seek to hinder its progress.

The Great Redeemer, who in pardoning the
adulteress, said, "He that is without sin among you,
let him first cast a stone at her," and the Prophet
who foretold the day when the wolf and the lamb

should dwell together and the lion should eat straw like the ox and should "not hurt nor destroy," divined perhaps this noble aim. If criminal anthropology is destined to lead mankind to this goal, it may well be pardoned all the harsh measures it has seen fit to suggest in order to realise the supreme end—social safety.

# PART III

CHARACTERS AND TYPES OF CRIMINALS

# CHAPTER I

## *EXAMINATION OF CRIMINALS*

CRIMINAL anthropologists are unanimous in insisting on the importance of the results to be gained from a careful examination of the physical and psychic individuality of the offender, with a view to establishing the extent of his responsibility, the probabilities of recidivation on his part, the cure to be prescribed or the punishment to be meted out to him; but besides furnishing the magistrate with a sound basis for his decisions, the anthropological examination will prove of great assistance to probation officers, superintendents of orphanages and rescue homes and all those who are entrusted with the destinies of actual offenders or candidates for crime. I have therefore decided to devote this part of my summary to a minute demonstration of the methods to be employed in these examinations, which should be conducted on the one hand with the scientific precision that distinguishes clinical

219

diagnoses of diseases and on the other with special
rules deduced from the long experience of criminologists in dealing with criminals and the insane, between
whom there is so much affinity.

## ANTECEDENTS AND PSYCHIC INDIVIDUALITY

The examination of a criminal or person of
criminal tendencies should, if possible, be preceded
by a careful investigation of his antecedents. Questions put to relatives and friends often bring
to light facts relating to his past life, and give an
idea of the surroundings in which he has grown up
and the illnesses suffered by him during childhood
(meningitis, typhus, convulsions, hemicrania, giddiness, *pavor nocturnus*, trauma). The prevalence of
disease in the family (parents, grandparents, uncles,
cousins, etc.) should be elicited and note taken not
only of nervous maladies, but of arthritic, tuberculous, pellagrous, and inebriate forms, including a
tendency to morphiomania. Even goitre should
not escape notice, since it may indicate cretinism or
any other form of degeneration. The existence of
criminality in the family is of still greater importance,
but it is extremely difficult to obtain any information
on this head, either from the patient himself or his
relatives. A certain amount of strategy must be
used in eliciting facts of this kind, by suddenly ask-

ing, for instance, whether a certain individual of the same name, already deceased or confined in such-and-such an asylum or prison, is any relation of the patient.

Next should be ascertained whether he is single or married, and in the latter case, whether his wife is still living; also what profession or professions he has exercised. In this connection it should be observed that although criminals are generally successful in everything they undertake, they are incapable of remaining constant to one thing for any length of time.

Many persons, cooks, tavern-keepers, confectioners, etc., exercise callings that have a deleterious effect on the nervous centres and encourage an abuse of alcohol; others like bakers, have night work, which is equally harmful. Professions which bring poor men, servants, secretaries, cashiers, etc., into close contact with wealth, are sometimes the cause of dishonesty in those who in the absence of special temptations, would have remained upright; others provide criminaloids with opportunities or instruments for accomplishing some crime, as in the case of locksmiths, blacksmiths, soldiers, doctors, lawyers, etc.

The time of the year and other circumstances under which the crime takes place should be elicited, and it should be borne in mind that the vintage season in countries of Southern Europe and extremes of heat and cold are favourable to seizures of an epileptic nature.

When the subject under examination is a recidivist, care should be taken to ascertain at what age and under what circumstances the initial offence was committed. Precocity in crime is a characteristic of born criminals, and puberty and senility have their peculiar offences, as have the extremes of poverty and wealth.

*Intelligence.* As we are not dealing with an ordinary patient, who is generally only too ready to talk about his troubles, but with an individual who has been put on his guard by constant cross-examination, his suspicions should first of all be allayed by a series of general questions on his native place or the town in which he is now living, his trade, etc. "Why did you leave your native town? Why do you not return? Are you married? How many children have you?" etc. Then an attempt should be made to gain an idea of his intellectual powers by asking easy questions: "How many shillings are there in a pound? How many hours are there in a day? In what year were you married?" etc.

*Affection.* The affections should be tested in an indirect way. "Is your father a bad man?" or

"Are your neighbours worthless people? Do they treat you with due respect? Has any one a spite against you? Are you fond of your parents? Are you aware that your brother (or mother) is seriously ill?" Questions concerning relatives and friends are of special interest, because they enable the examiner to ascertain whether they cause the patient emotion of any kind, whether he has any real affection for those beings to whom normal persons are attached, but towards whom born criminals and the insane in general do not manifest love. In the absence of instruments, we must judge of the feelings of patients by their answers and the facial changes caused by emotion, but medico-legal experts naturally prefer a scientific test by means of accurate instruments, by which the exact degree of emotion is registered. These instruments are the plethysmograph and the hydrosphygmograph.

It is well known that any emotion which causes the heart-beats to quicken or become slower makes us blush or turn pale, and these vaso-motor phenomena are entirely beyond our control. If we plunge one of our hands into the volumetric tank invented by Francis Frank, the level of the liquid registered on the tube above will rise and fall at every pulsation, and besides these regular fluctuations, variations may be observed which correspond to every stimulation of the senses, every thought and above all, every emotion. The volumetric glove invented by Patrizi (see Fig. 25), an improvement on the above-mentioned instrument, is a still more practical and convenient apparatus. It consists of a large gutta-percha glove, which is put on the hand and hermetically sealed at the wrist by a mixture

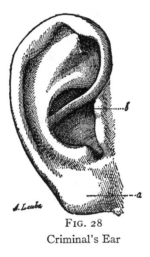

FIG. 28
Criminal's Ear

of mastic and vaseline. The glove is filled with air as the tank was with water. The greater or smaller pressure exercised on the air by the pulsations of blood in the veins of the hands reacts on the aerial column of an india-rubber tube, and this in its turn on Marey's tympanum (a small chamber half metal and half gutta-percha). This chamber supports a lever carrying an indicator, which rises and falls with the greater or slighter flow of blood in the hand. This lever registers the oscillations on a moving cylinder covered with smoked paper. If after talking to the patient on indifferent subjects, the examiner suddenly mentions persons, friends, or relatives, who interest him and cause him a certain amount of emotion, the curve registered on the

F IG . 26

F IG . 25

A V OLUMETRIC G LOVE
(see page 224)

H EAD OF A C RIMINAL
Epileptic
(see page 231)

revolving cylinder suddenly drops and rises rapidly, thus proving that he possesses natural affections. If, on the other hand, when alluding to relatives and their illnesses, or vice-versa, no corresponding movement is registered on the cylinder, it may be assumed that the patient does not possess much affection.

Thus when Bianchi and Patrizi spoke to the notorious brigand Musolino about life in his native woods, his mother, and his sweetheart, there was an immediate alteration in the pulse, and the line registered by the plethysmograph suddenly changed, nor did it return to its previous level until some time afterward.

My father sometimes made successful use of the plethysmograph to discover whether an accused person was guilty of the crime imputed to him, by mentioning it suddenly while his hands were in the plethysmograph or placing the photograph of the victim unexpectedly before his eyes.

*Morbid Phenomena.* When examining a criminal or even a suspected person, who is nearly always more or less abnormal, it is advisable to investigate the more common morbid phenomena he may be subject to, on which he is not likely to give information spontaneously because he is ignorant of their importance. He should be questioned about his sleep, whether he has dreams, etc. Mental

sufferers nearly always sleep badly and are frequently tormented by insomnia and hallucinations.
The inebriate imagines he is being pursued by
disgusting, misshapen creatures, from which he cannot escape. Epileptics, and frequently also hysterical persons have peculiar obsessions. They fancy
they cannot perform certain actions unless they are
preceded by certain words and gestures.

The susceptibility of the patient to suggestion
should also be tested, to determine what value can
be attached to his assertions. Sufferers from hysteria and general paralysis are like children, highly
susceptible to suggestion, not necessarily of an
hypnotic nature. If you tell an hysterical person
with conviction that he suffers pain in a certain part
of his body, is feverish or pale or something of the
sort, he will inform you spontaneously after a few
minutes that he feels pain or fever, etc. After a
crime of a startling nature has been committed by
some unknown person, it not unfrequently happens
that some hysterical subject, generally a youth, who
imagines he has been accused of the crime by the
neighbours or his acquaintances, becomes convinced
that he is really guilty and gives himself up to the
police.

*Speech.* Special attention should be directed during the examination to the way in which the

patient replies to questions and his mode of pronunciation. There may be peculiarities of pronunciation and stammering, characteristic of certain
forms of mental alienation, or at any rate of some
nervous anomaly; or articulation may be tremulous
and forced, as in precocious dementia and chronic
inebriety. In other cases the words are jumbled
and confused, especially if long and difficult. In
the first stages of progressive paralysis the letter *r*
is not pronounced. To test this anomaly, which is
of great importance in the diagnosis, the patient
should be requested to pronounce difficult words,
such as, corroborate, reread, rewrite, etc.

In order not to lose such valuable indications,
in cases where personal examination is impossible,
phonograph impressions of conversations between
the patient and some third person will serve as
a substitute.

The inquiry may reveal still more serious anomalies in the ideas, intelligence, and mental condition
of the patient. Sometimes the answers given are
sensible but are followed by nonsense. Other
patients, especially when afflicted with melancholia,
speak unwillingly, as if the words were forced
from them, one by one. Idiots, cretins, and demented persons are sometimes incapable of expressing themselves. Some patients who have had

apoplectic strokes substitute one word for another, "bread" for "wine," etc., or elide one part of the sentence and only repeat the last word.

*Memory.* To form an idea of the memory of the subject, questions should be put to him concerning recent and remote personal facts and circumstances, the year in which he or his children were born, what he had for his supper on the previous evening, etc., etc.

*Visual memory* may be tested by giving the patient a sheet of paper, on which are drawn various common objects, letters, or easy words. He should be allowed to look at these for five or ten seconds and requested to enumerate them after the paper has been withdrawn. In order to test the memory of sounds, the examiner should utter five or six easy words and ask the patient to repeat them immediately afterwards.

To test sense of colour, a picture on which various colours are painted is placed before the patient, as well as a skein of wool of the same shade as one of the colours in the picture, which he is requested to point out.

*Handwriting* is very important, particularly in distinguising a born criminal from a lunatic, and between the various kinds of mental alienation.

Monomaniacs and mattoids (cranks) who give

the police the most trouble often speak in a perfectly sane manner, but pour out all their insanity on paper, without an examination of which it is not easy to detect mental derangement. They write with rapidity and at great length. Their pockets, bags, etc., are always full of sheets of paper covered with small handwriting, sometimes scribbled in all directions. The matter is generally absurd or simply stupid, consisting of endless repetitions.

Individuals in the first stage of paralysis make orthographical errors, which coincide with their mistakes in pronunciation, like *Garigaldi*, instead of *Garibaldi*. Care must be taken to test this defect thoroughly. If the patient is fairly well-educated, his signature, which is the last to alter, is not sufficient; nor are a few lines a satisfactory test, since he can easily concentrate his attention on them, but he should be requested to write a page or two and be exhorted to make haste.

Alcoholism and paralysis generally give rise to tremulous handwriting with unsteady strokes, as in old people. After epileptic seizures and attacks of hysteria the writing is shaky. The slightest trembling of the hand is detected if Edison's electric pen be used.

In progressive general paralysis and some forms of dementia shakiness is so excessive that it becomes dysgraphy, with zigzag letters. The handwriting of persons subject to apoplectic strokes has often the appearance of copper-plate. Monomaniacs intersperse their writings with illustrations and symbols. They write very closely in imitation of print, as do mattoids, hysterical persons, and megalomaniacs, and use many notes of exclamation and capital letters. Their writings are full of badly-spelled words, scrolls, and flourishes.

Criminals guilty of sanguinary offences generally have a clumsy but energetic handwriting and cross their *t's* with dashing strokes. The handwriting of thieves can scarcely be distinguished from that of ordinary persons, but the handwriting of swindlers is easier to recognise, as it generally lacks clearness although it preserves a certain uniformity. The signature is usually indecipherable and enveloped in an infinite number of arabesques.

*Clothing.* The manner in which a patient is dressed often gives an exact indication of his individuality. Members of those secret organizations of Naples and Sicily, the Camorra and Mafia, are fond of dressing in a loud manner with an abundance of jewelry. Murderers, epileptics, and the morally insane, who lead isolated lives, attach no importance to dress and are frequently dirty and shabby. (See Fig. 26, A. D., a morally insane epileptic, the perpetrator of three murders.) Swindlers are always dressed in faultless style, the cinædus is fond of giving his costume a feminine air, and monomaniacs trick themselves out with ribbons, decorations, and medals: their clothes are generally of a strange cut. The cretin and the idiot go about with their clothes torn and in disorder and not infrequently emit a strong odour of ammonia.

## PHYSICAL EXAMINATION

Having carefully investigated the past history of the subject and made a minute study of his abnormal psychic phenomena, the expert should proceed to the examination of his physical characters.

Chapter I of Part I contains a detailed description of the principal physiognomical anomalies of the criminal that may be discerned by the naked eye. They will now be briefly recapitulated.

*Skin.* The skin frequently shows scars and (in the epileptic subject to seizures) lesions on the elbows and temples. Marks of wounds inflicted in quarrels and attempted suicide are frequent in habitual criminals. The forehead and nose must be examined for traces of acne rosacea frequent in drunkards, and for erythema on the back of the hands, characteristic of pellagra. Ichthyosis, psoriasis, or other skin

diseases are very common in cases of mental alienation, and scurvy often indicates long seclusion in
prison.

*Tattooing.* Great care must be taken to ascertain whether the subject is tattooed, and if so, on
what parts of his body. Tattooing often reveals
obscenity, vindictiveness, cupidity, and other characteristics of the patient, besides furnishing his name
or initials, that of his native town or village, and the
symbol of the trade he refuses to reveal (sometimes
such indications have been blurred or effaced).
(See Fig. 27.)

One of the chief proofs showing the untruthful-
ness of the statements made by the Tichborne
claimant was the fact that his person was devoid
of tattooing, whereas it was well known that Roger
Tichborne had been tattooed.

Tattooing often reveals the psychology, habits,
and vices of the individual. The tattooing on ped-
erasts usually consists of portraits of those with whom
they have unnatural commerce, or phrases of an
affectionate nature addressed to them. A pederast
and forger examined by Professor Filippi was
tattooed on his forearm with a sentimental declara-
tion addressed to the object of his unnatural desires; a criminal convicted of rape was covered with
pictorial representations of his obscene adventures.

From these few instances, it is apparent that these personal decorations are of the utmost value as evidence of hidden vices and crimes.

*Wrinkles.* We have already spoken of the abundance and precocity of wrinkles in born criminals. They are also a characteristic of the insane.

The following are of special importance: the vertical and horizontal lines on the forehead, the oblique and triangular lines of the brows, the horizontal or circumflex lines at the root of the nose and the vertical and horizontal lines on the neck. (The ferocious leader of a band of criminals at twenty-five, and a savage murderer under thirty years of age.)

*Beard.* The beard is scanty in born criminals and often altogether absent in epileptics. On the other hand, it is common in insane females and in normal women after the menopause. Degenerates of both sexes frequently manifest characteristics of the opposite sex in the distribution of hair on the body. A tuft of hair in the sacro-lumbar region, suggestive of the tail of the mythological faun, is frequently found in epileptics and idiots, and in some cases the back and breast are covered with thick down which makes them resemble animals.

The hair covering the head is generally thick and

dark, the growth is often abnormal with square or triangular zones growing in a different direction from the rest, or in small tufts like those inserted in a brush. Still more frequently do we find anomalies in the position of the vortex, or that point whence the hair-growth diverges circularly, which in normal persons is nearly always situated on the crown. In degenerates it is frequently on one side of the head and in cretins on the forehead. Precocious greyness and baldness are common in the insane criminals, and cretins, on the contrary, show these initial signs of senility at a much later period than normal persons.

*Teeth.* The greatest percentage of anomalies is found in the incisors; next come the premolars, the molars, and lastly the canines. In criminals, especially if epileptics, the middle incisors of the upper jaw are sometimes missing and their absence is compensated by the excessive development of the lateral incisors. In other cases the lateral incisors are of the same size as the middle ones, and sometimes the teeth are so nearly uniform that it is difficult to distinguish between incisors, canines, and molars, a circumstance which recalls the homodontism of the lower vertebrates. After the incisors, the premolars show the greatest number of anomalies. While in normal persons they are smaller than the molars, in degenerates they are frequently of the same size or even larger. Supernumerary teeth, amounting sometimes to a double row, are not uncommon. In other cases there is extraordinary development of the canines. Inherited degeneracy from inebriate, syphilitic, or tuberculous parents frequently manifests itself in rickety teeth with longitudinal and transverse *striæ* or serration of the edges, due to irregularities in the formation of the enamel. In idiots and epileptics, dentition is often backward and stunted; the milk-teeth are not replaced by others, or are almond-shaped and otherwise of abnormal aspect.

*Ears.* The ears of criminals and epileptics exhibit a number of anomalies. They are sometimes of abnormal size or stand out from the face. Darwin's tubercle, which is like a point turned forward when the helix folds over, and turned backward when the helix is flat, is frequently encountered in the ears of degenerates. The lobe is subject to a great many anomalies, sometimes it is absent altogether, in some cases it adheres to the face or is of huge dimensions and square in shape. Sometimes the helix is prolonged so as to divide the concha in two. Idiots often show excessive development of the anti-helix, while the helix itself is reduced to a flattened strip.

*Eyes.* The eyebrows are generally bushy in murderers and violators of women. Ptosis, a species of paralysis of the upper lid, which gives the eye a half-closed appearance, is common in all criminals; but more frequently we find strabismus, a want of parallelism in the visual axes, bichromatism of the iris, and rigidity of the pupils.

*Nose.* In thieves the base of the nose often slants upwards, and this characteristic of rogues is so common in Italy that it has given rise to a number of proverbs. The nose is often twisted in epileptics, flattened and trilobate in cretins.

*Jaws.* Enormous maxillary development is one of the most frequent anomalies in criminals and is related to the greater size of the zygomæ and teeth. (See Fig. 27.) The lemurian apophysis already alluded to is not uncommon.

*Chin.* This part of the face, which in Europeans is generally prominent, round and proportioned to the size of the face, in degenerates as in apes is frequently receding, flat, too long or too short.

These anomalies may be studied rapidly with the naked eye, but height, weight, the proportions of the various parts of the body, shape of the skull, etc., should be measured with the aid of special instruments.

*Height.* Criminals are rarely tall. Like all degenerates, they are under medium height. Im-

Fig. 27

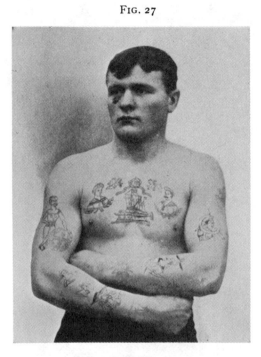

Anton Otto Krauser
Apache
(see page 236)

beciles and idiots are remarkably undersized. The span of the arms, which in normal persons about equals the height, is often disproportionately wide in criminals. The hands are either exaggeratedly large or exaggeratedly small.

The height of a patient must be compared with the mean height of his fellow-countrymen, or, to be more exact, of those inhabitants of his native province or district who are, needless to say, of the same age and social condition. The average height of a male Italian of twenty is 5 feet 4 inches (1.624 m.), that of a female of the same age, 5 feet (1.525 m.). The distances from the sole of the foot to the navel

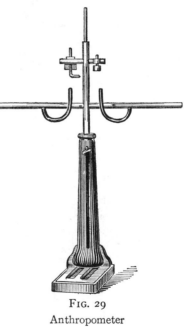

Fig. 29
Anthropometer

and from the navel to the top of the head are in ratio of 60 to 40, if the total height be taken as 100.

These measurements may be effected very rapidly by using the tachyanthropometer invented by Anfossi (see Fig. 29). It consists of a vertical column against which the subject under examination tion places his shoulders, a horizontal bar adjustable vertically until it rests on the shoulders, and can be used at the same time for ascertaining the length of

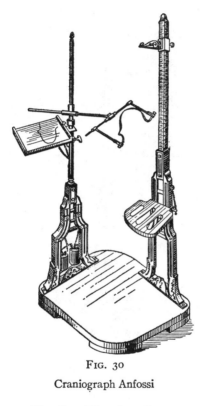

the arms and middle finger: a graduated sliding scale in the vertical column for rapid measurements of the other parts of the body and a couple of scales at the base for measuring the feet.

*Weight.* In proportion to their height, criminals generally weigh less than normal individuals, whose weight in kilogrammes is given by the decimal figures of his height as expressed in metres and centimetres.

Fig. 30

Craniograph Anfossi

*Head.* The head, or rather the skull, the shape of which is influenced by the cerebral mass it contains, is rarely free from anomalies, and for this reason the careful examination of this part is of the

utmost importance. We have no means of studying
subtle cranial alterations in the living subject, but
we can ascertain the form and capacity of his skull.
This is rendered easy and rapid by means of a very
convenient craniograph invented by Anfossi (see
Fig. 30), which traces
the cranial profile
on a piece of spe-
cially prepared card-
board.

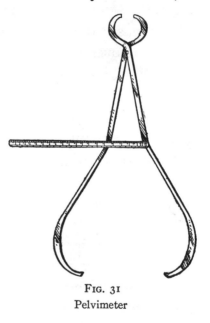

Fig. 31
Pelvimeter

In the absence of a
craniometer, measure-
ments may be taken
with calipers, the arms
of which are curved
like the ordinary pel-
vimeters used in ob-
stetrics (see Fig. 31),
and a graduated steel
tape.

The following are the principal measurements:

1. Maximum antero-posterior diameter, which is
obtained by applying one arm of the instrument above
the root of the nose just between the eyebrows and
sliding the other arm over the vault of the skull till
it reaches the occiput. The distance between the two
arms furnishes the maximum longitudinal diameter.

2.  The maximum transverse diameter or breadth of the skull is measured by placing the arms of the calipers, one on each side of the head on the most prominent spot.

3.  The antero-posterior curve is obtained by fixing the graduated tape at zero on the root of the nose (on the fronto-nasal suture) and passing it over the middle of the forehead, vertex, and occiput to the external occipital protuberance.

4.  The transverse, or biauricular curve is obtained by applying the steel tape at zero to a point just above the ear, and carrying it over the head in a vertical direction till it reaches the corresponding point on the other side.

5.  The maximum circumference is obtained by encircling the head with the steel tape, touching the forehead immediately above the eyebrows, the occiput at the most prominent point, and the sides of the head more or less at the level, where the external ear joins the head, according to whether the position of the occipital protuberance is more or less elevated.   (See Figs. 32, 33.)

6.  The cranial capacity is obtained by adding together these five measurements, the antero-posterior diameter, maximum transverse diameter, antero-posterior curve, transverse curve, and maxi-

mum circumference. For a normal male the capacity is generally 92 inches (1500 c.c.).

7. The cephalic index is obtained by multiply-
ing the maximum width by 100 and dividing the

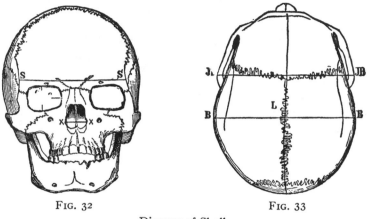

FIG. 32          FIG. 33

Diagram of Skull

product by the maximum length, according to the
following formula:

$$\frac{W \times 100}{L} = X \text{ (cephalic index)}.$$

If the longitudinal diameter is 200 and the
transverse diameter 100, the cephalic index is 10,000
divided by 200 = 50.

The cephalic indices of degenerates, like their
height, have only a relative importance; that is, when
they are compared with the mean cephalic index

prevalent in the regions of which the subject is a native. The cephalic index of Italians varies between 77.5 (Sardinians) and 85.9 (Piedmontese).

Skulls are classified according to the cephalic index, in the following manner:

| | | |
|---|---|---|
| Hyperdolichocephalic | under | 66 |
| Dolichocephalic | | 66–75 |
| Subdolichocephalic | | 75–77 |
| Mesaticephalic | | 77–80 |
| Subbrachycephalic | | 80–83 |
| Brachycephalic | | 83–90 |
| Hyperbrachycephalic | above | 90 |

We shall find among criminals frequent instances of microcephaly, macrocephaly, and asymmetry, one side of the head being larger than the other. Sometimes the skull is pointed in the bregmatic region (hypsicephaly), sometimes it is narrow in the frontal region in correlation to the insertion of the temporal muscles and the excessive development of the zygomatic arches (stenocrotaphy, see Fig. 5, Part I., Chapter I.), or depression of the bregmatic region (cymbocephaly).

*Face.* We have already remarked on the excessive size of the face compared with the brain-case, owing chiefly to the high cheek-bones, which are one of the most salient characteristics of criminals, and to the enormous development of the jaws, which gives them the appearance of ferocious animals (see Fig. 5). To these peculiarities may be added progeneismus, the projection of the lower jaw beyond the upper, a characteristic found only in 10% of normal persons, receding forehead as in apes, and the lemurian apophysis already mentioned.

*Arms and Hands.* With the exception of the excessive length as compared with the stature, anomalies in the arms are rare, but the hands show some interesting characteristics, which have already been described in the first chapter of Part I, an increase or decrease in the number of fingers and syndactylism or palmate fingers. Also the lines in the palm and those on the palmar surfaces of the finger-tips show deviations from the normal type resembling characteristics of apes.

*Feet.* Degenerates and more especially epileptics, frequently have flat or prehensile feet and an elongated big-toe with which, like the Japanese, they are able to grasp objects.

All these anomalies vary in number and degree according to whether the subject examined is a born criminal or a criminaloid, and according, also, to the special type of crime to which he is addicted. Thieves commonly show great mobility of the face and hands. Their eyes are small, shifty and obliquely placed, and glance rapidly from one object to another. The eyebrows are bushy and close together, the nose twisted or flattened, beard scanty, hair not particularly abundant, forehead small and receding, and the ears standing out from the head. Projecting ears are common also to sexual offenders, who have glittering eyes, delicate physiognomy excepting the jaws, which are strongly developed, thick lips, swollen eyelids, abundant hair, and hoarse voices. They are often slight in build and humpbacked, sometimes half impotent and half insane, with malformation of the nose and reproductive organs. They frequently suffer from hernia and goitre and commit their first offences at an advanced age.

The cinædus is distinguished by his feminine air. He wears his hair long and plaited, and even in prison his clothing seems to retain its feminine aspect. The genitals are frequently atrophied, the skin glabrous, and gynecomastia not uncommon.

The eyes of murderers are cold, glassy, immovable, and bloodshot, the nose aquiline, and always voluminous, the hair curly, abundant, and black. Strong jaws, long ears, broad cheek-bones, scanty beard, strongly developed canines, thin lips, frequent nystagmus and contractions on one side of the face, which bare the canines in a kind of menacing grin, are other characteristics of the assassin.

Forgers and swindlers wear a singular, stereo-typed expression of amiability on their pale faces, which appear incapable of blushing and assume only a more pallid hue under the stress of any emotion. They have small eyes, twisted and large noses,

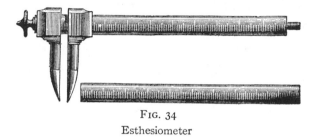

FIG. 34
Esthesiometer

become bald and grey-haired at an early age, and often possess faces of a feminine cast.

### SENSIBILITY

This external inspection of the criminal should be followed by a minute examination of his senses and sensibility.

*General Sensibility and Sensibility to Touch and Pain.* Tactile sensibility should be measured by Weber's esthesiometer, which consists of two pointed legs, one of which is fixed at the end of a scale graduated in millimetres, along which the other slides (see Fig. 34). After separating the two points three or four millimetres, they are placed on the finger-tips of the patient, who closes his eyes and is asked to state whether he feels two points or one.     Normal individuals feel the points as two when they are only 2 mm. or 2.5 mm. apart; when, however, tactile sensibility is obtuse (as in most criminals) the points must be separated from 3 to 4.5 mm. or even more, before they are felt as two.     Obtuseness varies with the type of crime committed habitually by the subject; in burglars, swindlers, and assaulters, being approximately double, while in violators, murderers, and incendiaries it stands in the ratio of 5 to 1 compared with normal persons.

In the absence of an esthesiometer, a rough calculation may be made by using an ordinary drawing compass or even a hairpin, separating the two points and measuring with the eye the distance at which they are felt to be separate.

*General Sensibility and Sensibility to Pain* are measured by a common electric apparatus (Du Bois-Reymond), adapted by Lombroso for use as an algometer.     (See Fig. 35.)     It consists of an induction coil, put into action by a bichromate battery. The poles of the secondary coil are placed in contact with the back of the patient's hand and brought slowly up behind the index finger, when the strength of the induced current is increased until the patient feels a prickling sensation in the skin (general sensibility) and subsequently a sharp pain (sensibility to pain). The general sensibility of normal individuals is 40 and the sensibility to pain, 10–25: the sensibility of the criminal is much less acute and sometimes non-existent.

*Sensibility to Pressure.* Various metal cubes of equal size but different weight, are placed two by two, one on each side, on different parts of the back of the hand. The patient is then asked to state which of any two weights is the lighter or heavier. This sense is fairly acute in criminals.

*Sensibility to Heat.* Experiments are made by placing on the skin of the patient various receptacles filled with water at different temperatures. If great exactitude is desirable, Nothnagel's thermo-esthesiometer should be used. This is an instrument very similar to Weber's esthesiometer, but the points are replaced by receptacles filled with water of varying heat and furnished with thermometers. The patient must state which is the colder, and which the hotter spot. Sensibility to heat is less acute in criminals than in normal individuals.

*Localisation of Sensibility.* After the patient has been requested to close his eyes, various parts of his body are touched with the finger and he is asked to point out the exact spot touched. Should he not be able to reach it with his finger, a statuette should be placed before him on which he should mark with a pencil the part touched. Normal persons are always able to localise the sensation exactly: inability to do so signifies disease of the brain or some kind of anomaly.

*Sensibility to Metals* is tested by placing discs of different metals, copper, zinc, lead, and gold, or the poles of a magnet, on the frontal and occipital parts of the patient's head. Sometimes he feels pricking or heat, giddiness, somnolence, or a sense of bodily well-being. In general, criminals show great sensibility to metals; in hysterical persons this sensibility reaches an extraordinary degree of acuteness. By applying a magnet to the nape of the neck, the sensations of such individuals become polarised, that is, what appeared white to them before becomes black; bitter, what was formerly sweet, or vice versa. This is an excellent way of distinguishing between bonafide cases of hysteria and sham ones. My father once detected simulation in a *soi-disant* hysterical patient by means of a piece of wood shaped and coloured to represent a magnet. On application of either magnet, the real or sham one, the patient's sensations were identical, whereas hysterical persons experience very diverse sensations and are able to distinguish

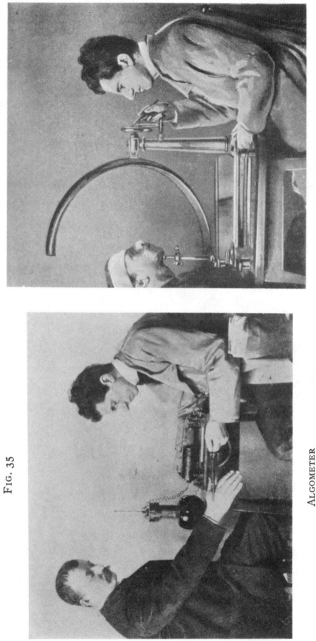

FIG. 35

ALGOMETER
(see page 246)

FIG. 36

CAMPIMETER OF LANDOLT
(Modified)
(see page 249)

very sharply between the contact, not only of wood and metal, but of the different kinds of metal, and are particularly sensitive to the magnet.

*Sight—Acuteness of Vision—Chromatic Sensibility —Field of Vision.* Visual acuteness is tested by holding letters of a specified size at a certain distance. Sight is generally more acute in criminals than in normal persons; not so, chromatic sensibility, which is tested by giving the patient a number of skeins of different coloured silks, and requesting him to arrange them in series. Persons afflicted with dyschromatopsia confuse the different colours and the different shades of the same colour. Colour-blind people confuse black and red.

Especially important is the examination of the field of vision, as the seat of one of the most serious anomalies discovered by the Modern School, the presence of peripheral scotoma, frequently found in epileptics and born criminals. To test this anomaly, use should be made of Landolt's apparatus (Fig. 36). This consists of a semicircular band, which can revolve around a column. The patient rests his chin on a support placed in front of the semicircle in such a manner that the eye under examination is exactly in the centre, and looks directly at the middle point of the semicircle, corresponding to o in the scale: the testing object, a small ball, is passed backwards or forwards along the semicircle. A graduated scale, placed on the semicircle, marks the point limiting the field of vision, and the result is registered on a diagram. The average limit of the normal field of vision is 90 mm. on the temporal side, 55 mm. on the nasal side, 55 mm. above and 60 mm. below (see

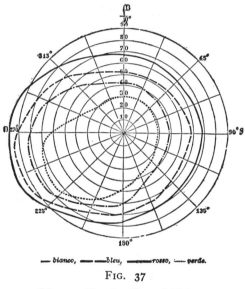

— *bianco,* — — *bleu,* — — *rosso,* ·—·· *perde.*

FIG. 37

Diagram Showing Normal Vision

Fig. 42). If a suitable instrument is not available, a series of concentric circles may be traced on a slate and the patient placed at a certain distance with one eye covered. The examiner then touches the different points of the circles with his hand and asks the patient whether he can see it when his eye is fixed on the central point. In this way the various points limiting the field of vision are noted and furnish, when united, the boundary line.

*Hearing* is generally less acute in the criminal than in the normal individual, but does not show special anomalies. It may be tested by speaking in a low voice at a certain distance from the patient, or by holding an ordinary watch a little way from his ear.

*Smell.* Olfactory acuteness is tested by solutions of essences of varying strength, which the patient should be requested to place in order, indicating the one in which he first detects an odour. Ottolenghi has invented a graduated osmometer which is easy to use. The criminal generally shows olfactory obtuseness.

*Taste* is tested in the same way as smell, by varying solutions of saccharine or strychnine dropped on to the patient's tongue by means of a special medicine dropper. The mouth should be rinsed out each time. Normal persons taste the bitterness of sulphate of strychnine in a solution 1:600,000; the sweetness of saccharine in a solution 1:100,000. The sense of taste is less acute in criminaloids than in normal persons, and is specially obtuse in born criminals, 33% of whom show complete obtuseness.

*Movements.* Normal individuals in a state of repose remain almost motionless, and their gestures are always appropriate. Lunatics and imbeciles have a habit of speaking and gesticulating even when they are not interrogated. Nervous diseases manifest themselves in facial contortions or slight spasmodic contractions. In melancholia and all forms of depression, the patient does not gesticulate but remains immovable like a statue with his eyes cast down. Degenerates manifest a fairly varied series of involuntary motions,—twitchings of the muscles, as in chorea, tonic and clonic convulsions and tremors. In senility, chorea, and Parkinson's disease, the tremors are incessant and continue even when the body is in a state of repose; in sclerosis, goitre, and chronic inebriety they accompany voluntary movements, and in this case they are easily detected by making the patient lift the tip of his finger to his nose or a filled glass to his lips. The nearer the hand approaches its goal, the more intense the oscillations become. Above all, the examiner should not fail to ask the patient to put out his tongue. If it protrudes on one side, it is a sign of a serious nervous alteration and nearly always denotes the beginning or remains of paralysis, or partial apoplectic strokes.

*Muscular Strength* is measured by a common dynamometer (Fig. 38), which the patient is requested to grasp with all his might. Compressive strength is tested by compressing the oval. In order to test tractive strength, the dynamometer is fastened to a nail at the point C, and the patient pulls with all his strength at D. The effort is registered on a graduated scale and is of importance for detecting left-handedness and measuring the

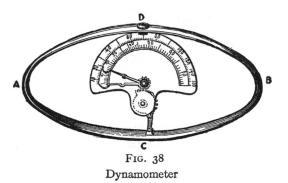

FIG. 38
Dynamometer

extraordinary force that is displayed in certain states of excitement.

*Reflex Action* consists of movements and contractions produced by an impression exciting the nerves of the cutis (cutaneous reflex) or tendons (tendinous reflex).

*Cutaneous Reflex Movements* may be tested by placing the patient in a recumbent position and stroking methodically certain parts of the body, the sole of the foot (plantar reflex), the under side of the knee-joint (popliteal reflex), the abdcminal wall (abdominal reflex). Certain reflex movements are of special importance: the cremasteric reflex, on the inner side of the thigh (obtuse in old people and individuals addicted to onanism), the reflex action of the mucous membrane covering the cornea (suspended during stupor, coma, and epileptic convulsions), and the pharyngeal reflex along the isthmus of the fauces (absent in hysterical persons).

The dilatation and contraction of the pupil in accommodation to the distance of the object viewed or in response to light stimuli is undoubtedly the most important cutaneous reflex movement. It may be tested by requesting the patient to look at a distant object and immediately afterwards at the examiner's finger, placed close to his eye, or bringing him suddenly from semi-darkness into the light. If the pupil reacts very slightly to the light, it is called torpid: if it does not react at all, it is called rigid. Rigidity of the pupil always denotes some serious nervous disturbance. In certain diseases, especially tabes, the pupils do not respond to light stimuli, but accommodate themselves to objects.

*Tendinous Reflex Action* may be tested in every part of the body, but the rotular reflex movement is generally sufficient. The patient is asked to sit on the edge of the bed or on a chair with his legs crossed. If he is healthy, the reflex movement is fairly strong,

Fig. 39

HEAD OF AN ITALIAN CRIMINAL

but in some illnesses spastic movements may be provoked and extend to the abdomen (exaggerated reflex action); in others no reflex is forthcoming. This is one of the first symptoms of tabes.

*Urine* and *Feces.* As the functions are anomalous, the chemical changes must also be anomalous, owing to the correlation of organs. In born criminals there is a diminished excretion of nitrogen, whereas that of chlorides is normal. The elimination of phosphoric acid is increased, especially when compared with the nitrogen excreted. Pepton is sometimes found in the excretions of paralytic persons in whom there is always an increased elimination of phosphates and calcium carbonate.

The temperature is generally higher than in normal persons, and, more important still, varies less in febrile illnesses.

---

For the reader's convenience, I have drawn up a list of the different points that should be noted in a careful examination.

*Table showing the Anthropological Examination of Insane and Criminal Patients (drawn up by Tamburini, Strassmann, Benelli, and Mario Carrara).*

A—*Anamnesis.* Name—surname—nationality—domicile— profession—age—education.
  Economic and hygienic conditions of native place.
  Family circumstances—pre-natal conditions—infancy— puberty.

Causes to which decease of parents may be attributed.

Cases of insanity—neurosis—imbecility—perversity—suicide—crime—or eccentricity in the family.

Progressive diseases or trauma in the subject.

Offence and causes thereof.

B—*Physique.* Skeletal development—height—span of the arms.

C—*Physical Examination.* Muscular development.

Colour of hair and eyes.

Quantity and distribution of hair.

Tattooing.

Craniometry: Antero-posterior diameter—transverse diameter—antero-posterior curve—transverse curve—cephalic index—type and anomalies of the skull—circumference—probable capacity—semi-circumference (anterior, posterior)—forehead—face, length, diameter (bizygomatic and bigoniac)—facial type—facial index—anomalies of conformation and development in the skull, in the face, in the ears, in the teeth, in other parts.

D—*Functions.*

E—*Animal Life.* Sensibility: meteoric—tactile—thermal—dolorific and muscular—visual—auditory—of the other senses.

Motivity: Sensory left-handedness—motory left-handedness—voluntary and involuntary movements—reflex action (tendinous or muscular, abnormal, chorea).

F—*Vegetative Life.* Muscular strength.

Circulation.

Respiration.

Thermo-genesis.

Digestion: Rumination—bulimy—vomiting—dyspepsia—constipation—diarrhœa.

Secretions: Milk—saliva—perspiration—urine—menstruation.

Dyscrasia: poisoning.

G—*Psychic Examination.* Language—writing—slang.

    Attention—perception.

    Memory (textual)—reason.

    Dreams—excitability—passions.

    Sentiments: Affection—morality—religion.

    Instincts and tendencies.

    Moral character—industry.

    Physiognomical expression.

    Education—aptitudes.

H—*Morbid Phenomena.* Illusions—hallucinations—delusions—susceptibility to suggestion.

I—*Offences.*

    Cause of first offence: Environment—occasion—spontaneous or premeditated—drunkenness.

    Conduct after the offence: Repentance—recidivation.

# CHAPTER II

*SUMMARY OF THE CHIEF FORMS OF CRIMIN-
ALITY TO AID IN DISTINGUISHING BETWEEN
CRIMINALS AND LUNATICS AND IN DETECT-
ING SIMULATIONS OF INSANITY. A FEW
CASES SHOWING THE PRACTICAL APPLICA-
TION OF CRIMINAL ANTHROPOLOGY*

THE cases described in this chapter show the necessity of being able to estimate correctly accusations made against insane persons by criminals or
normal individuals. Since, moreover, criminals are
prone to sham insanity in order to avoid punishment,
I sum up the characteristics that distinguish the
various types of criminals. With regard to insane
criminals, it must be remembered that every form of
mental alienation assumes a specific criminality.

The idiot is addicted to bursts of rage, savage
assaults, and homicide. His unbridled sexual appetite prompts him to commit rape. He is sometimes
guilty of arson in order to gratify a childish pleasure
at the sight of the flames.

The imbecile or weak-minded egotist is a frequent though unnecessary accomplice in nearly every crime, owing to his susceptibility to suggestion and incapability of understanding the gravity of his actions.

Melancholia is often the cause of suicide or homicide (as a species of indirect suicide). The sufferer generally confesses and gives himself up to the police. Delusions that he is being poisoned or insulted are often the cause of the murders committed by this type of lunatic.

Maniacs commit robbery, rape, homicide, and arson, and behave indecently in public.

Stealing is common among those afflicted with general paralysis, who believe everything they see belongs to them, or do not understand the meaning of property.

Dementia causes general cerebral irritation, which frequently results in murder and violence.

Hysterical persons invent slanders, especially of an erotic nature. They are given to sexual aberrations and delight in fraud and extravagant actions to make themselves notorious.

Persons subject to a mania for litigation offend statesmen and others.

Epileptics, of whom born criminals and the morally insane are the most dangerous variety, are

familiar with the whole scale of criminality. Their
special offences are assault and battery, rape, theft,
and forgery. The first offences are committed in-
termittingly at the prompting of attacks of cortical
irritation, the last two almost continuously owing
to a state of constant irritation.

To distinguish between genuine insanity and simulation, it must be remembered that exaggeration
of the symptoms is one of the chief characteristics of
shamming. The simulator exaggerates the morbid
phenomena and manifests a greater inco-ordination
of ideas than does the genuine lunatic who gives
sensible replies to simple questions, whereas the
simulator talks nonsense. For instance, if a simulator is asked his name, his answer will show no
connection with the question. He will say, perhaps:
"Did you bring the bill?" or if asked how old he
is, will answer: "I am not hungry."

Above all, in order to distinguish between dementia,
idiocy, cretinism, and an imitation of these forms,
a minute somatic examination is necessary. It
should be remarked that in idiots, imbeciles, and
cretins we generally find hypertrophy of the con-
nective tissues, earthen hue, scanty beard, *stenocrotaphy*, malformations of the skull, ears, teeth, face,
and especially jaws, and there are invariably anomalies in the field of vision, lessened sensibility to

touch and pain (which cannot be simulated since pain invariably produces dilatation of the pupils), meteoric sensibility, attacks of hemicrania, neuralgia, hallucinations, and even convulsions, epileptic fits, tremors disposing to propulsive forms, and, psychologically, absence of natural feeling, sadism, and the inability to adopt a regular occupation.

When dealing with a simulation of epilepsy, it must be borne in mind that the epileptic always manifests salient degenerate characteristics, especially asymmetry of the face, skull, and thorax; and a careful investigation reveals neurosis of some kind in the family and trauma or serious illness in childhood. During the seizure, the pupil does not react (this cannot be simulated) or there is excessive mydriasis. The sudden pallor, and the exhaustion which follows the fit, are absent in the simulator, nor does he bite his tongue or injure himself in other ways. Furthermore, he reacts at the application of ammonia, and as he is not in that state of asphyxia in which the epileptic lies during the fit, the closing of his mouth and nostrils likewise produces a reaction.

*Hysteria.* Here the detection of shamming is more difficult, since deceit is a characteristic of this disease. Tests with metals, to which hysterical persons are extremely sensitive, suggestion and hypnotism should be resorted to. The character of the crime should be specially considered, because, as we stated, the foundation of hysteria is an erotic one, and offences committed by the hysterical are nearly always of this nature in the means or the end.

An examination of sensibility with suitable instruments, and of reflex action, is to be recommended in all cases.

## PRACTICAL APPLICATION OF CRIMINAL ANTHROPOLOGY

The minute study of the criminal admits of infinite applications. It is generally used in deciding to which category of crime a particular offender belongs, whether he is a born criminal, a morally insane subject, an occasional criminal, or a criminaloid; but in certain cases the examination may be of value in establishing the innocence of an accused person, or in recognising in an accuser an insane individual whose accusation originates in some delusion and not in a knowledge of the facts.

## AN ACCUSED MAN PROVED INNOCENT BY THE ANTHROPOLOGICAL EXAMINATION

On the 12th of January, 1902, a little girl of six, living at Turin, suddenly disappeared. Two months later, the corpse was discovered hidden in a case in a cellar of the very house the little victim had inhabited. It bore traces of criminal violence and the clothing was in disorder. Various persons were arrested, among them a coachman named Tosetti, who had been seen joking and playing with the child on several occasions.

Tosetti was of honest extraction, his grandparents and parents having died at an advanced age (between sixty and ninety) without having manifested nervous anomalies, vices, or crimes. Tosetti himself, although fond of drinking, was rarely, if ever, intoxicated, and was an individual of quiet, peaceful aspect with a benevolent smile and serenity of look and countenance. His hair had become grey at an early age, and he was devoid of any degenerate characteristics except excessive maxillary development. [Height 5 feet, 7 inches (1.70 m.); weight, 158 lbs. (72 kilogrammes); cranial capacity, 93 inches (1531 c.c.); cephalic index, 84 (brachycephaly; characteristic of the Piedmontese); tactile sensibility, 3 mm. left, 2.5 mm. right; general sensibility, 83 right, 78 left; sensibility to pain, 55 right, 45 left. The sensibility was, therefore, almost normal without any trace of left-handedness. Analysis of urine—absence of earthy phosphates common to born criminals. Tendinous reflex action feeble, few cutaneous reflexes, no tremors. The field of vision was not much reduced but manifested a few peculiarities, due no doubt to the abuse of alcohol.]

Psychologically, Tosetti appeared to be a man of average or perhaps slightly less than average intelligence. He was quiet, very respectful, not to say servile, entirely devoid of impulsiveness of any form, and averse to quarrels, on which account he was rather despised by his companions. His natural affections were normal, and he was a good son and brother; he was excessively timid and disconcerted by the slightest reproof from his employer. He was rather fond of wine, though not of liquors. His sexual instincts he had lost very early, a fact which caused his companions to indulge in many jokes at his expense. His stinginess bordered on avarice, and he had never changed his trade.

During his trial he showed no resentment against anyone, not even the police and warders, of whom he said on one occasion, "They have treated me like a son."

The examination proved beyond a doubt that Tosetti was not a born criminal, and was incapable of committing the action of which he was suspected —the murder of a child for purely bestial pleasure.

To obtain stronger proof, my father adopted the plethysmograph and found a slight diminution of the pulse when Tosetti was set to do a sum; when, however, skulls and portraits of children covered with wounds were placed before him, the line registered showed no sudden variation, not even at the sight of the little victim's photograph.

The results of the foregoing examination proved conclusively that Tosetti was innocent of a crime which can only be committed by sadists, idiots, and the most degenerate types of madmen, like Vacher and Verzeni and all bestial criminals, who have reached the summit of criminality and unite in their persons the greatest number of morbid physical and psychic characteristics.

A few months after my father had diagnosed this case, an assault of the same nature was committed on another little girl living in the same house. In this case, however, the victim survived and was able to point out the criminal—an imbecile, afflicted with goitre, stammering, strabismus, hydrocephaly, trochocephaly, and plagiocephaly, with arms of disproportionate length, the son and grandson of drunkards, who confessed the double crime and entreated pardon for the "trifling offence" since he had always done his duty and swept the staircase, even on the day he committed the crime.

Other cases of this kind might be cited, but one instance will suffice. I may, however, mention a case in which my father demonstrated the innocence of an unfortunate individual who had been sentenced to ten years' penal servitude and released at the expiration of his sentence. By means of a thorough examination, which showed a complete absence of criminal characteristics, my father declared the man to be innocent of the crime for which he had been imprisoned; and subsequent investigations resulted in his rehabilitation and the discovery of the actual culprit.

## ACCUSATION PROVED TO BE FALSE BY THE ANTHROPOLOGICAL EXAMINATION

An individual named Ferreri suddenly disappeared, and ten days later his corpse was found down a well. The evidence of several persons led to the arrest of the owner of the well, a certain Fissore, a man of very bad reputation, with whom Ferreri had been seen on the day of his disappearance.

On being arrested, Fissore admitted having committed the crime, but not alone, and named as his accomplices three others, Martinengo, Boulan, and a prostitute, named Ada. All three strenuously denied their guilt. They all appeared perfectly normal.

But after a month of investigations, Martinengo, a tipsy porter of thirty-five, the son and grandson of drunkards, who at first had advanced an alibi, after being confronted several times with Fissore, admitted his complicity, and in the latter's absence added various details to his (Fissore's) version.

The four accused persons were examined anthropologically with the following results:

Boulan had the appearance of an honest country notary with broad forehead, precocious grey hairs and baldness, small jaws and a well-shaped mouth. He was a quiet man and had only once come into conflict with the law, but for an action which is not a crime in the eyes of an anthropologist (striking a carabinier who had ill-treated his father). He worked hard at his trade, which was that of a journeyman baker, and showed his kindly nature by substituting for sick comrades. He showed great attachment to all his companions, relatives, and family, and was generally beloved. In short, he was an honest, hard-working man. His alibi was corroborated by several persons who had been playing cards with him on the evening of the crime.

The second prisoner, Ada, although a prostitute, had never shown other criminal tendencies; she had adopted her calling in order to maintain her father and children, of whom she was very fond.

Martinengo, who had admitted his complicity, had no previous convictions. He was, however, an individual of earthy hue, with precocious wrinkles. Height, 5 feet, 3 inches (1.60 m.); span of the arms,

5 feet, 7 inches (1.70 m.); flattened, nanocephalous head, normal urine (phosphates 3.1), but anomalous reflex action and senses. Rigid, unequal pupils, tongue and lips inclined towards the right, shaky hand, astasia, aphasia, strong rotular reflex action, absence of cutaneous and cremasteric reflexes, illegible handwriting—a defect of long standing, since it was also found in writing dating back nine months before his arrest, uncertainty and errors of pronunciation (bradyphasia and dysarthria), complete insensibility to touch and the electric current, which gave him no sensation of pain. On the other hand, he was subject to unbearable pains in various parts of the body.

He was in the habit of laughing continually, even when reprimanded, or when sad subjects were mentioned. In spite of sharp pains in the epigastric region, he appeared to be in a strange state of euphoria or morbid bodily well-being, which prevented him from realising that he was in prison. He manifested regret when taken from his cell, where he said he had enjoyed himself so much in passing the hours in reading. Occasionally he had hallucinations of ghosts, lizards, mice, etc.

At night, he seemed to suffer from acute mental confusion, which caused him to spring out of bed.

Sometimes he was seized by a fit of chorea, followed by deep sleep.

These phenomena led my father to the conclusion that Martinengo was an inebriate in the first stage of paralytical dementia.

The demented paralytic and the imbecile, like children, are easily influenced by the suggestions of others or their own fancies. Mere reading may produce a strong impression on such minds, as in the case of the little girl who accused the Mayor of Gratz of assault, because she had listened to the account of a similar case; and the impression is intensified when, as in the case of Martinengo, it is preceded by arrest, seclusion in a cell, the remarks of magistrates, warders, etc.

In order to test Martinengo's susceptibili y to suggestion, my father told him that his cell was a room in the "Albergo del Sole," the name of a hotel in his native town. At first the idea amused him, but after a few days he began to mention it to other persons and at last he firmly believed in it. A few months later, he was transferred in a state of paralysis to the asylum, and there he was fond of boasting of the "Albergo del Sole" where he had been staying a few months before, and where they had treated him to choice dishes, etc.

We now come to Fissore, the accuser of the other

three.   Investigation of his origin showed that a male cousin had died raving mad, a female cousin had died in an asylum, a great-uncle on the maternal side had been crazy and had committed suicide; another cousin was weak-minded and subject to fits; another, a deaf-mute, had died in an asylum; another great-uncle was a drunkard and a loafer; one sister was an idiot, the other had run away from home, and a brother had been convicted several times.

Giuseppe Fissore had suffered from somnambulism and *pavor nocturnus* (fear of darkness) when quite a child; when a little older, he used to get up in the night, walk about and try to throw himself out of the window.   At school he shunned the company of other boys and grew violently angry when called by his name.   When ten years old, he was bitten by a mad dog and while being tended in Turin by the wife of an inn-keeper, had an epileptic seizure. At thirteen, he was seized by another fit, and in falling broke his arm.   His restless and capricious character led him to change his occupation a great many times; he became, in turn, baker, carpenter, forester, and farm-labourer.   He appeared to have little affection for his mother and still less for his father, with whom he had come to blows on one occasion.   At the age of twenty, in a quarrel with some companions, one of them struck him with a sickle and fractured his skull. He had been convicted several times of theft, assault, etc.

He manifested only a few physical anomalies,— exaggerated facial asymmetry, due to the disproportionate development of the left side of his skull, Carrara's lines in the palm of his hands, and a scar resulting from the fracture of his skull; but the convulsions, the *pavor nocturnus*, the two fits, and other characteristics showed him to be an epileptic and an abnormal individual, and explained how he could have accomplished a murder single-handed, which was moreover rendered more easy by the fact that the victim had been drinking heavily. Nor was the crime without a motive, since the murdered man had been robbed of a large sum of money. The total lack of moral sense that distinguished Fissore explains why he should have sought to implicate three persons who had never wronged him for the pleasure of harming and enjoying the sufferings of others. In fact, during his trial he made many false accusations against the police merely for the sake of lying, which is characteristic of degenerates.

Irrefutable alibis and a mass of evidence in favour of the three others corroborated the anthropological diagnoses and led to their acquittal, while Fissore was convicted of the crime.

## Simulation of Dementia and Aphasia by Morally Insane Subject

In August, 1899, a certain E. M. (see Fig. 44) was removed from prison to an asylum. Although only eighteen, he had been convicted several times of theft and robbery. As a child he had always shown a strong dislike to school and was given to inventing strange falsehoods. In one instance, he asserted that he had killed and robbed a man, although it was known that he had not left the house during the time.

After six months in prison, he began to show signs of mental alienation, with insomnia, loss of speech, and coprophagy. Whenever the cells were opened, he made wild attempts to escape by climbing up the grating. He was often seized with epileptic convulsions.

On the 30th of August, 1899, he was examined medically with the following results:

Stature, 5 ft., 1 in. (1.55 m.); weight, 130 lbs. (59 kilogrammes). Other measurements could not be obtained, owing to the subject's obstinate resistance. His skeletal constitution appeared to be regular and his body well nourished. His skull was brachycephalic, with strongly developed frontal sinuses, and fine, long, dark-brown hair. In the parieto-occipital region were a scar and lesion of the bone, the marks cf a wound received during one of his dishonest adventures. He had a normal type of face with frequent contractions of the mimic muscles; the hair-growth on the face scanty for his age. Extremely mobile eyes of vivacious expression, slight strabismus. An examination of the mouth showed a slight obliqueness of the palate, and the mucous membrane was rather pale. The colourless skin was inclined to sallowness.

The functions showed an extraordinary degree of cutaneous anæsthesia and analgesia. In winter and summer the patient wore only a pair of trousers and a thin jersey covering his chest and leaving the arms bare; these he was fond of adorning with ribbons and medals. He was in the habit of slipping pieces of ice between his clothing and skin, and pricking himself on the chin with a needle for the purpose of inserting hairs in the holes. On one occasion, one of the doctors came quietly behind him and thrust a needle rather deeply into the nape of his neck, apparently without producing any sensation. Various tests were made by pricking him with a needle when asleep, but without causing the slightest reflex movement on his part.

*Psychology.* He was subject to strange impulses, which appeared to be irresistible. On one occasion he was caught cutting off the head of a cat, and at times he would devour mice, spiders, nails, excrements, and the sputum of the other patients. He committed acts of self-abuse publicly, with ostentatious indecency; was in the habit of snatching at bright objects and frequently tore his clothes. His obstinate mutism procured him the nickname of "the mute," but he talked in his sleep and replied to questions by signs.

At first, medical men judged him to be in the first stages of dementia, but the course of the symptoms and certain biological and psychic data obtained from the examination led them to the conclusion that the case was one of simulation by a morally insane individual.

In the first place, the patient's look expressed a certain amount of confusion and constant distrust; furthermore, it was noticed that the filthy, indecent, and cruel acts practised by him were committed only when he knew he was being observed. The warders often saw him retire to a quiet spot and vomit all the nauseous substances he had swallowed publicly. As soon as he believed himself to be secure from observation, the usual apathetic look on his face was replaced by one of vivacity and intelligence.

In November of the same year, although he had not discarded his air of imbecility, he gave abundant proofs of intelligence. He helped the asylum barber, and showed skill and neatness in the way he soaped the other patients' faces, but if a doctor appeared on the scene, he would daub the soap clumsily in their eyes and mouths. In playing cards he showed no lack of skill and never missed an opportunity of cheating.

All these facts pointed to shamming, and the suspicions of medical men were amply confirmed by his escape on the 26th of November. The manner in which he had prepared and executed this plan showed great astuteness on his part. Some time before, he had completely changed his clothes and dressed with a certain amount of elegance. He left a note bidding an affectionate farewell to everyone. Later on, he confessed to a fellow-prisoner that he had prepared everything beforehand for his escape as soon as he should have sufficient money. He also asserted that he had felt pain when pricked.

Some of the peculiarities manifested in this case, aphasia, insensibility, and coprophagia, have been noticed in other simulators, and it is easy to see why morally insane persons, who are naturally insensible and filthy in their habits, should adopt these peculiarities as traits of their insanity. The stubborn resistance offered by the subject to all attempts to apply diagnostic instruments, except those for measuring insensibility, may be explained by fear lest the simulation should be detected.

Simulators of insanity are generally psychophysiologically, and often anatomically, degenerate, and their inferiority obliges them to resort to violence and trickery—the traits of savage races—to counterbalance their natural disadvantages. The simulation of insanity resembles in its motive the mimicry of certain insects which assume a protective resemblance to other and noxious species. Naturally inferior individuals tend to imitate characters of a terrifying nature (psychic in this case) which serve to protect them and enable them to compete with others who are better equipped for the battle of life.

## Mental Derangement and Criminal Monomania Demonstrated by the Anthropological Examination

In June, 1895, Michele Balmi, aged 30, was arrested for stabbing Maria Balmi in the neck and hands. The deed had been committed in broad daylight and apparently without any motive, but the accused asserted that it was done in revenge, because the girls were always jeering at him.

From evidence given, it appeared that far from insulting Balmi, the girls of the village were in the habit of avoiding him as much as possible on account of his lubricity. The testimony of other witnesses, including the mayor of the place, showed that he was looked upon generally as a semi-insane person, because in a very short time he had squandered all his inheritance and had quite ceased to work.

*Somatic Examination.* Body fairly well nourished, height 5 ft., 3 in. (1.60 m.), weight 150 lbs. (68 kilogrammes). Shape of the skull apparently normal but more exaggeratedly brachycephalic than the mean cephalic index of the Piedmontese, which is 85; probable capacity 90 cu. in. (1475 c.c.), or slightly below that of a normal male skull, but proportioned to the low stature.

General sensibility and sensibility to pain and touch more obtuse on the left, the general sensibility of the right hand being 68 and the left 81. Dolorific sensibility, 35 right and 41 left; tactile sensibility, 1.5 right, 3.5 left. The strength tested by the dynamometer showed 47 on the right and 54 on the left, which proved that the subject was left-handed.

The field of vision manifested extraordinary irregularities, with serious scotoma on the inner side of the right eye; on the left side the eye showed only slight scotoma but there was myopia on the inner side.

*Psychic Examination.* The behaviour of the subject was very strange. From the very first day of his imprisonment he seemed to be perfectly calm and composed, as though nothing had happened. When asked how he found prison life, he only remarked: "I certainly thought the food was better."

When asked why he had committed the crime, he replied:

"Crime indeed! I have only done my duty. Those women were always annoying me. Even in the night, they would come tapping at my window and calling me [acoustic hallucinations] and they insulted me because they wanted me to marry them."

"Did they insult you during your absence from Italy?"

"Yes, they worried me all the time I was in America. It was no use changing my occupation. I tried everything; first I was a musician, then a barber, then I tried weaving, but they went on just the same, until I lost my situations through them and had to leave the country."

"Have you ever been insane or suffered from pains in the head?"

"At Chicago, all of a sudden, a doctor called on me, but I have never been mad and should be all right if those women would leave me alone. After all, I only wanted to give them a lesson."

He showed a profound and unshaken belief in his

own assertions, such as is rare in simulators or in sufferers from melancholia, but is peculiar to mono-maniacs, especially if subject to delusions and convinced that they are the object of general persecution.

Careful investigation of the crime showed that it was entirely without motives and had been committed openly without any attempt to escape or to establish an alibi. It bore no resemblance to ordinary crimes and was clearly a case of monomania with hallucinations. This diagnosis was confirmed by the fact of the anomalies in the field of vision and sensibility, the acoustic hallucinations, and, psychologically, the anomalous nature of the affections and moral sense.

It was impossible to suppose that any of these peculiarities had been simulated, because the subject was far too ignorant to be aware of the importance of hallucinations and alterations in the senses and affections. Moreover, his whole bearing was that of a man profoundly convinced that he had done his duty, and he had no motive for shamming to escape punishment, since it evidently never entered his head that he ran any risk of incurring it. He was sent to an asylum.

# APPENDIX

# WORKS OF CESARE LOMBROSO (BRIEFLY SUMMARISED)

## I

## *The Man of Genius (L' Uomo di Genio)*

IN 1863, my father was appointed to deliver a series of lectures on psychiatry to the University of Pavia. His introductory lecture, "Genius and Insanity," showed the close relationship existing between genius and insanity; and the theme proved so absorbingly interesting to him that he threw himself into the study of the problem with all the ardour of which he was capable.

Those who have never come into contact with mentally deranged persons may deem it absurd to mention genius and insanity in the same breath, and still more absurd to seek to demonstrate the existence of flashes of inspiration in insane persons. In the minds of most people, the word *lunatic* has from earliest childhood conjured up the vision of an incoherent, stupid, or demented being, with wildly streaming hair, raging in paroxysms of maniacal fury, or sunk in imbecile apathy; not, certainly, a sharp-witted individual capable of reasoning logically. But the briefest of visits to an ordinary asylum will make it plain to any observer that such extreme types form only a very small minority. The greater number, when drawn outside the small circle of their delusions, often reason with greater acumen than normal persons; and their ideas, unhampered by stale prejudices which

283

hinder freedom of thought, are remarkable for their originality. Fine fragments of prose and poetry and really beautiful snatches of melody, the work of inmates of lunatic asylums, were collected by my father and published, as special monographs, in *The Man of Genius;* and his museum at Turin contains specimens of embroidery of marvellously beautiful design and execution, and carvings of extreme delicacy.

The well-known cases of mathematical, musical, and artistic prodigies and somnambulists with prophetic gifts, who nevertheless appear to be perfectly imbecile apart from their special talents, are interesting examples of the transition from madness to genius. The solving of equations of the fourth and fifth degree or mental calculations involving the multiplication or division of a large number of figures, are difficult operations for normal persons; yet individuals barely able to read and write, and often afflicted with insanity or imbecility, have been known to possess marvellous mathematical faculties. Imualdi was a cretin, and Dase, Juller, Buxton, Mondeur, and Prolongeau, men of feeble intellect. Among the inmates of asylums, we may find cretins and idiots that are able to play on a whistle any melody they have heard. The drawings of cats, executed by a Norwegian cretin, have been deemed worthy of a place among the treasures of art-galleries and museums. Such cases prove that the possession of one highly developed faculty does not imply a corresponding development of all the intellectual powers. Unintelligent, unbalanced, or even mentally deficient women, when in a somnambulistic or hypnotic state, are able to predict future events, an impossible feat for normal persons, or to discover the whereabouts of objects hidden at a distance, a marvellous phenomenon, which can be explained only by presuming the existence of a far-seeing vision, and the working of a powerful synthetic process resembling the inspirations of genius.

Although not a difficult task to prove the existence of traits of genius in mentally diseased persons, the bringing to light of instances of insanity in men of genius was a much simpler matter.

These instances, carefully classified, form the longest and most important part of *The Man of Genius*, but it is not necessary to give space to any of these instances here. The proofs of the connection between genius and insanity were supplemented by data supplied by the physical examination of a number of geniuses, compared with insane subjects, and a careful investigation of the ethnical, social, and geographical causes which influence the formation of both types. All the facts elicited demonstrated their complete analogy.

But my father's studies did not stop short at the discovery of this analogy, or that of the sources whence the diverse varieties of genius spring, which is perhaps the most interesting part of the book, or even at the application of the new doctrines for the purpose of clearing up obscure points in history and shedding light on the lives of great men. He pursued his investigations until he found the keystone of the edifice reared by insanity and genius—epilepsy.

It is a well-known fact that a great many men of genius have suffered from epileptic seizures and a still greater number from those symptoms which we have shown to be the equivalent of the seizure. Julius Cæsar, St. Paul, Mahomet, Petrarca, Swift, Peter the Great, Richelieu, Napoleon, Flaubert, Guerrazzi, De Musset, and Dostoyevsky were subject to fits of morbid rage; and Swift, Marlborough, Faraday, and Dickens suffered from vertigo.

But it is in the descriptions written by men of genius of their methods of working and creating that we find the strongest resemblance to the different phenomena of epilepsy, which have already been described in detail in this work, in the part treating of the connection between epilepsy and crime. While writing his poems, Tasso appeared to be out of his senses; Alfieri felt everything go dark around him; Lagrange's pulse became irregular; Milton, Leibnitz, Cujas, Rossini, and Thomas could work only under special conditions. Others have encouraged inspiration by using those stimulants which provoke epileptic attacks. Baudelaire made use of hashish; and wine evoked the creative spirit in Gluck, Gerard de Nerval, Verlaine, De Musset, Hoffmann, Burns, Coleridge, Poe, Byron, Praga, and Carducci. Gluck was wont to declare that he valued money only because it enabled him to procure wine, and that he loved wine because it inspired him and transported him to the seventh heaven. Schiller was satisfied with cider; and Goethe could not work unless he felt the warmth of a ray of sunlight on his head. Many have asserted that their writings, inventions, and solutions of difficult problems have been done in a state of unconsciousness. Mozart confessed that he composed in his dreams, and Lamartine and Alfieri made similar statements. The *Henriade* was suggested to Voltaire in a dream; Newton and Cardano solved the most difficult problems in a similar manner; and Mrs. Beecher Stowe, George Eliot, and George Sand asserted that their novels had been written in a dreamlike state, and that they themselves were ignorant of the ultimate fate of their personages. In a preface to one of her books Mrs. Beecher Stowe even went to the length of denying her authorship. Socrates and Tolstoi declared that their works were written in a condition of semi-unconsciousness; Leopardi, that he followed an inspiration; and Dante described the source of his genius in those beautiful lines:

> ". . . quando
> Amore spira, noto, ed a quel modo
> Che detta dentro, vo significando."

> "When love inspires, I write,
> And put my thoughts as it dictates in me."

"I call inspiration," says Beethoven, "that mysterious state during which the whole world seems to form one vast harmony, and all the forces of Nature become instruments, when every sentiment and thought resounds within me, a shudder thrills through my frame, and every hair on my head stands on end."

These expressions show that when a genius attains to the fulness of his development and, consequently, to the widest possible deviation from the normal, he is more or less in that condition of unconsciousness which characterises psychic epilepsy and is represented by a series of unconscious psychic activities.

Having demonstrated the frequent existence of a spice of insanity in the genius and flashes of genius in the insane, and, further, that geniuses are subject to a special form of insanity, my father, who was no mere theorist, but an admirer of facts and eager to turn them to account, considered next the possibility of making practical use of these discoveries. This he had no difficulty in doing.

The prevalence of insanity in men of genius explained innumerable contradictions and mad traits in their lives and works, the true meaning of which had hitherto escaped biographers, who either ignored them altogether or covered reams of paper with vain attempts to represent them as inspirations or, at any rate, reasonable actions. It also explained the origin of some of the extraordinary errors committed by great men; for example, the absurdly contradictory actions of Cola di Rienzi, who, after making himself master of Rome when the city was in a state of chaos, restoring peace and order, reorganising the army and conceiving the vast idea of a united Italy, ended his patriotic mission with a series of extravagances worthy of a madhouse.

The fact that traits of genius are so often found in mentally unsound persons and *vice versa*, permits us to suppose that lunatics have not infrequently held the destinies of nations in their hands and furthered progress by revolutionary movements, of which by reason of their natural tendencies and marked originality they are so often the promoters.

It may seem a simple idea to class great men, who have exercised such an enormous influence on civilisation, with wretched beings, to whom no brilliant part has been allotted, and to estimate mad ideas at their true worth; yet it had never occurred to any one before.

It is in the minor works of geniuses that the greater number of absurdities abound, but they are little known to the general public, who are acquainted only with the master-pieces. Critics either ignored the absurdities and heresies contained in these works, or, dazzled by the genius of the author, made them the subject of infinite studies, in the conviction that they were merely allusions or symbols demanding interpretation. All the defects of great men, all the extravagant notions written or spoken by them were covered with the magic veil of glory; and there was no innocent little child, as in Andersen's charming story, to tell the world of the nakedness of geniuses.

Thus idiocy, epilepsy and genius, crimes and sublime deeds were forged into one single chain; and the brilliant lights of some of its links, and the gloomy shadows thrown by others, were reduced to a play of molecules, like those which transform carbon into a refulgent diamond or a sombre lump of graphite.

## II

## *Criminal Man* (*L' Uomo Delinquente*) *considered in relation to Anthropology, Jurisprudence, and Psychiatry*

Although my father's theories on the male criminal have already been set forth in the volume now presented to the public, I feel that it would not be inappropriate to add to the descriptions of his other important works a brief survey of the original book for the use of readers desirous of studying the subject more thoroughly.

The first volume is devoted to an investigation of the atavistic origin of crime among plants, animals, savages, and children. This is followed by an exhaustive study of the physical nature of the born criminal and the epileptic, modern craniology, the anomalies connected with the different classes of offences, the spine, pelvis, limbs, and physiognomy. The data given are based on the results obtained from the examination of about 7000 criminals.

In the study of the brain, the macroscopic anomalies in the convolutions and histological structure of the cerebral cortex of criminals and epileptics are the object of special consideration, since these anomalies solve the problem of the origin of criminality.

Certain additional degenerate characters, the prehensile foot, wrinkles, lines on the finger-tips, the ethmoid-lachrymal suture, anomalies of dentition, the existence of a single horizontal line on the palm of the hand, etc., are further described, and a careful examination made of the field of vision and olfactory and auditory sensibility.

The psychological examination of the criminal includes psychometry, the discovery of new characteristics, such as neophily, lack of exactitude, frequent existence of traits of genius, pictography, hieroglyphics, gestures, and the arts and crafts peculiar to the criminal.

Finally, the different types of offenders—epileptic and morally insane criminals, political and passionate offenders, inebriate, hysterical, and mentally unbalanced (mattoid) criminals—are described separately and compared with each other, their diversities and analogies being thrown into relief. Around these types are grouped juridical figures of crimes, reproduced from psychiatric forms. These are followed by an examination of occasional or pseudo-criminals, criminaloids, latent criminals, and geniuses.

The second volume treats of epileptics, and discusses, among other things, their ergography, psychology, graphology, and anomalies of the field of vision. The studies on criminals of passion are supplemented by observations on suicides and political offenders, those on the insane include investigations of their age, psychology, sex, tattooing, heredity, and the difference between insane and ordinary criminals with respect to the motives that prompt their crimes, and the manner in which these are carried out, thus furnishing a new theory of sexual psychopathy.

The third volume of the fifth edition treats of the etiology and cure of crime.

In the part dealing with the etiology of crime, the geological, ethnical, political, and economical factors determining or influencing criminality, as well as other causes,—density of population, food, alcoholism, sex, heredity, instruction, religion, etc., are examined statistically and sifted with critical care. For the first time, light is thrown on the influence exercised by criminality and wealth on the increase or decrease of emigration.

My father demonstrates by means of data, contributed for the most part by Bodio and Cognetti, that the importance attributed to poverty as a factor of criminality, especially by certain socialistic schools, has been largely exaggerated; while, at the same time, the fact that both wealth and education have their specific crimes, has been ignored by these schools.

In dealing with collective criminality, my father merely repeats the original theories on the subject, expressed by him in 1872 and constantly confirmed since then. These theories have been utilised and illustrated by a number of writers: Ferri, Sighele, Ferrero, Le Bon, and Tarde.

In the prophylaxis and cure of crime, not content with mere criticism of present methods, the new doctrines suggest practical and efficacious means of repressing crime.

In view of the fact that criminality is assuming a changed aspect, adapted to the conditions of modern life and civilisation, it should be combated by the very means furnished by progress,—the telegraph, press, all measures for fighting alcoholism, popular places of recreation, etc.

For the prevention of crime, besides those measures designed to minimise the influence of physical and economic factors,—baths, sanitary regulations, clearing of forests, prevention of over-crowding, social legislation, limitation of wealth, graduated system of taxation, collective services, expropriation, etc.,—my father suggests special measures for diminishing certain kinds of crime,—divorce for sexual offences, affiliation orders for infanticide and government of a truly liberal character, with freedom of the press and public opinion to combat political crime. He also emphasises the importance of provident and charitable institutions, specially for orphan and destitute children, to aid in suffocating germs of criminality, in view of the fact that it is to ragged schools and similar institutions that the decrease of crime in England is certainly due.

Finally, with regard to the direct repression of crime, the new methods of identification devised by Bertillon and Anfosso, and all modern aids for the detection and apprehension of criminals, such as rapid communication and publicity, should be utilised in all countries where the police aspire to be considered scientific in their methods.

A minute and intelligent individualisation of penalties is suggested as being far more efficacious than the uniform and injurious punishment of detention in prison; so that while society defends itself, it tends to improve the perverted faculties of criminals, or where improvement is impossible, to utilise them in their natural state, following the example set by nature in the transformation of injurious parasitical relationships into pacific and mutually beneficial symbioses.

## III

### *The Female Offender (La Donna Delinquente); The Prostitute and the Normal Woman*

#### (In Collaboration with Guglielmo Ferrero)

The first part of this book is devoted to a study of the normal woman, or rather the female of every species, beginning with the lowest strata of the zoölogical world and working upwards through the higher mammals and primitive human races to civilised peoples.

As a result of this study, it is shown that although in the lower species, the female is the superior in intelligence, strength, and longevity, among the higher mammals she is surpassed in strength, intelligence, and beauty by the male, who is developed and perfected by the struggle for the possession of the female; while on the other hand, owing to her maternal functions, the female tends to a perpetuation of her physical and psychic characters; and this prevents variation and evolution.

The same phenomenon is encountered in the human race. After a careful examination of the normal woman (height, weight, brain, nervous system, hair, senses, physiognomy, and intellectual and moral manifestations), the authors arrived at the conclusion that the physical, anatomical, physiological, functional, and sensory characters of the female show a lower degree of variability than those of the male.

In the same way, cases of monstrosity, degeneration, epilepsy, and insanity are less frequent in the female of the human race; and the percentage of genius and criminality is decidedly lower. The examination of the senses showed that the normal human female possesses a lower degree of tactile, olfactory, auditory, and visual sensibility than the male, and also, contrary to the hitherto accepted opinion, a diminished moral and dolorific sensibility. Among savage peoples, the female appears to be less sensitive,—that is, more cruel than the male and more inclined to vindictiveness.

But when we consider woman from the point of view of her maternal functions, her physiological, psychological, and intellectual nature assumes an entirely changed aspect; for maternity is the natural function of the female, the end to which she has been created. Lofty sentiments, complete altruism, and far-sighted intelligence develop all of a sudden when she becomes a mother. Maternity neutralises her moral and physical inferiority, pity extinguishes cruelty, and maternal love counteracts sexual indifference. Maternity stimulates her intelligence and sharpens her senses, explains and exalts those characteristics which have hitherto constituted her inferiority until they become signs of superiority when considered from the point of view of the reproduction of the species.

A lessened sensibility enables woman to bear with greater ease the pains inherent to childbirth; her refractoriness to all kinds of variation—also that of a degenerate nature—serves to correct morbid heredity and to bring back the race, which owes its continuation to her, to its normal state.

Women commit fewer crimes than men; and offenders of the female sex, generally speaking, exhibit fewer degenerate characteristics. This is due in part to the tenacity with which the female adheres to normality, but also to the deviation caused in her criminality by prostitution. The history of this social phenomenon, and an examination of the anatomy and functions of the types representing this variation of criminality show that the prostitute generally exhibits a greater number of degenerate and criminal characters than the ordinary female offender.

Prostitution is therefore the feminine equivalent of criminality in the male, because it satisfies the desire for licence, idleness, and indecency, characteristic of the criminal nature.

In addition to prostitutes and ordinary offenders, who constitute the larger part of female criminality, there exists a small number of born criminals of the female sex, who are more ferocious and terrible even than the male criminal of the same type. The criminality of this class of women develops on the same foundation of epilepsy and moral insanity. The physical characters are those peculiar to the male born criminal—projecting ears, strabismus, anomalies of dentition, and abnormal conformation of the skull, brain, etc.; in addition, an absence of feminine traits. In voice, structure of the pelvis, distribution of hair, etc., she tends to resemble the opposite sex and to lose all the instincts peculiar to her own.

From this brief description it may be gathered that this work on the female offender owes much of its interest to the light it throws on the normal woman. It is true that it casts doubt on many of the postulates of feminism; but, on the other hand, it lays stress on and exalts the many invaluable qualities characteristic of the female sex.

The preface to the work concludes with the following remarks:

"Not one of the conclusions drawn from the history and examination of woman can justify the tyranny of which she has been and is still a victim, from the laws of savage peoples, which forbade her to eat meat and the flesh of the cocoanut, to those modern restrictions, which shut her out from the advantages of higher education and prevent her from exercising certain professions for which she is qualified. These ridiculous, cruel, and tyrannical prohibitions have certainly been largely instrumental in maintaining or, worse still, increasing her present state of inferiority and permitting her exploitation by the other sex. The very praises, not always sincere, alas, heaped on the docile victim, are often intended more as a preparation for further sacrifices than as an honour or reward."

## IV

### Political Crime (*Delitto Politico*)

#### (In Collaboration with Rodolfo Laschi)

The law of inertia governs nature. Every organism tends to adhere indefinitely to the same mode of life and will not change unless forced to do so.

In the depths of the ocean, where existence, comparatively speaking, is uniform and undisturbed, we still find organisms allied to the species of pre-historic epochs. Those stars and suns, which are outside the sphere of action of other worlds, continue eternally their vertiginous gyrations in the trajectories assigned to them at the beginning of all things.

Every progress in nature is the result of a struggle between the tendency to immobility, manifested by misoneism, or the hatred of novelty, and a foreign force which seeks to conquer this tendency.

As in nature, misoneism dominates every human community. It is most invincible in children and neuropathic and insane individuals, very powerful among barbarous peoples, and more or less disguised among civilised nations. But the world progresses: every day new conditions and new interests arise to combat the law of inertia and render impossible the realisation of the much-desired invariability; and progress, unwelcome yet inevitable, prevails.

By political crime we understand every action which attacks the laws, the historical, economical, political and social traditions of a nation or, in fact, any part of the existing social fabric, and which comes into collision with the law of inertia.

Any attempt to obtain forcibly a change in existing systems, to enforce by violence, for instance, the claims of free trade in a protectionist country, to plunge a nation into war or to incite workers to strike—all such actions represent the first steps in political crime, which reaches its climax in revolts and insurrections, and which victory alone can exalt above a host of blameworthy and base deeds, and crown with glory.

Revolution is the struggle between the tendency to immobility innate in a community, and the force which urges it to move. Revolution is the historical expression of evolution and has always great and sublime ends in view. It is the struggle against an institution or a system which hinders the progress of a nation, never against any temporary oppression, no matter how unbearable it may be. The French revolution was not a struggle against an individual king or even a dynasty, but against the institutions of monarchy and feudalism; nor was Lutheranism a revolt against any pope, but against the corruption that had invaded the Roman Catholic Church.

The Italian revolution was not directed against foreign rule, which indeed was mild and generous in some parts of the country, but it voiced an imperious demand for independence indispensable to every people that desires to become truly civilised.

A revolution is therefore a slow, constant effort towards progress, preceded by propaganda. In some instances, it may last for years; in others, for centuries, until an entire nation, from the humblest citizen to the most wealthy patrician, is convinced of the necessity of the proposed change, and the habitual misoneism of the masses overcome, the existing order of things being defended by only a few, whose personal interests are bound up in the old system. The ultimate triumph is inevitable, even when the leaders of the movement perish and the first risings are suffocated in blood; nay, death and martyrdom serve only to kindle greater enthusiasm for an ideal, if it be worthy to live. This becomes apparent when we consider the impulse given to Christianity by the crucifixion of its Leader, and to Italian independence by the death of the two brothers, Emilio and Attilio Bandiera.

But bloody episodes are not always essential to the march of a revolution. The triumph of Hungary over Austria was almost a bloodless one, and that of Free Trade in England was effected practically without violence.

Since a revolution implies a change in the ideas of the masses and not of a minority, be this of the elect or merely of turbulent spirits, revolutions are rare occurrences in history and their effects are lasting. In fact, after the death of Cromwell, feudalism was extinct in England.

Like the pear which falls in autumn when the process of ripening has caused the gradual reabsorption of the juices in the stalk, revolution triumphs and the ancient system perishes when an entire people is persuaded of the necessity for a change. The fall of the pear, however, is not always the result of a slow physiological process, but may be caused by a gust of wind, which dashes it to the ground before the pulp has developed the sweet juices that are the sign of its maturity. In the same way, a revolt or an armed rising of men, whose demands are enforced by threats, may result in the carrying into effect of some programme of reform which is nevertheless too progressive or reactionary, or otherwise unsuited to the country.

In fact, nearly every revolution is preceded by an insurrection, which is suppressed by violence, because it seeks to realise premature ideals, and on this account is frequently followed by a counter-revolution, provoked by reactionary elements.

Unlike revolutions, insurrections are always the work of a minority, inspired by an excessive love or hatred of change, who seek forcibly to establish systems or ideas rejected by the majority. Unlike revolutions, also, they may break out for mere temporary causes—a famine, a tax, the tyranny of some official, which suddenly disturbs the tranquil march of daily life; in many cases they may languish and die without outside interference.

In practice, however, it is extremely difficult to distinguish a revolt from a revolution since the results alone determine its nature, victory being the proof that the ideas have permeated the whole mass of the people.

Political offenders, insurrectionists, and revolutionists are the men who seize the standard of progress and contest every inch of the ground with the masses, who naturally incline towards a dislike of a new order of things. The army of progress is recruited from all ranks and conditions—men of genius, intellectual spirits who are the first to realise the defects of the old system and to conceive a new one, synthesising the needs and aspirations of the people; lunatics, enthusiastic propagandists of the new ideas, which they spread with all the impetuous ardour characteristic of unbalanced minds; criminals, the natural enemies of order, who flock to the standard of revolt and bring to it their special gifts, audacity and contempt of death. These latter types accomplish the work of destruction which inevitably accompanies every revolution: they are the faithful and unerring arm ready to carry out the ideas that others conceive but lack the courage to execute.

Finally, there are the saints, the men who live solely for high purposes and to whom the revolution is a veritable apostolate. They rank high above the mass of mankind, from whom they are frequently distinguished by a singular beauty of countenance, recalling ancient paintings of holy men. They are consumed by a passion for altruism and self-immolation, and experience a strange delight in martyrdom for their ideals. These men sweep the masses along with them and lead to victory with their propaganda, their inspired songs, and thrilling accents. Tyrtæus was not the only poet who led soldiers to war: every insurrection has had its own songs, in which the love of a whole people is crystallised.

Lunatics, unbalanced individuals, and saints are the promoters of progress and revolutions. These types have one thing in common—their passionate devotion to a sublime ideal and their love for humanity, which torments and crushes them in every case where they fail to attain that for which they have fought. But whether victorious or defeated, on the throne or on the scaffold, their efforts are not lost. Love is the spiritual sun of mankind. A ray shed by a human heart may spread far and wide, traversing unknown regions and sojourning with unknown races; and if powerless to revive some timid flower that has been numbed by the chilly night, it may still be stored up in the songs of a people, like the sunlight in green plants, to be retransformed at some future time into light and warmth.

## V

### *Too Soon! (Troppo Presto!)*

#### (A Criticism of the New Italian Penal Code)

In this book, which was written during the interval between the publication of the new Penal Code and its sanction by the

Italian Parliament, my father makes a rapid criticism of the Code, which he considered premature. Only a few decades had elapsed since the proclamation of Italian Unity; and the widely differing races that people the provinces constituting the kingdom of Italy had not been able in that brief period to acquire sufficient uniformity of customs to make a single code of laws desirable.

But the book is not merely a criticism. It also contains an exposition of the fundamental principles that, according to my father, should underlie every serious and efficacious code of laws. It is this part that makes this somewhat hastily written book of such importance to criminologists; because it sets forth under the chief heads the juridical desiderata of the New School.

The following brief extract gives an indication of the nature of these principles:

1. The legislation of a country should always be regulated by the customs of the people whom it is to govern; and although a system of different penal codes to suit the varying races and customs in the different regions of one State may offer certain disadvantages, they are always of less importance than the difficulties caused by a uniform code.

2. The object of every code should be the attainment of social safety, not the careful weighing of guilt and individual responsibility. The worst and most dangerous criminals should be treated with the greatest severity; but indulgence should be shown towards minor offenders. The former should be segregated for life in prisons or asylums; the latter should never be allowed to become acquainted with prison life, but should be corrected by means of other penalties, which would not bring them into contact with true criminals, nor necessitate their temporary retirement from civil life.

3. Certain reprehensible actions (abortion, infanticide, suicide or complicity therein, passionate crimes, duelling, swearing, adultery, etc.), which are not considered criminal

by the general public, should be non-criminal in the eyes of the law.

4. Born criminals, the morally insane, and hopeless recidivists, whose first convictions are not followed by any signs of improvement, should be regarded as incurable and confined for life in criminal lunatic asylums, relegated to penal colonies, or condemned to death.

A second edition of this book was published shortly afterwards with the title *Notes on the New Penal Code*. In this edition, each of the most notable adherents of the new doctrines: Ferri, Garofalo, Ballestrini, Rossi, Masé Dari, Carelli, Caragnani, and others, discussed one special point of the code and suggested the necessary modifications.

## VI

### *Prison Palimpsests (I Palimsesti del Carcere)*

(A Collection of Prison Inscriptions for the Use of Criminologists)

"Ordinary individuals, and even scientific observers, are apt to regard prisons, especially those in which the cellular system prevails, as mute and paralytical organisms, deprived of speech and action, because silence and immobility have been imposed on them by law. Since, however, no decree, even when backed up by physical force, avails against the nature of things, these organisms speak and act, and sometimes manifest themselves in brutal assaults and murders; but as always happens when human needs come into conflict with laws, all these manifestations are made in hidden and subterranean ways. Walls, drinking-vessels, planks of the prisoners' beds, margins of books, medicine wrappers, and even the unstable sands of the exercise-grounds, and the uniform in which the prisoner is garbed, supply him with a surface on which to imprint his thoughts and feelings."

With this paragraph my father begins the introduction

to his book *Prison Palimpsests*, a collection of inscriptions and documents revealing the inmost thoughts of prisoners.

In the first part, these inscriptions are classified under different headings: opinions on prison life, penalties, morality, women, etc., and according to the surface on which they are inscribed—books, walls, pitchers, clothing, paper, etc.

For the psychologist and the student of degenerate types of humanity, this collection is of the greatest interest. The inscriptions are followed by a series of poems, autobiographies, and letters written by intending suicides, and criminals immediately before their execution. The comments made by criminals on the margins of books belonging to the prison library are especially interesting, because they enable the student to compare the effect produced on criminals by certain works with the impressions of normal individuals. The poems written by prisoners are equally interesting, since, like popular songs, they represent the intimate expression of the poet's desires and aspirations.

In the second part, these prison inscriptions are compared with the remarks commonly found scribbled in the streets, on school benches, and on the walls of public buildings of all kinds—courts of justice, places of worship, and even those edifices in which the legislation of the State is framed. All the inscriptions are classified according to the sentiments they express and the sex of the writer, distinction being made between the writings of prisoners and those of the ordinary public.

The book closes with practical suggestions regarding the use to which similar collections might be put, as critical hints on the present methods of dealing with criminals and as an aid in investigating the characters of accused persons.

All offenders, except the most degenerate types, born criminals or the morally insane, desire work or occupation of some kind, and books of an interesting character. This demand emanates from innumerable inscriptions on the walls of cells and the margins of prison books: "How unbearable is enforced idleness for a man who has always been accustomed to work and study, and in whom activity and the desire of some ennobling pursuit are not quite extinct!" . . . "The nun of Cracow cried, 'Bread, bread!' but my voice pleads from my solitary cell, 'Work, work!'"

"If jurists would leave their desks and libraries," says my father in conclusion, "put aside all pre-conceived notions, enter the prisons and study the problem of criminality not on the walls of the cells, but on the living documents they enclose, they would speedily realise that all reforms evolved and applied without the aid of practical experience are only dangerous illusions."

## VII

### Ancient and Modern Crimes (*Delitti Vecchi e Delitti Nuovi*)

"This volume contains a collection of facts, sometimes valuable, at other times merely curious, that I was able to glean during long years of study in the field of criminal anthropology and psychiatry. They all tend to show the great difference that exists between ancient and modern crimes."

With these words my father begins the preface to this book, in which cases of recent crimes are described and compared with those committed in by-gone ages.

It is divided into three parts. The first part contains a comparative and statistical study of criminality in Europe, Mexico, the United States, and Australia.

The second part describes the careers of typical criminals of former times, such as the Tozzis of Rome, a family of anthropophagous criminals, and Vacher, Ballor, and other assassins of the Jack-the-Ripper type, whose perverted sexual instincts prompted them to murder a number of women and mutilate the corpses in a horrible fashion.

The third part treats of those modern criminals, like Holmes and Peace, who accomplish their misdeeds in a refined and elegant manner, substituting for the more brutal knife or hammer, the resources of chemistry, physics, and modern toxicology. In other cases, some product of modern times, such as the motor-car or bicycle, forms the motive for the crime, or is of assistance in its accomplishment.

"From the data we have been able to gather relating to crime in by-gone ages," continues my father in his preface, "we are led to conclude that crimes of a violent and bloody nature predominated exclusively in more barbarous times, and that fraudulent offences are characteristic of modern communities. Violence is more primitive than trickery and must always precede it, exactly as a more barbarous state in which property is gained or maintained by force, at the point of the sword, precedes a state in which ownership is regulated by means of contracts; and crime always adapts itself to the prevailing customs.

"The admirable work of Coghlan shows criminality in Australia to be of this latter type, as contrasted with its semi-barbarous nature in states like Mexico, and gives us a picture of the character it will assume a century or two later in Europe.

"As the fundamental nature of the criminal has not changed, his actions are still of the same character; and violence and cunning are mingled or alternate in modern crime. But though the individual remains unchanged, he is subordinated to a more powerful factor than himself—modern progress. It is true that many modern crimes are facilitated by modern contrivances; but the same contrivances often furnish means for their defeat; and so we may foresee a time, perhaps not very remote, when such anti-social elements shall partially, if not totally, have disappeared."

## VIII

### *Diagnostic Methods of Legal Psychiatry (La Perizia Psichiatrica Legale)*

This work was not intended to introduce the doctrines of modern criminology to the general public, but as a text-book for the guidance of jurists, doctors, experts—in short, all those whose professions bring them into contact with criminals.

It consists of two parts, the first of which contains about fifty cases diagnosed according to the new methods, and collected by the author of the work and his followers. These cases include all types of delinquents: born criminals, morally insane individuals, hysterical, insane, inebriate, and epileptic criminals, criminaloids, criminals of passion, etc.

In each case, as the diagnosis was intended to serve a practical purpose, the criminal is examined physically, psychologically, and psychiatrically; and his antecedents are investigated with great care.

In the second part, "The Technical Aspect of Criminal Anthropology," a detailed description is given of the methods to be employed in the examination of a supposed criminal, the rules for determining to what class he belongs, the manner in which the physical examination should be conducted, a list of the necessary measurements, a description of the most suitable apparatus, and the mode of using them, the methods of procedure in the interrogation of a criminal, in order to elicit useful information, and instructions for analysing his intellectual manifestations (handwriting, drawing, and work), movements, attitude, and gestures.

Thanks to the methodical instruction imparted by this book, the inexperienced student is enabled to progress gradually until he is in a position to conduct a complete psychiatric and medico-legal examination.

The third part treats of the methods for discriminating between criminals and lunatics. The various forms of mental alienation are described in detail; and an examination of cases of feigned insanity shows that simulators of lunacy are generally mentally unsound.

In the concluding part are discussed the various uses to which a careful diagnosis may be applied.

The Appendix contains studies on the application of mental tests in medico-legal practice, and a glossary, alphabetically arranged, of the terms commonly employed in criminal anthropology, compiled by Dr. Legiardi-Laura.

## IX

## *Anarchists (Gli Anarchici)*

The book opens with an examination of the theories of anarchists, from which the author arrives at the conclusion that in view of the importance generally conceded to economic ideals to-day and the universal abuse of power, these theories in reality are not so absurd as they are supposed to be. It is the methods adopted by anarchists for the realisation of their ideals that are both absurd and dangerous.

"However valuable many of the proposals of anarchism may be," says the author, "they become absurd in practice; because all reforms should be introduced very gradually in order to escape the inevitable reaction which neutralises all previous efforts."

The crimes of anarchists tend to mingle with ordinary crimes when certain dreamers attempt to reach their goal by any means possible—theft, or the murder of a few, often innocent, persons. It is easy to realise, therefore, why, with a few exceptions, anarchists are recruited from among ordinary criminals, lunatics, and insane criminals. Investigations made by the author showed that 12 per cent. of the communards were of a criminal type, and this percentage was still higher in anarchists (31 per cent.). Of forty-five anarchists examined at Chicago, 40 per cent. had faces of a criminal cast. The majority of anarchists possess the passions and vices peculiar to ordinary criminals: impulsiveness, love of orgies, lack of natural affections and moral sense; and similar intellectual manifestations, such as slang, ballads, tattooing, hieroglyphics. But there are a greater number of genuine epileptic and hysterical subjects, lunatics, and indirect suicides among anarchists than among ordinary criminals; greater, too, is the proportion of criminals from passion. These truly heroic natures, profoundly convinced that the remedy for so many social evils lies in the murder of certain personages of high standing, who appear to bear the greatest share of responsibility for the existing system, do not hesitate to have recourse to violence when they deem it necessary; although it is distasteful to them and although they have hitherto disassociated themselves from the excesses of their companions. The anarchists Caserio and Bresci were of this type. The crimes of these passionate criminals are always accomplished single-handed; they always surrender to the police immediately afterwards and make no attempt to defend themselves. On the contrary, when in court, they frequently give a lucid explanation of the motives that have induced them to commit their crimes and affront the penalty with stoicism.

Such being the origin, and such the promoters of anarchism, it is evident that the methods for curing crimes deriving from this source should differ greatly from those used in suppressing ordinary crime.

In spite of the fact that anarchists are frequently criminals, their ideas, although often absurd, imply a greater elevation of character than the cynical apathy in which the worst types of criminals are sunk.

Instead of combating violence by violence and dealing out death sentences with a prodigality almost rivalling that of anarchists themselves, the authorities should segregate the most dangerous types or relegate them to distant islands, and adopt exile as a penalty for genuine criminals of passion. However, political liberty and some safety-valve, whereby lawless instincts may be turned into harmless channels, are the best methods for preventing anarchism. Constitutional government and freedom of speech and the press may go a long way towards combating anarchism; but the restoration of popular tribunates, like those to which Rome owed her balance and tranquillity, would be still more efficacious. If the governing bodies were to favour, instead of hindering, the

formation of such institutions, which tend to spring up everywhere and to voice the grievances of the people, just causes
would not be abandoned exclusively to the advocacy of
extremists.

## X

## *Lectures on Legal Medicine (Lezioni di Medicina Legale)*

This book, as the preface explains, was an attempt to
present in a concise and popular form the theories of criminal
anthropologists, on which the author had previously delivered
a series of university lectures, and which he feared might have
been erroneously or imperfectly understood by those of his
hearers who were diffident or insufficiently prepared.

It is divided into three parts, criminal anthropology, mental alienation, and the relation of serious offences (assault,
murder, poisoning, etc.) to legal medicine.

The first part contains a summing-up of the author's
ideas on the atavistic and pathological origin of the criminal.
He examines the equivalents of crime among plants, animals,
savages, and children, describes the pathological causes which
call forth atavistic instincts and alludes to other special kinds
of degeneration peculiar to criminals. Finally, the anatomy,
functions, and internal organs of the criminal are examined, and
a careful study made of his intellectual manifestations and psychology. Similar studies on epileptics and the morally insane
show that the three forms are only variations of the same
degeneration.

We have an examination of occasional, habitual, and latent criminals, who represent an attenuated type of delin-
quency, following on the investigations of these serious forms,
admitting of correction, prevention, or cure. It develops
much later in life than the vicious propensities of instinctive

criminals or may even remain latent; yet at the root we always find the same anatomical and pathological anomalies, although less marked and fewer in number.

The origin of passionate and political criminals is entirely diverse. Their criminality springs from an excess of noble passions, the impetuosity of which prevents them from exercising sober judgment and urges them to unpremeditated actions that afterwards cause them the deepest remorse.

After a rapid survey of feminine criminality and its equivalent, prostitution, the author discusses juridical and social methods of curing crime.

In the second part, 'mental alienation in relation to legal medicine, the author examines the anthropological and psychic characters of lunacy, which he divides into various classes: congenital mental alienation (cretinism, idiocy, imbecility, eccentricity); acquired mental alienation (mania, melancholia, paranoia, circular insanity, dementia); mental alienation in conjunction with neurosis (epilepsy, hysteria, progressive general paralysis); alienation resulting from toxic influences (alcoholism, including forms produced by indulgence in absinthe and coca, saturnine encephalopathy, pellagra). An investigation is made into the etiology of these various forms with special reference to their juridical importance.

The third part is devoted exclusively to medico-legal questions, to an examination of the various forms of violent death: by heat, electricity, starvation, hanging, strangulation, asphyxia, and poisoning, the symptoms which distinguish each type being carefully defined. This is followed by a study on wounds produced by firearms, pointed weapons or blades, on living and dead bodies, in order to determine the exact situation of the wound and the manner in which it has been inflicted. Finally, we have an examination of the different forms of poisoning.

A separate lecture treats of sexual psychopathy and offences against morality; and other lectures discuss questions of legal obstetrics: abortion, infanticide, and matrimonial questions.

## XI

*Recent Discoveries in Psychiatry and Criminal Anthropology and the Practical Application of these Sciences*

This volume was published in 1893. It contains a complete summary of the latest research of criminologists in jurisprudence, psychiatry, and anthropology, during the interval between the publication of the fifth and that of the last edition of Prof. Lombroso's *Criminal Man*.

The research includes anthropological discoveries in the skull, skeleton, internal organs, and brains of criminals, as well as others of a biological and functional nature. They are followed by a study of the methods to be employed for the cure and punishment of crime.

# BIBLIOGRAPHY OF THE CHIEF WORKS OF CESARE LOMBROSO

Archivio di Psichiatria, antropologia criminale e scienze affini (Archives of Psychiatry, Criminal Anthropology and Kindred Sciences). Thirty-two volumes. Published by Fratelli Bocca, Turin and Lausanne.

L'Uomo Delinquente (Criminal Man). Fifth Edition. Vols. I, II and III of xxxv + 650, 576, and 677 pages respectively, with separate volume of plates, maps, etc. Bocca, Turin, 1906, 1907.

*Translations:*

L'Hommea criminel. Vols. I and II published 1895, Vol. III (Le crime, ses causes et remèdes) 1907, by F. Alcan, Paris.
Die Ursachen und Bekämpfung des Verbrechens. Bermuheler Verlag, Berlin, 1902.
El Delito, sus causas y remedios. Librería de Victoriano Suárez, Madrid, 1902.

La Donna Delinquente, la prostituta e la donna normale. (With Guglielmo Ferrero.) New Edition. Bocca, Turin, 1903.

*Translations:*

Das Weib als Verbrecherin und Prostitute. Verlagsanstalt und Druckerei, Hamburg, 1894.
The Female Offender. Fisher Unwin, London, 1895.

Il Delitto Politico e le Rivoluzioni. (With R. Laschi.) Bocca, Turin, 1890.

*Translations:*
Das politische Verbrechen und die Revolutionen. Two vols. 1890.
Le Crime politique. Two vols. Félix Alcan, Paris, 1890.

Le piu recenti scoperte ed applicazioni della psichiatria ed antropologia criminale. Bocca, Turin, 1893.

*Translations:*
Neue Fortschritte in den Verbrecherstudien. Wilhelm Friedrich, Leipzig. 1894.
Neue Fortschritte der kriminellen Anthropologie. Marhold, Halle, 1908.
Neue Verbrecherstudien. Marhold, Halle, 1908.
Nouvelles recherches de Psychiatrie et d'Anthropologie criminelle. Alcan, Paris, 1890.

Gli anarchici. Bocca, Turin, 1894.

*Translations:*
Die Anarchisten. Verlagsanstalt und Druckerei, Hamburg, 1895.
Les Anarchistes. E. Flammarion, Paris, 1896.

La Perizia psichiatrico-legale. Bocca, Turin, 1905.
Lezioni di Medicina legale. Bocca, Turin, 1900.
Troppo Presto! Appunti al nuovo codice penale. Bocca, Turin, 1888.
Palimsesti del carcere. Bocca, Turin, 1888.

*Translations:*
Kerker Palimpsesten. Hamburg, 1899.
Les Palimpsestes des prisons. Stock, Lyon.

La Delinquenza e la rivoluzione francese. Treves, Milan, 1897.

Criminal Anthropology. (Twentieth Century Practice of Medicine, Vol. XII, pp. 372-433.) New York, 1897.
Luccheni e l'antropologia criminale. Bocca, Turin, 1899.
Il caso Olivo. (With A. G. Bianchi.) Libreria Editrice Internazionale, Milan, 1905.
Ricerche sui fenomeni ipnotici e spiritici. Unione Tip. Edit. Turin, 1909.
L'Uomo di genio. Sixth Edition. Bocca, Turin, 1894.

*Translations:*
L'Homme de génie. Alcan, Paris, 1889.
The Man of Genius. Walter Scott, London, 1891.

Genio e degenerazione. Second Edition. Remo Sandron, Palermo, 1908.

*Translations:*
Entartung und Genie. Wiegand, Leipzig, 1894.

Nuovi studi sul genio. Two vols. Sandron, Palermo, 1902.

*Translations:*
Neue Studien über Genialität (Schmidt's Jahrbücher der gesammten Medizin, 1907).

Pazzi e anormali. Lapi, Citta di Castello, 1890.
In Calabria. Niccolo Giannotta, Catania, Sicily, 1898.
L'Antisemitismo e le scienze moderne. Roux, Turin, 1894.

*Translations:*
Der Antisemitismus und die Juden. Wiegand's Verlag, Leipzig, 1894.
L'Antisémitisme. Giard et Brière, Paris, 1899.

Problèmes du jour. Flammarion, Paris, 1906.
Il momento attuale in Italia. Casa Editrice Nazionale, Milan, 1905.

Grafologia. Ulrich Hoepli, Milan, 1895.

*Translations:*
Graphologie. Reclam, Leipzig.

Trattato profilattico e clinico della pellagra. Bocca, Turin, 1890.

*Translations:*
Die Lehre von der Pellagra. Oscar Coblenz, Berlin, 1898.

# INDEX

315

Gipsies, 140
Goitre, 220, 244

**H**

Habitual criminals, 44, 110–115, 198
Hallucinations, 30, 82–84
Hamburg, percentage of illegitimates among prostitutes, 144
Handwriting, 228–230
Harwick, quoted, on sense of right and wrong, 33
Hebrew Sheltering Guardian Society in New York City, 160–164
Heredity, indirect, 137
—direct, 57, 137–139
—influence of, 144, 220, 235
Hieroglyphics, 43, 44
Homicide, among criminaloids, 121
—in Italy, 140
—relation of temperature to, 145
—in Massachusetts, 173
—and melancholia, 259
Hydrosphygmograph, 223
Hypnotism, 101
Hysteria, 92–99
—relation to epilepsy, 92
—physical and functional characteristics, 93
—psychology, 94
—susceptibility to suggestion, 95, 226
—and delirium, 98
—sensibility to metals, 248, 261
—special offences of, 259
—simulation of, 261

**I**

Idiots, impulses, 74, 258
—speech, 227
—physical characteristics, 235, 260
Idleness, 40, 150
Illegitimates, percentage of, among criminals, 144
Imbeciles, 75, 259, 260, 269
Imitation, 146
Immigration and its relation to crime, 147, 148
Imprisonment, 154, 186, 187
Impulsiveness, 36, 85
Incendiaries, 26
Indemnity, 191

India, infanticide in, 126
—theft in, 129
Industrial Homes of the Salvation Army, 168
Inebriates, crimes peculiar to, 85–86
—hallucinations of, 226
Infanticide, 121, 126, 127
Insane, the morally, relation to born criminals, 53, 57, 58
—cases, 53 *ff.*
—relation to epileptics, 61, 65 *ff.*
—professional characteristics, 71
—institutions for, 206
—dress, 230
—special offences, 259, 260
Insane criminals, 74–99, 234
—characteristics distinguishing them from habitual criminals, 77, 78
—antecedents, 78
—motives, 78
—typical cases, 79
—institutions for, 205 *ff.*
—two classes, 208
Insanity, moral, 56, 65–69, 272 *ff.*
—criminal, 74–99
—genuine and simulation of, 260, 276. *See also* Lunacy
Institutions, for destitute children, 156
—for destitute adults, 167
—for women criminals, 180
—for minor offenders, 185
—for habitual criminals, 198
—for born criminals and the morally insane, 205. *See also* Reformatories, Penitentiaries
Intellectual manifestations of born criminals, 42–44
Intelligence, of born criminals, 41
—of criminaloids, 106
—examination, 222
Invulnerability of criminals, 64
Italy, hot-beds of crime in, 140
—percentage of illegitimates among criminals, 144
—percentage of women among criminals, 151
—institutions for orphans, 157

**J**

Jackson, on epileptic fits, 60

PATTERSON SMITH REPRINT SERIES IN
CRIMINOLOGY, LAW ENFORCEMENT, AND SOCIAL PROBLEMS